D1082901

WITHDRAWN

Annie Ernaux

New Directions in European Writing

. . . .

Editor: John Flower, Professor of French, University of Kent at Canterbury.

As the twentieth century draws to a close we are witnessing profound and significant changes across the new Europe. The past is being reassessed; the millennium is awaited with interest. Some, pessimistically, have predicted the death of literature; others see important developments within national literature and in movements cutting across frontiers. This enterprising series focuses on these developments through the study either of individual writers or of groups or movements. There are no definitive statements. By definition the books in this series are introductory and set out to assess and explore the full spectrum of modern European writing on the threshold of a new age.

ISSN 1350-9217

Annie Ernaux: An Introduction to the Writer and Her Audience

Lyn Thomas

Oxford • New York

First published in 1999 by
Berg
Editorial offices:
150 Cowley Road, Oxford, OX4 1JJ, UK
70 Washington Square South, New York, NY 10012, USA

Berg is the imprint of Oxford International Publishers Ltd.

Library of Congress Cataloging-in-Publication Data

A catalogue record for this book is available from the Library of
Congress.

British Library Cataloguing-in-Publication Data

A catalogue record for this book is available from the British Library.

ISBN 1 85973 207 0 (Cloth)

Typeset by JS Typesetting, Wellingborough, Northants.
Printed in the United Kingdom by WBC Book Manufacturers,
Bridgend, Mid Glamorgan.

For my parents, Betty and Arthur Thomas

Contents

Acknowledgements

I would like to express my very sincere thanks to my friend Nicki Hitchcott for making the connection between my work on Ernaux and Berg's interest in publishing a book on the writer in their New Directions in European Writing series. I owe to her and to Kathryn Earle at Berg the invaluable opportunity of writing this book.

Without my sabbatical in 1997, granted by the Research Committee of the Faculty of Humanities and Teacher Education at the University of North London (UNL), the book would have taken many more years to complete. The four trips to Paris to research the book were also possible thanks to the support of the Committee. I am particularly grateful to Alistair Ross, the former Faculty Research Director, for his support and encouragement over several years. My students at UNL, particularly those who took my two units on contemporary French women writers, have made an important contribution to this book. Their enthusiasm for Annie Ernaux's writing confirmed and strengthened my own, and discussions in class were always stimulating.

In Paris, a number of people assisted me in my work: the keeper of the archives at Gallimard, Madame Liliane Phan, and the staff at the Institut National de l'Audiovisuel and the Bibliothèque Marguerite Duras were exceptionally helpful. I would also like to thank Hélène de Saint-Hippolyte, Ernaux's attachée de presse at Gallimard, for giving me some of her valuable time in May 1997, and for providing me with crucial information on translations and sales figures. I am grateful to Diana Knight for her helpful comments on the manuscript, and to Duncan Fraser for help with the bibliography and for the cover photograph.

Annie Ernaux herself in many ways made the full realisation of the project possible: I am indebted to her for access to the readers' letters which form the basis of chapter 5, for articles, books and videocassettes, which provided otherwise unobtainable information, and for interviews in March, May and November 1997. Throughout she has taken an active interest, reading and commenting on draft chapters, and facilitating my work in every way. I would like to thank her for her generosity of spirit, and for her support and friendship.

I am deeply grateful to Duncan Fraser, without whose intellectual, emotional and domestic support the past year's intense writing and research would not have been possible.

Translations

In chapter 1 I provide English translations for the titles of Ernaux's works at the beginning of the main presentation of each text; the format is either: 'translated as' followed by the published title/s, or, where no translation has been published, I simply provide my own version. Thereafter, the titles are given in French. A full list of translations with dates, authors and publishers is provided in the bibliography. Again here, I have added my own translation into English of the titles of the untranslated texts.

I would like to thank Carol Sanders and Dalkey Archive Press for their kind permission to use *Cleaned Out*, Professor Sanders's translation of *Les Armoires vides*, for quotations. All other quotations from French texts are my own translations. Except for *Les Armoires vides*, where I have provided page references both for the original and the published translation, all page references are to the original French texts. In this way I hope to have accommodated (and encouraged) readers who would like to consult the original texts, whilst simultaneously making them accessible to a wider English-speaking audience.

I would like to thank Annie Ernaux, Gallimard and the editor of *L'Infini*, Philippe Sollers, for permission to reproduce my translation of 'Fragments autour de Philippe V.' in appendix 1. I would also like to thank the *Feminist Review* collective, who are publishing this translation in *Feminist Review* 61, Spring 1999, for their permission to include it here.

Abbreviations

IN = my unpublished interview with Ernaux, 21 March 1997.

Preface

In France Annie Ernaux's popularity and success are rarely disputed; within weeks of its publication in January 1997 Ernaux's *La Honte* was near the top of the bestseller lists in magazines and newspapers as diverse as *Elle, Le Nouvel Observateur, Le Point, L'Express* and *Aujourd'hui Le Parisien*. By February Marie-Françoise Leclère in *Le Point* spoke of the book's sales as an 'astonishing result'; 68,000 copies had been sold by April 1997 (Leclère, 1997, p. 94; Gallimard, unpublished summary sheet, April 1997). The sales figures for some of the earlier works are even more striking: to date 459,179 copies of *La Place* have been sold in France, whilst the figure for *Passion simple* is 274,014 copies. *La Place* and *Passion simple* have so far been translated into sixteen and fourteen languages respectively (Gallimard, April 1997). The significance of these statistics is reinforced by the fact that, particularly since 1984, each of Ernaux's publications has been followed by invitations to appear on radio and TV, including the prestigious television discussion programme *Bouillon de Culture*. However, despite this success, and the award of the Prix Renaudot for *La Place* in 1984, Ernaux's literary status in France is controversial, and she has received more academic attention outside France, particularly in Britain, Canada and America. In America, Ernaux has also acquired a following among the general reading public: she was interviewed by *Publishers Weekly* in December 1996, and to date six of the nine texts are available in translation in the United States. In Britain and Ireland, although translations of three of the texts are available, Ernaux is not widely known outside university French departments.

This book aims to provide a critical discussion of Ernaux's writing for existing readerships, particularly academics, undergraduate and postgraduate students in university French departments, and students and teachers of French in schools. I also aim to introduce Ernaux's works to a wider English-speaking public than they have so far reached, and to provide an introduction to Ernaux's work for the general reader. The first part of the book focuses on the nine texts Ernaux has published to date. In chapter 1 I provide a chronological account of Ernaux's development as a writer, indicating the broad variations in narrative structure, language and to a lesser extent, theme, which distinguish each text. Chapter 2 looks at Ernaux's approach to auto/biographical writing and the development of her auto/biographical voice.[1] A more detailed discussion of the themes of Ernaux's writing follows in chapters 3 and 4. After the general survey of the key themes of Ernaux's work in chapter 3 – gender, sexuality and class – chapter 4 provides a psychoanalytical reading of representations of identity, femininity and loss in Ernaux's writing. In all of these chapters my analysis indicates the profound modernity of Ernaux's work, even in the texts which focus on her experiences in the 1940s and 1950s. In her literary exploration of the boundaries between self and other, between writer and reader, Ernaux points to a definition of auto/biography based on relationality, a critical term highlighted by Sidonie Smith and Julia Watson in their account of contemporary and prospective approaches to autobiography by women (Smith and Watson (eds), 1998). The self, like the text, exists as part of a network; it is, as Ernaux argues in *La Honte,* both fragmented and historical. It is this relational and unstable self which Ernaux's writing project explores.[2]

In part 2 of the book I look beyond the texts themselves in order to provide an account of Ernaux's place in contemporary French culture. I have chosen to do this for a number of reasons. Partly, I am mirroring one of Ernaux's central concerns: as the title of *La Place* indicates, she is preoccupied by the different places occupied in French society by working-class and middle-class culture – her culture of origin and her acquired culture. Her writing is in some ways a search for a space where she can bring these two cultures together, and feel *à sa place,* or at home. If this awareness of social hierarchies is inscribed in the texts themselves, its reception by the French literary establishment generates a further struggle, this time to place the texts, both generically and in a system of values. To use Isabelle Charpentier's term – 'réceptions croisées' ('intersecting receptions') – I am looking at the cross-over between these two projects: Ernaux's depictions of French society, and the latter's reception of those depictions; the place or role she claims for herself, and the place which is attributed to her by critics and readers (Charpentier, 1994). In this I believe that my project is entirely consistent with the aims of a writer who has insisted on the social and communicative function of literature (see chapter 2). The second part of the book is in effect exploring the nature of the social impact which Ernaux's writing may have.

However, the main reason for the approach adopted in part 2 is my own conviction that the definition of literary criticism as the study of texts in isolation from their reception is no longer appropriate. Following on from Barthes, postmodern critical theory emphasises the polysemy of the text and the power of the reader, yet, with the notable exception of some feminist work, literary criticism is still generally based on the notion of the privileged reading of the critic, and almost invariably provides only one authoritative reading of the text.[3] Inevitably, in a work such as this, my own readings of Ernaux's writing are in the end dominant; nonetheless, in the second part of the book, I attempt to open up the critical text to other readings – by 'lay' readers and professional reviewers. There is a parallel between Ernaux's questioning of the notion of a unitary identity, and my own interrogation of the authoritative, unique reading of the critic. In chapter 5, I present a study of letters which Ernaux has received from readers over more than twenty years. As I have already suggested, my interest in these appropriations of Ernaux's work stems in part from my understanding of contemporary critical theory: if meaning is the result of a negotiation between reader and text, then the study of these negotiations seems to be a crucial aspect of the analysis of the significance and significations of a work. Secondly, the wide popularity of Ernaux's works seems in itself to justify or even demand this approach: what, in Ernaux's writing, permits these appropriations? Why do Ernaux's texts speak to, and perhaps even for, so many readers? In exploring these questions I am analysing the literary text as a social rather than purely aesthetic phenomenon. Again, this seems a particularly appropriate strategy for the study of a writer who eschews narrow aesthetic definitions of literature, and defines the place of her work as 'between literature, sociology and history' (*Une femme*, p. 106).

The intense mediatisation of the work of a successful writer such as Ernaux in the contemporary period means that the literary text simply cannot exist in a pristine, isolated form: it gives rise to a circulation or network of meanings which influence and inform each other, and from which it can only be artificially separated. In chapter 6, I attempt to introduce the reader to the critical discourses which Ernaux's texts generate, and which constitute a further manifestation of their place and significance in contemporary French society. The contradictory and ambivalent nature of these discourses and their intermittent contestation of Ernaux's status as a writer inevitably lead to some insights into the workings of the French literary establishment. The study of these mediatisations of Ernaux's works also calls into question the traditional primacy of the literary work, its privileged and prestigious role as the site where a culture is mysteriously distilled and symbolically preserved. As a result, this chapter particularly is theoretically underpinned by the work of the sociologist Pierre Bourdieu (Bourdieu, [1979] 1984). I am also indebted to Isabelle Charpentier, who has provided an illuminating study of the reception of Ernaux's work by critics and librarians (Charpentier, 1994). Finally, in chapter 7, I return to my own reading of Ernaux, in an attempt to uncover its subjective basis, and to explore my own dialogue with Ernaux's texts. In this final chapter, I have aimed to disrupt the unity of the impersonal academic voice which I have inevitably adopted in the book as a whole, and to subject my own reading to the kind of analysis applied to the readings of others in chapters 5 and 6; in this task, Nancy K. Miller's concept of 'personal criticism' and the example of other scholars who have made links between academic analysis and personal experience were my reference point and inspiration (Miller, 1991a; Dawson, 1994, Pearce, 1997). Finally I must acknowledge how much I have gained, both personally and academically, from Ernaux's writing, which has inspired and necessitated this attempt at reading *in the first person*.

Notes

1. In some of Ernaux's works, particularly *La Place* and *Une femme*, the boundary between autobiography and biography is unclear. Because of this, following Laura Marcus and Liz Stanley, I will use the spelling 'auto/biographical' throughout in referring to Ernaux's texts; in this way I hope to signal that they cannot easily be placed within conventional generic definitions (Marcus, 1994; Stanley, 1992; see chapter 2). Liz Stanley's commentary on the term is relevant here: 'My aim in this book is to contribute to the groundwork of a feminist approach to auto/biography which rejects conventional generic distinctions and separations, instead showing how the same analytic apparatus is required

for engaging with all forms of life writing, for the same question and problematics demand critical inquiry' (Stanley, 1992, p. 3).

2. Ernaux herself has coined the term 'the transpersonal I' to describe this aspect of her auto/biographical writing (Ernaux, 1994b).

3. Whilst this is still largely true of 'mainstream' literary criticism, particularly in the field of French Studies, feminist critics have pioneered approaches which, like mine, explore a range of readings. In French Studies the work of Elizabeth Fallaize and Toril Moi on the reception of Simone de Beauvoir immediately springs to mind, whilst in the wider field of feminist work on literary texts, Sara Mills and Lynne Pearce have combined empirical readership study with their own analyses (see chapter 5).

Part 1

1

A Writing History

Introduction

*I*n this chapter my presentation of Ernaux's work takes the conventional form of chronology; this seems to be a necessary basis for the other types of analysis which follow, and like several of the texts themselves, allows a narrative of formation or development, in this case as a writer, to emerge. (A chronological list of Ernaux's works is provided in the bibliography.) The parallels between this process, or mode of analysis, and Ernaux's literary reconstructions of her life are clear; in both cases a number of alternative versions inevitably suggest themselves, and the final selection, presented here, makes no claims to be the definitive truth. A further complication, or perhaps enrichment, is the fact that Ernaux, as a highly self-aware and self-reflexive writer, has her own versions of this history, which at the very least deserve serious attention.

In this narrative, the publication of the first novel, *Les Armoires vides,* is clearly a highly significant moment, representing a turning away from the generic and stylistic conventions of the literary canon and Ernaux's discovery that her strength as a writer lies in the reworking of her own experience. The publication of *La Place* is also an important turning point, since, as I will argue below, this work can be seen as the first example of Ernaux's mature style. One of the main characteristics of this style is economy: from *La Place* onwards Ernaux's texts are short, and very clearly focused; even the spacing on the page conveys meaning, as I will demonstrate in my discussion of the individual texts. Within this economy, there is a creative tension between statement and suggestion, authorial absence and presence: the texts combine direct address to the reader (where Ernaux comments on content, form and the writing process itself) and the technique of implying or suggesting meanings through the impersonal description of events, experiences or material objects. I would argue that the technique of suggestion through 'objective' description of the material world is reminiscent both of nineteenth-century realist writing, particularly Flaubert, and of Camus's *L'Étranger* (*The Outsider*), itself the subject of a passage of Ernaux's second novel, *Ce qu'ils disent ou rien* (pp. 32–3).[1] Despite the strong sense of the emergence of a characteristic mature style, it is also true that Ernaux's writing remains consistently experimental: *Passion simple* and *Journal du dehors* are thematically and formally innovative, whilst *'Je ne suis pas sortie de ma nuit'*, published in 1997, seems to question many of the aims expressed in the earlier texts and, through its disordered and impressionistic form, the careful structuring and selections of the earlier work.

A thematic account of Ernaux's work might identify two strands in the corpus published to date: the texts which foreground Ernaux's own development, from childhood to young adulthood, and the narratives of loss or bereavement. These strands or categories are clearly not exclusive: the narratives of loss are also concerned with Ernaux's own life history, whilst the theme of loss is omnipresent, even in the novels of development.[2] However, broadly speaking, there is a strong focus on Ernaux's own early life in the first three novels, and in *La Honte*, published in 1997, which interestingly represents a recent return to this theme. All of these texts refer to the tradition of the novel of development, or *Bildungsroman*, though they are highly subversive, both of the conventional genre, and even of the feminist *Bildungsroman* of the 1970s and 1980s as defined by Rita Felski (Felski, 1989; see the discussion of *La Femme gelée*, below). *La Place*, *Une femme* and *'Je ne suis pas sortie de ma nuit'* are concerned with the lives and deaths of Ernaux's mother and father, and thus clearly belong to the second category I have constructed – the narratives of loss. *Passion simple* in some ways stands alone in Ernaux's work, but the themes of loss and grief or 'separated love', Ernaux's own words to describe her feelings for her father, link it with these texts (*La Place*, p. 23). *Journal du dehors*, even more than *Passion simple*, stands alone as the only Ernaux text to date which focuses on the contemporary social context. In some ways it is a link between the two groups: it presents the subjectivity which has been observed in formation in the early works, temporarily free of the overwhelming sense of loss which emanates from the narratives of bereavement. However, both strands are present as subtexts: memories of childhood are triggered through the encounters with the urban reality of the 1980s and 1990s, which also prompt philosophical reflection on the themes of loss, death and time.

Nine Texts, Nine Lives

Les Armoires vides (translated as *Cleaned Out*) was Ernaux's first novel to be published, though it was not her first attempt at writing. In an earlier novel, influenced by the *nouveau roman*,[3] she had experimented with an avant-garde, anti-realist style. It is, however, with *Les Armoires vides*, written during her years as a mother, wife and teacher in Annecy, that Ernaux seems to have found her own voice. Finding this voice meant allowing herself to write a realist novel based on her own experience, predominantly of the change of class which her education had engendered. *Les Armoires vides* begins with a crisis – the heroine, Denise Lesur, is waiting for an abortion to take its course in her room in a university hall of residence. The description of this crisis leads to the question of how and why she finds herself in this situation, which becomes a pretext (in both senses) for the rest of the novel. This short introduction is then followed by a long 'flashback' which constitutes most of the text. The opening crisis is returned to in the final pages, with Denise reaffirming her determination to survive at the end. This circular structure, consisting of crisis – explanatory flashback – return to, or resolution of, the initial crisis, is fundamental to Ernaux's writing, and at least a further four of the nine texts clearly constitute variations on this theme (*Ce qu'ils disent ou rien, La Place, Une femme, La Honte*).[4] In *Les Armoires vides*, the desire for knowledge expressed by the narrator becomes a powerful motivating force in the ensuing narrative. In some ways this is an obviously artificial device, since it seems unlikely that the heroine, Denise, would choose this particular moment to write her life-history. Nonetheless, a narrative structure based on epistemophilia, or the search for knowledge, is particularly compelling, as is evidenced by the popularity of crime fiction (see chapter 2, p. 34).

As Ernaux herself has explained, the language and tone of *Les Armoires vides* were abandoned when she began to write her father's life-history in *La Place*, and from that point on, they have never been returned to (see chapter 2, pp. 31–2). The violent and angry tone of *Les Armoires vides* is set by the nature of the initial crisis: the heroine is in the process of rejecting not only the foetus, but also the middle-class culture which she has acquired through education. She reflects on her adolescent rejection of her parents' culture, and actively rejects the new culture during the course of the writing. The abortion is clearly symbolic: at her moment of need her middle-class boyfriend has abandoned her, just as the cultural baggage she has acquired (the empty cupboards of the title)[5] has proved to be a useless sham. The foetus is the physical manifest-ation of her taking in, and being taken in by, middle-class culture: 'It's important to remember that it's through the body – via the pregnancy and the abortion – that the encounter with the middle class and its rejection take place. The symbolic value of the abortion is enormous, even if I was not aware of it at the time of writing' (Ernaux in Vilain, 1997a, p. 69). *Les Armoires vides* can be seen as a *Bildungsroman* in reverse, or *anti-Bildungsroman*, in that it describes the negative aspects of an education: instead of gradually assim-ilating the culture to which she is exposed, Denise is violently expelling it, the upward trajectory of *Bildung* replaced here by the downward spiral which culminates in abortion.

After the *entrée en matière* which is provided by the abortion, the narrative proceeds at a hectic pace, uninterrupted by the authorial interventions and comments on the writing process which characterise Ernaux's writing from *La Place* onwards. Similarly, the spaces on the page which interrupt the narratives of all the texts after *La Place* are absent here, replaced by a continous flow of words. The predominant use of the present tense provides a sense of immediacy, and reinforces the colloquial register. As Carol Sanders has pointed out, the sentences are long and loosely structured, and there is often an 'accumulation of near synonyms', as if Ernaux is struggling to find the words to express hitherto repressed or culturally unacceptable experiences (Sanders, 1993, p. 21). If in *La Honte* Ernaux declares that she will 'never know the delights of the metaphor', in *Les Armoires vides*, on the contrary, metaphors abound (*La Honte*, p. 70). Sanders provides a detailed account of Ernaux's use of metaphors, which she categorises into three main types: the elemental (fire, water, movement, light, depth), animal imagery and 'basic sensory imagery' – references to the senses of smell and taste (Sanders, 1993, p. 21). As Christine Fau's analysis of the problem of language in Ernaux's writing suggests, colour can be added to this list. In her article Fau comments on the almost physical, concrete nature which Ernaux attributes to language in her first novel, where the mother's words are described as 'dense and black' and school is 'an orange word' (Fau, 1995, p. 502). I will return to the question of imagery in *Les Armoires vides* below, and in my discussion of the representation of the female body in chapter 4. Now, it is sufficient to note the gulf between this linguistic and metaphorical profusion and the pared down, minimalist style of the later texts.

The mixed register of *Les Armoires vides* is also particular, in that whilst literarity in the form of the metaphor is not rejected as it will be later, it is combined with slang expressions, the familiar language both of Denise's culture of origin and of the student world she is now part of. Indeed, as Denise herself points out, there is no clear dividing line between the two: 'Marc. I admire everything he says, even when he swears, which he does because he hasn't had to put up with his parents doing it all day long like me' (*Les Armoires vides*, p. 170; trans. p. 115). Just as the linguistic register ranges from the metaphorical to the everyday, many voices are heard in the text:[6]

> I was on the table, all I could see between my legs was her grey hair and the red snake she was brandishing with a pair of forceps. It disappeared. Unbearable pain. I shouted at the old woman, who was stuffing in cotton wool to keep it in place. Shouldn't touch yourself down there, it'll get damaged . . . let me kiss the little sweeties, there between the lips. Mauled, battered, plugged up, will it ever be usable again, I wonder. (*Les Armoires vides*, p. 11; trans. p. 7)

In this passage it is possible to observe the animal imagery ident-ified by Sanders – the probe becomes a snake – and the emphasis on colour (grey, red) which Fau has noticed in Ernaux's descriptions of words. The colour red recurs in *Les Armoires vides*, and is assoc-iated with both violent emotion and the female body; at the end of the novel, the process of abortion is described as having to 'empty out all alone the little bag of hatred, reddish, messed up from the start' (*Les Armoires vides*, p. 180). If the red snake could be seen as a poetic version of this harsh reality, the word 'engueuler' (to shout or yell at) in the next sentence reinstates the colloquial register. Then we hear the voice of the mother, warning the daughter about the dangers of sexual pleasure, then her lover, encouraging her to indulge in them. The combination of colloquial, everyday language, vivid imagery and the slippage from one voice to another successfully conveys a woman's experience of alienation from her own body, and is typical of Ernaux's writing in *Les Armoires vides*.

Published in 1977, *Ce qu'ils disent ou rien* (*What They Say Goes*) describes the disenchantment of an even younger heroine, Anne. The novel is written from a position of hindsight: in the autumn term of her *seconde* at school, aged fifteen, Anne reflects on the end of the previous school year and the summer holidays. The circular structure is again adopted, as at the end we return to the diegetic present, and to Anne's autumnal melancholy. In this case, however, the structure is less clearly demarcated; unlike *Les Armoires vides*, the narrative of *Ce qu'ils disent ou rien* is not triggered by a specific crisis, and it seems to drift from the present to the recent past, from October to June. The textual markers indicating the start of the flashback section found in *Les Armoires vides* – the statement of the narrator's intentions, and the opening of a new chapter – are absent here, as is the expressed desire for explanation and understanding of the narrator's disillusionment. However, whereas in *Les Armoires vides* the present tense is the main tense of the narrative, here, more conventionally, the perfect and imperfect tenses are used to situate the main account in the past. In the first few pages there is a continual shift from the present moment of writing, and present tense, to the events of the previous summer which constitute the substance of the novel:

> What do I look like. I wish I was still at the end of the school year, in June, it was boiling hot, my father would stand outside after the news, saying it's about time the weather turned, for the sake of the garden. Yesterday I saw myself in a shoe-shop window, it was pouring with rain, my hair was all over the place, the holidays really are over. I'm ugly with my glasses on. (*Ce qu'ils disent ou rien*, p. 12)

Ce qu'ils disent ou rien deals with a similar trajectory to *Les Armoires vides*, in that the narrator, Anne, is simultaneously changing class through education and discovering her sexuality. There are, however significant differences – of time-scale, setting, thematic emphasis and language. The narrative of *Ce qu'ils disent ou rien* focuses on a period of about six months of Anne's adolescence, whereas *Les Armoires vides* covers the whole of Denise's childhood, adolescence and early adulthood. The representation of the move from working- to middle-class culture is altered by the different perspectives and ages of the fictional narrators. Denise analyses the process from the vantage-point of early adulthood, and the account traces the development of her conflicting and difficult emotions over time, whereas Anne appears to be writing from within the experience of adolescence, just one of the points on the emotional spectrum described by Denise. As a result, *Ce qu'ils disent ou rien* encompasses a narrower range of experience, focusing mainly on the narrator's sexual discoveries, and her alienation from her parents. The linguistic register is also more narrow, in that the novel lacks the sensuous language of the descriptions of childhood of *Les Armoires vides*, and in general is written in a style which although colloquial is less colourful and dramatic than the language of the earlier text. Ernaux has also chosen to set this novel in a small suburban house, which Anne's parents are struggling to buy, and to change the parents' professions: here, the father leaves early in the morning to work as a foreman in a factory, and the mother works part-time in a café in town. *Ce qu'ils disent ou rien* is thus exceptional in the group of texts based on Ernaux's experiences of growing up and changing class, in that it has a clearly fictional setting, and a heroine whose adolescent viewpoint creates a more obvious distance between narrator and author than is the case for the slightly older Denise. If *Les Armoires vides*, as Ernaux's first novel, is an outpouring of the negative experiences and emotions which the change of class has entailed for the writer, *Ce qu'ils disent ou rien* is a variation on the theme, a fictionalised case-study of a particular phase of that experience.

The change from the working-class milieu depicted in all of the other works dealing with childhood and adolescence to a more petit-bourgeois context combines with the adolescent disaffection of the narrator, Anne, to emphasise the mediocrity of the parents. As Lucille Cairns has pointed out, Anne lacks the ability to analyse how material circumstances have curtailed her parents' horizons, demonstrated both by Denise Lesur and to an even greater extent by the auto/biographical first-person narrator of *La Place*, *Une femme* and *La Honte*, and as a result shows them little mercy (Cairns, 1994, p. 73). Although Anne's surroundings are relatively luxurious – her parents' house has a bathroom and television – they lack the contact with the outside world provided by the café and the colourful and sensuous delights of the shop in *Les Armoires vides*. The difference is partly age-related, in that the positive descriptions of the home environment in *Les Armoires vides* are part of the evocation of the more idyllic aspects of the narrator's childhood. However, at adolescence, the problem of excessive proximity is just as great for Anne in her thinly partitioned house as for Denise, and Anne's discomfort is compounded by the dull and mediocre nature of her surroundings. Home for Denise may be a source of shame, but it is less tedious than the silent suburban house in which Anne finds herself imprisoned. Ernaux has perhaps chosen this setting specifically in *Ce qu'ils disent ou rien* in order to emphasise the strong feelings of claustrophobia experienced by Anne. It may also have been easier to express extreme disaffection from the milieu of origin and the parents in a more obviously fictionalised form. Certainly, the effect is to convey an intense impression of a typical adolescent dilemma – the combination of energy, vitality and burgeoning sexuality with lack of material resources and dependency on the confining structures of home and family.

La Femme gelée (translated as *The Frozen Woman*), Ernaux's third novel, published in 1981, describes the heroine's trajectory from a working-class childhood to middle-class femininity. This gendered life-history is recounted more or less chronologically, but although the text lacks the circular structure of the first two novels, the narrator's interventions and commentary ensure that the strategy of writing from a position of hindsight is maintained. Here, as in the previous works, class, gender and sexuality are seen to be closely linked, but the emphasis in *La Femme gelée* is very clearly on the analysis of how Beauvoir's famous phrase 'one is not born, but becomes a woman' is played out in a particular life-history (Beauvoir, 1949, vol. 2, p. 13). Like much women's writing of the 1970s and 1980s, *La Femme gelée* can be read as a literary version of the consciousness-raising group, also typical of the period. It has affinities with the feminist *Bildungsroman*, as defined and discussed by Rita Felski, in that it depicts a gradual process of self-awareness, and the development of feminist understanding of her individual experience by the narrator (Felski, 1989). In this sense the analytical perspective is even more clearly foregrounded than in the previous two novels, as the reader is consistently reminded that the narrator is specifically concerned with the social construction of femininity: 'But I'm following my line of development as a girl and a woman and I know that at least one shadow did not hover over my childhood, the idea that little girls are sweet, weak creatures, inferior to boys. That there are differences in roles' (*La Femme gelée*,

p. 31). As this quotation illustrates, *La Femme gelée* offers a more positive image of working-class women than the previous texts, since it associates the negative aspects of femininity – subservience to the needs of others, imprisonment in domesticity and so on – specifically with middle-class culture (see chapter 3, p. 67). This is reinforced by the chronological narrative structure, which begins with the strong images of womanhood of the narrator's childhood and ends with her full assumption of the role of middle-class wife and mother, providing three meals a day and polishing the furniture. In this sense it can be seen as the beginning of Ernaux's reconciliation with and rehabilitation of her culture of origin. Ironically, in some senses, it is also the point where Ernaux begins to move away from the colloquial register and slang expressions which typify the earlier works, and to adopt a more neutral and classical style.

Unlike the *Bildungsroman* as analysed by Felski, however, *La Femme gelée* is not the history of a liberation. Felski comments that the feminist novel of self-discovery typically begins 'at the stage when the traditional plot of women's lives breaks off, with the attainment of a male sexual partner' (Felski, 1989, p. 128). This stage is described by Felski as 'an image of female alienation', and the subsequent narrative is driven by the desire to overcome this initial, oppressive state of affairs (Felski, 1989, p. 129). The heroine of the feminist *Bildungsroman* typically moves out from the domestic sphere, and after a series of intense and often painful new experiences of the world and of relationships, emerges as a stronger and more self-sufficient person. Ernaux's novel, as its title might suggest, remains frozen in the initial, alienated stage; at the end, the heroine recognises herself as the archetypal frozen woman – 'happily married', mother of two small children, about to resume her career, and the double shift of paid and unpaid work. She sees her future only in terms of the onset of the ageing process, dreading the moment when she will resemble the tired faces of the women she meets at the hairdresser's. Self-awareness, in this case, leads to no moment of triumph. Near the end of the novel, the narrator decides to combat the tedium of her existence, by embarking on 'the only enterprise permitted by everyone, blessed by society and the parents-in-law', a second child. Her comment at this point, 'I will never sink any lower than this', confirms the downward trajectory which the novel depicts (*La Femme gelée*, p. 177). Like the previous two novels, *La Femme gelée* is concerned with denunciation, not reconstruction; as yet there is no way out for the heroines of Ernaux's narratives.

La Place (translated as *A Man's Place* or *Positions*), published in 1984, marks a turning point in Ernaux's writing, in terms of both content and form. A discussion of the change of tone and mode of representation of working-class culture, as well as the full adoption of the auto/biographical voice, is provided in chapter 2. P. M. Wetherill's account of the slow genesis of *La Place* indicates the significance of the narrative structure finally arrived at (Wetherill, 1987). Because of this, and the importance of *La Place* in the development of Ernaux's writing, the structure of the text merits some attention here. Again, circularity is a notable feature, with the text beginning and ending at the same point – the father's death. As in *Les Armoires vides*, the main body of the text, in this case an account of the father's life, is in some way explanatory of the emotional disjuncture and physical crisis described in the opening section; towards the end of the introduction, Ernaux comments on her feelings in the train on the way home, and during the months immediately following her father's death, commenting that the cultural and social distance between them could be compared to separation from a loved one. The text which follows is both an attempt to understand and explain this distance, and an expression of Ernaux's desire for love and closeness to her father. It is, as she says 'too late' and perhaps too difficult for the relationship to become close again, but the text, which unlike real life is able to focus almost entirely on the positive aspects, can become a substitute, an idealised reconstruction. The fact that descriptions of the narrator's experience of his final days and of her relationship with him are 'wrapped round' the account of the father's life, seems to justify fully the use of the term 'auto/biographical' to describe *La Place* (see note 2 and chapter 2, p. 30). Although I would not agree with Warren Motte, who argues that Ernaux has written her father 'out of the story', it can be argued that *La Place* tells us as much about Ernaux's own life as it does about her father (Motte, 1995, p. 65).[7]

Further features which distinguish *La Place* from its precedents are brevity, economy and the spacing of the text on the page. Both the narrative structure and the language have been pared down, and in *La Place* Ernaux finally abandons the slang and colloquialisms of the first two novels. Even in comparison with the already more classical French of *La Femme gelée*, the register is more neutral and impersonal and the detailed descriptions more factual in tone. The colloquial phrases and expressions used by the parents are marked out by the use of italics or quotation marks.[8] Whilst the first three texts are characterised by a dense and continuous narrative, in *La Place* Ernaux develops the technique of leaving spaces at significant points in the text. Thus, at the beginning of the work, there is a long gap after the initial section which describes Ernaux's success in the practical test for the C.A.P. E.S. (secondary level teaching qualification). The section which follows describes how, two months later, her father died. Here a paragraph is followed by a space, then a single sentence: 'It was on a Sunday, in the middle of the afternoon.' This sentence is isolated by a second space, followed by a section recounting the events of the afternoon of her father's death. The isolation on the page of the sentence giving the precise time of her father's death emphasises how this event effectively cuts Ernaux's life into two halves, how after this loss nothing will ever be the same; in the final pages of *La Place* she describes herself reading de Beauvoir's *Les Mandarins* during her father's illness: 'I couldn't get involved in my reading, at a certain page of this thick book my father would no longer be alive' (p. 108). From *La Place* onwards Ernaux is increasingly concerned with the subjective experience of time, the attempt to record the significance of particular dates and times (see the discussion of *Passion simple* below, and chapter 4). The description of the days which followed her father's death, the funeral and the apparent resumption of normality (pp. 15–22) is divided into sections by spaces, the most significant of which separates this narrative from Ernaux's reflections in the train on the way home. A gap of almost half a page separates Ernaux's statement of her intention to write in a simple, unadorned style ('l'écriture plate') from the start of the narrative of her father's life: 'The story begins a few months before the start of the twentieth century, in a village of the pays de Caux' (*La Place*, p. 24). This technique, the separation of the narrative from the metatext commenting on the writing process by the insertion of spaces on the page, is consistent throughout *La Place*, as well as becoming a hallmark of Ernaux's style, reproduced in later texts such as *Une femme* and *Passion simple*.

The narrative of the father's life ends on page 100 with the poignant phrase: 'He enjoyed life more and more.' After a space, the writing resumes with commentary on the present moment of writing, which slips almost imperceptibly into the account of the father's final days. Here Ernaux recounts the period immediately preceding the death, thus completing the narrative of the death and funeral at the beginning of the text. This account ends with the repetition of her mother's phrase 'It's over', which reinforces the impression of circularity. Ernaux concludes in a sentence which again is isolated on the page that she too has finished 'unearthing the inheritance which I had to leave at the threshold when I entered the middle-class, educated world' (*La Place*, p. 111). There follows a series of anecdotes, which share the theme of education; in the first Ernaux recounts a visit to the town library with her father at the age of twelve. Her father allows her to pronounce the request for books, but both of them are taken aback when asked what kind of books they would like to borrow. Without elaborating on the shame and discomfiture which this lack of *savoir-faire* induced, Ernaux notes with characteristic economy: 'We never returned to the library. My mother had to return the books, perhaps, late' (*La Place*, p. 112). Then, after a space, three sentences, separated on the page, create three images: the first, the father taking his daughter to school on his bicycle, like Charon conveying travellers from one bank of the river Styx to the other. Then, her father's pride that she could belong to the world which had scorned him. Finally, a popular song he used to sing about a rowing boat going round and round.[9] On the next page Ernaux remembers her discouragement when trying to read a difficult, metaphysical text. The sentence which follows returns us to the present moment of writing, as Ernaux notes the feeling of unreality generated by her work as a teacher, correcting students' work and providing model essays. After a large space, the final anecdote, dated October of the previous year, closes the book; Ernaux encounters an ex-pupil working at the till of a supermarket. The girl assumes incorrectly that Ernaux remembers which vocational course she had taken, and comments that 'it didn't work out' (*La Place*, p. 114). As Ernaux says goodbye, the girl resumes her work, picking up the items purchased with her left hand, tapping in the prices with the right.

The cumulative effect of these anecdotes is twofold: the story of the library, the cycling to school, the song, and Ernaux's dispirited feelings faced with a difficult book, or her current educational work, all serve to emphasise the indelible links between her and her father and culture of origin. In these images, she is either physically close to her father, and socially categorised with him, or experiencing the same difficulties which he had in relation to education: feelings of discouragement and unreality. This sense of unity is underlined by the parallel between the father, physically conveying his daughter from one culture to another, and Ernaux herself who, in writing *La Place*, is providing a passage from one (cultural and social) place to another.[10] However, the final story cuts through these images of wholeness and solidarity, to emphasise the distance between Ernaux, her ex-pupil, and by extension her father and class.[11] Ernaux returns in this passage to the professional status as a teacher which she acquired in the opening passage of the book. The last line of *La Place* leaves the reader with the image of the girl's hands, carrying out a tedious and repetitive task, and a strong sense of the difference between Ernaux's status as an intellectual and the oppressive nature of manual work.[12] In this choice of closure, Ernaux is true to her expressed desire to emphasise the social rather than the personal, the material reality of oppression (see chapter 2, p. 38). Thus *La Place* begins and ends with two losses, two deaths: just as her father has given up the life 'he enjoyed more and more', Ernaux has left behind the culture she appreciates more and more, in order to enter another world, that of the educated, professional bourgeoisie. In both cases, there is no possibility of return; the circle is closed.

In contrast to the long gestation of *La Place*, Ernaux wrote *Une femme* (published in 1988 and translated as *A Woman's Story*) in the ten months after her mother's death. *Une femme* can be seen as a parallel text to *La Place*, in that it deals with her mother's life, and Ernaux's grief for her mother. The circular structure of *La Place* is repeated here, with the mother's death opening and closing the text. In contrast to the preamble recounting an episode of Ernaux's own life which opens *La Place*, *Une femme* begins with an abrupt and shocking sentence – 'My mother died on Monday, the seventh of April in the geriatrics unit of the Pontoise hospital, where I had placed her two years previously' (*Une femme*, p. 11). The description of the funeral which follows maintains this neutral and detached tone, forming a kind of first chapter. This is followed by a second, shorter section (pp. 20–3) where Ernaux describes her emotional response in more detail, and finally, her intentions in writing *Une femme*. The main narrative begins, as in *La Place*, with a marker of location; whilst in the former case the father's life is located in time, here the mother's existence is situated geographically in the small Normandy town of Yvetot, 'a cold town, built on a windswept plateau between Rouen and Le Havre' (*Une femme*, p. 24). At the end of the account, after a single sentence, isolated on the page ('now everything is connected'), Ernaux notes the time of writing, the end of February 1987. A series of images follows: Ernaux herself as a geriatric patient in the next century, a dream where she is floating in a river, physically merged with her mother, moments of believing that her mother is still alive, sewing in the living-room. On the penultimate page Ernaux then describes her unwillingness to accept any new information about her mother, whom she remembers as the 'large, white shadow' of her childhood. The penultimate paragraph discusses the nature of the text, and its effect of making Ernaux feel 'less alone and artificial in the world of words and ideas' (*Une femme*, p. 106). Ernaux concludes that she has lost not only her mother but 'the last link with the world I came from'.

As this account makes clear, *Une femme* is similar to *La Place* in that the story of the parent's life is enclosed by descriptions which foreground the writer herself, and the writing process. Again the circular structure emphasises the inevitability of death, and of the cultural separation which the text recounts. There are, however, significant differences. The intensity of the mother–daughter relationship is a constant theme of *Une femme*, so that the account of the mother's life is interspersed with powerful images of the closeness and hostility between the two women. The result is a difference in tone, and thematic emphasis: *Une femme* is perhaps inevitably the more personal of the two texts, since the mother figure is too psychologically important to be depicted on a purely social level. Whereas *La Place* begins and ends with Ernaux in her professional role as a teacher, *Une femme* begins with the depiction of the narrator in an intensely private moment, her mother's funeral. As I have indicated above, the closure is marked by a series of images from dreams and fantasies, in contrast to the memories of real events which conclude *La Place*, emphasising the primordial place of the mother in the writer's subconscious (see chapter 4). The titles are in this sense appropriate: *La Place* is concerned with social place – that which is imposed, and that which, with a resulting sense of guilt and betrayal, is chosen. *Une femme*, on the other hand, describes not only the separation of social and cultural hierarchies, but the connections between women, in this case through the mother–daughter bond. In this sense it is concerned both with the mother as 'histoire' and as an ahistorical image of maternity and the feminine. In Ernaux's own words: 'Of course she was my mother so it's autobiographical. But at the same time I did not simply want to recount my mother's story. This is exactly why it's called *Une femme* and not *ma mère*' (Bacholle, 1998, p. 143). These many levels of contradiction, invoked by the opening quotation from Hegel, close the text: 'everything is connected' (p. 103), and yet Ernaux has *lost* the last link with her world of origin (p. 106).

The publication of *Passion simple* (translated as *Simple Passion* or *Passion Perfect*) in 1992 can be seen as a second turning point in Ernaux's writing, in that here she abandons her own and her parents' histories, in order to focus on a phase of her life as a mature adult. In *Passion simple* Ernaux leaves behind the small Normandy town in which she grew up, and which has figured with varying degrees of fictionalisation in all the texts up to this point. The first-person narrator of *Passion simple* is a teacher, living in the Paris region, in effect the person whose development has been traced from various points of view in the previous five texts. The topic – passionate and obsessive love – in its adult, rather than adolescent form, is also new, and as the study of Ernaux's critical reception in chapter 6 will indicate, daring, in an auto/biographical text by a French woman writer in her fifties (see also chapter 2, p. 51). However, there are continuities on the level of both theme and form. *Passion simple*, like *La Place* and *Une femme*, is concerned with separation from a significant other, and with the process of grieving. A discussion of the extent to which *Passion simple* can be read as a more positive representation of female desire than *La Femme gelée* is provided in chapter 3 (pp. 67–72).

The narrative structure of *Passion simple* is broadly chronological, rather than circular, in that it follows the course of the relationship depicted. However, the emphasis is on continuity of a state of mind rather than chronology, since there are few actual events. The short introduction, a kind of prologue describing a pornographic film seen on a satellite channel, is not causatively linked to the main narrative in the same way as the introductions to *Les Armoires vides* or *Ce qu'ils disent ou rien*. Unlike *Les Armoires vides*, the narrative of *Passion simple* is not motivated by an expressed desire to understand or explain an initial crisis, but rather by the project of 'objective' description also enunciated in *La Place* and *Une femme*: 'I don't want to explain my passion – this would mean seeing it as a mistake or a disorder which I would have to justify – but simply to describe it' (*Passion simple*, p. 32). The introduction itself is, however, thematically linked to the main body of the text, in that it raises the question of the representation of the erotic, and of the links between the experience of sexual passion and literature (see Ernaux's 'Fragments autour de Philippe V.', 1996; translated in appendix 1). It also contains the statement of authorial intention, and recommendation of a particular mode of reading, which since *La Place,* and the full adoption of the auto/biographical voice, have become *de rigueur* for Ernaux (see chapter 2). In this case, Ernaux argues, perhaps optimistically, that writing should aspire to produce a suspension of moral judgement.

The narrative which follows, like those of *La Place* and *Une femme,* is punctuated by spaces on the page and reflections on the writing process. Again, the language is plain and classical, and flowery or metaphorical description is avoided; even the lover is referred to simply as 'A.'. The emphasis is on the almost clinical depiction of nuances of feeling and their links with, or location in, material reality. The text can be divided into three main sections: the time of the passion – pages 13 to 51, the time of grief – pages 52 to 66, and the time of recovery and writing – pages 66 to 77. There are overlaps, in that the time of writing is referred to at earlier stages, such as the passage quoted above, and the final section includes the description of A.'s final, unexpected visit. Apart from the reflections on writing which mainly use the present tense, the first two sections use the imperfect tense almost exclusively, emphasising the duration of a particular state of affairs – here, passionate love. In her stimulating analysis of *Passion simple* Marrone refers to Ernaux's use of the imperfect as the 'passion tense', associating it with the attempt both 'to break out of grammatical and narrative boundaries', and the boundaries of time itself (Marrone, 1994, pp. 81–2). The separation of this phase of life and state of mind from 'normality', as well as the attempt to step outside the experience in order to describe, or enumerate, are further emphasised by the use of lists, indented on the page and in lower case, describing Ernaux's habitual behaviour at the time (pp. 14, 27–30, 54). In the final section, A.'s isolated final visit, which occurs outside the time of the passion, is recounted in the tense used for single events in the past – the perfect. The use of tense, along with the spacing on the page, and narrative structure as a whole, seem to create two temporal and thematic levels – the stages, and time of the passion, and the process and time of writing. In this sense, both the form and content of *Passion simple* can be seen as an intensified version of the reflection on the relationship between writing and experience which begins with *La Place*. The subjective experience of time is a crucial aspect of this reflection. Within the passion, time is either, in the lover's absence, to be filled with aimless activity, or in his presence, impossible to hold on to, already lost. In the process of writing, on the contrary, this double-edged loss of time is to be combated in a hopeless but determined struggle to save, to preserve: 'The imperfect tense which I used spontaneously from the opening lines is the tense of duration, of a period of time which I did not want to end' (*Passion simple*, p. 61).

The desire to preserve and record can also be seen as a motivating force in *Journal du dehors* (translated as *Exteriors*), published in 1993, though in this case, in yet another new departure, it is contemporary social reality, rather than her own close relationships, history and emotional life which Ernaux seeks to save from oblivion. The text is a record of an everyday life, its material location in Paris and Cergy, a nearby new town, and its social context, depicted through encounters with others, in the supermarket or the metro. The diary form which is adopted, with the text divided into years (from 1985 to 1992), is also a new departure, in that *Journal du dehors*, even more than the three previous texts, foregrounds the present and the writing self, the subjectivity which 'like a prostitute' is traversed by 'people, their existence' (*Journal du dehors*, p. 69). The diary form also entails an abandonment of the careful structuring of a single narrative which characterises the earlier texts, particularly from *La Place* onwards: in *Journal du dehors* the reader is presented with a series of fragments, some of which simply recount a story or describe a scene, whereas others lead to analysis and commentary of an almost Barthesian kind.[13]

In *Passion simple* Ernaux described how the experience of passion had made her more able to identify with the vulnerabilities and follies of others (*Passion simple*, p. 76). *Journal du dehors* can be seen as the literary consequence of this experience, in that the exploration of the boundaries, or lack of them, between self and other which began in *Passion simple* is here pursued in relation to the public, rather than private sphere. A further continuity with *La Place*, *Une femme* and *Passion simple* is the concern with memory and the subjective experience of time. In *Journal du dehors* Ernaux suggests that the narrative of a life can be divided into phases, not only by life events themselves, but by the social and material context in which the life is lived: 'This morning I was looking at

Saint Lazare station, its glass roof, the birds which criss-cross it. Nine years of my life will be closed by a change in the route from Cergy to Paris, there will be the time of the Cergy–Paris train, and the time of the RER line A' (*Journal du dehors*, p. 75). As in *La Place*, memory is also described as located in or triggered by present realities; in a passage where she describes how the sight of an adolescent young man and a woman with a small boy in the train take her back to two different moments of her life, Ernaux concludes: 'So it's outside, in the passengers on the metro or the RER, the people on the escalators of the Galeries Lafayette and Auchan that my past existence is contained' (*Journal du dehors*, p. 107).[14] In this sense the diary of a life 'from the outside' which is constructed in *Journal du dehors* is also a diary of the inside; it could be argued that the question of boundaries, in space and time, between self and other, inner life and external social reality – in fact, the nature of subjectivity itself – is the link between the apparent fragments (see note 6). I will develop this point in my analysis of Ernaux's representations of space and the body in chapter 3, and of identity, femininity and loss in chapter 4.

Journal du dehors is also an expression of the general importance of social context in Ernaux's writing, and her diary of 'the outside' is as sensitive to social injustices and inequalities as the texts describing her own and her parents' experiences as members of the dominated class. Here the poor and destitute are brought into literature, but from the perspective of someone who has herself experienced deprivation, and whose present material security at times seems rather unreal.[15] The narrating voice always identifies with those whose public behaviour is outside the norms of bourgeois politeness, and indicative of a level of powerlessness where these norms become irrelevant. On the other hand, middle-class culture, including its more bohemian expressions, is subjected to acerbic irony, particularly when the language and self-representations of members of the milieu are contradicted by their evident material privileges. Thus Ernaux observes a woman writer at a book launch in central Paris announcing that 'writing is a choice to lose every-thing'; the absurdity of this statement is implied by its juxtaposition with a description of the woman's material, physical and social accoutrements – red curly hair, violet shawl, bangles and rings – to say nothing of loyal publisher at her side and attentive audience (*Journal du dehors*, p. 94). As in this instance, the importance of the material reality of people's lives, 'la matérialité de la vie' (p. 56), is never underestimated; detailed observation of the interaction between individuals and the contemporary urban environment serves not only to create a strong impression of the latter, but also to reveal the mythical and symbolic importance attributed to material objects. It is in this sense, and in the consistent analysis of the ideological subtexts of contemporary cultural phenomena, that a continuity with Roland Barthes's *Mythologies* can be observed. Buying meat at the butcher's, for example, becomes 'a ritual consecrating the conviviality of this food heavy with blood, the family, the repeated happiness of Sundays spent round the table' (*Journal du dehors*, p. 41).

After a gap of four years Ernaux published two texts in January 1997: *La Honte* (*Shame*) and *'Je ne suis pas sortie de ma nuit'* (*'My Night is not Over'*). There is also a thematic gap between these two texts and the two which immediately precede them, since both return to the subject matter of earlier works: *'Je ne suis pas sortie de ma nuit'* to *Une femme*, and *La Honte* particularly to *Une femme* and *La Place*, but arguably also to *Les Armoires vides*. As the title suggests, *La Honte* is a systematic exploration of the feelings of shame and inferiority described in all of these earlier works. Here, however, Ernaux reveals their most profound cause as the event which triggers the narrative, and which hitherto has been perhaps the most significant absence of Ernaux's work: her observation, at the age of twelve of an argument between her parents, which led to her father attempting to kill her mother. In this sense *La Honte* can be read as an answer to the question posed in *Les Armoires vides*: 'Good God, at what point in time, on which day did I start to think the walls looked shabby, the chamber pot stank, the old men were nothing more than drunks, the dregs?' (*Les Armoires vides*, p. 50; trans. p. 33). The structure of *La Honte* can also be seen as a revisiting of earlier work, since it combines the circularity of *La Place* and *Une femme*, and the crisis followed by explanation structure of *Les Armoires vides*. However, *La Honte* also represents a development, in that its structure seems to differentiate it as far as possible from fictional narrative, and on the contrary, to resemble the systematic review of information and critical perspectives found in an academic essay. In his review of the book, Vilain comments: 'Thus the narrative does not simply follow the chrono-logical order – as was the case for *La Place* and *Une femme* – but digs through stratified layers where memories of shame, images of childhood and the archives of the year 1952 are superimposed on each other, like a palimpsest' (Vilain, 1997b, p. 112). *La Honte* is divided into four chapters; the first describes the scene which triggers the narrative, and which for a long time Ernaux believed to be the source of all her writing (*La Honte*, p. 30). It then goes on to investigate the 'traces matérielles' (photographs, postcards and so on) which Ernaux retains of the year in question, as well as the local newspaper (*Paris-Normandie*) of the time. At this point, the search for the past through data is abandoned; Ernaux states her aims in writing *La Honte*, and the technique she will adopt: in the face of the inadequacies of memory and of material remains, she will attempt to find her twelve-year-old self by describing the codes and values which defined the school, home and milieu in which she existed, and by which she lived at the time.

Chapters 2 and 3 are the fulfilment of this aim. Chapter 2 begins with a systematic investigation of the space which the twelve-year-old Ernaux inhabited, with a gradual narrowing of focus: from the region to the town – Yvetot – to the part of the town inhabited by the family (*le quartier*), to the home itself – the parents' grocery shop and café (see chapter 3, p. 59). Ernaux then turns from the spatial to the linguistic and cultural universe – the language of the milieu, the codes governing the behaviour of men and women, the popular understanding of time with its emphasis on passive acceptance of routine, and the self-imposed policing of behaviour and manners. The movement into increasingly narrow and confined space of the first part of the chapter reflects and reinforces the sense of claustrophobia created by the description of the culture in the second part, compared by Ernaux to 'that indefinable heaviness, the impression of closure which I feel in my dreams' (*La Honte*, p. 69). In chapter 3 she turns to the world of the private Catholic school which she attended, beginning again with a description of its spaces and their social functions and meaning. This is followed by a list of the school rules, and a discussion of the merging of education and religion which was the hallmark of the school. The relationship to time created by the events of the school calendar parallels the description of popular customs and routines in chapter 2. Again the same narrowing of focus can be observed: from the school, its spaces, customs and codes to the class and class teacher, and finally to the twelve-year-old herself, her desires for the body and dress style of a woman, and her mother, who bases the child's upbringing on the precepts of religion and the school.

The final chapter is both the narrative and analytical conclusion of the work: in the first sense, it returns to the period immediately following the initial crisis, describing the events of the time which are coloured by the newly acquired sense of shame. In particular, Ernaux describes a coach trip to Lourdes with her father, omitted from *La Place*, perhaps being too closely linked to the then indescribable scene of one Sunday in June 1952. In some ways this account is a development of the library visit recounted at the end of *La Place*. Again, father and daughter are united by feelings of helplessness and shame in the face of customs and contexts which make them aware of the inferiority reflected by their clothes and manners. On the level of analysis, Ernaux concludes that her investigation of the codes and conventions of home and school has demonstrated how the scene she witnessed simply could not fit in, or be contained by, either universe:

> We ceased to belong to the category of respectable people, who don't drink or fight, who put on clean clothes to go into town. It was no good having a new overall at the start of each school year, a beautiful missal, being first in everything and saying my prayers, I wasn't like the other girls in the class any more. I had seen what I should not have seen. (*La Honte*, p. 108)

The final paragraphs of the work are a typical closure for Ernaux, in that they bring the reader back to the writing self, and to the time of writing. The commentary on contemporary events developed in *Journal du dehors* is again deployed here, as Ernaux remarks on the superficial use of the word 'shame' by journalists describing the quickly forgotten tragedies of Sarajevo and Rwanda. The final paragraph returns to the photograph taken of Ernaux and her father on the trip to Lourdes, and in a passage reminiscent of the closure of *Une femme*, to the attempt to make links between present and past which is fundamental to Ernaux's writing and identity.

In *'Je ne suis pas sortie de ma nuit'* (*'My Night is not Over'*), after a short contextualising introduction which gives a rationale for their publication, Ernaux has published the notes she wrote during her mother's slow decline and death from Alzheimer's disease. They are presented in diary form and, Ernaux claims, 'as they were written' (*'Je ne suis pas sortie de ma nuit'*, p. 13). Ernaux's technique of invoking emotional and symbolic meanings through the detailed description, *sans commentaire*, of material reality, leads here to the inclusion of every aspect of this decline, and of the institutionalised context in which her mother ended her life. The shocking nature of some of these descriptions, delivered in Ernaux's plain and unadorned style, caused some disquiet among critics (see chapter 6, p. 149). In the introduction Ernaux describes how she is quite intentionally disrupting the coherence arrived at in *Une femme* by this publication: 'I now believe that the unity, the coherence arrived at by a work – regardless of the extent to which there has been a desire to take into account contradictory elements – must be threatened whenever the opportunity arises' ('*Je ne suis pas sortie de ma nuit*', p. 12). This view in itself contradicts earlier statements (see chapter 2), and is perhaps a reflection, not only of Ernaux's awareness of contemporary critical theory, but also of her position as an established author with an impressive corpus of work behind her: the need to attain perfection in a single text is perhaps mitigated by a greater sense of freedom, manifested in part by the intertextual links and self-referential commentary which are now possible. Ernaux's own comments seem to confirm this: 'And afterwards, [after *La Place* and *Une femme*] I felt a great sense of freedom, which I still have, in relation to existing literary forms' (IN). *La Honte* can be read, similarly, as a 'disruption' of *La Place* and *Une femme*, and as I have already argued, as an answer to some of the questions posed by *Les Armoires vides*.

The introduction to '*Je ne suis pas sortie de ma nuit*' also includes the customary indication of an appropriate or desired mode of reading: 'These pages will in no case be read as an objective, eye-witness account of long-term geriatric care, even less as a denunciation (the majority of the nurses were caring and attentive), but simply as the remaining traces of the pain' ('*Je ne suis pas sortie de ma nuit*', p. 13). In the main body of the text, comments on the writing process are relatively rare, but significant when they do occur. At one point Ernaux comments that this is not literature, and that it is different from the other books she has written; she then corrects herself, concluding that all her writing is motivated by the same desire to save, to preserve ('*Je ne suis pas sortie de ma nuit*', p. 94; see also chapter 2, p. 46). This desire, both in writing and in lived experience, is, as I will argue in more detail in chapters 2, 3 and 4, fundamental to Ernaux's work; in '*Je ne suis pas sortie de ma nuit*' it perhaps reaches its most acute form, since the life which Ernaux describes herself nurturing and cherishing has reached a humiliating level of debilitation. The title itself is illustrative of this poignant and hopeless struggle, since these were the last words written by Ernaux's mother in a letter to a friend, Paulette (p. 18). Although clearly lacking the tight structure of its precedents, *'Je ne suis pas sortie de ma nuit'* is drawn together by this and other significant themes: the mother–daughter relationship, time, memory, ageing and death. The image of herself as an old woman, which concludes *La Femme gelée* and figures in *Journal du dehors* (p. 83), is here omnipresent, and in *'Je ne suis pas sortie de ma nuit'*, more than in any of the other texts of bereavement, Ernaux contemplates not only her mother's but her own death. Appropriately, in the light of this, there can be no neat closure: the text ends abruptly in the midst of overwhelming grief.

In chapter 2 I will focus on the authorial interventions in the text which, as is clear from this analysis, are characteristic of Ernaux's writing, particularly from *La Place* onwards. The version of the auto/biographical 'I' which they construct, as well as the modes of reading which they implicitly recommend, will be the focus of this discussion.

Notes

1. See chapter 3, pp. 57–58. For a discussion of realism in Ernaux's writing, particularly *La Place* and *Une femme*, see McIlvanney, 1992. McIlvanney enumerates the realist features of the texts, finding some similarities with nineteenth-century realism. In her conclusion, however, she notes that Ernaux's writing differentiates itself from the latter through its awareness of the class hierarchies expressed through literary forms. In anthologies/ histories of women's writing, such as Holmes, 1996, Ernaux is often classified as a realist. This is perhaps in part determined by the dominance of feminine writing (*écriture féminine*) in anglophone discussions of contemporary French women's writing (see Thomas and Webb, 1999). A binary opposition between the latter's revolutionary approach to language and 'realist' writers is constructed. In fact, Ernaux consistently problematises the concept of realism (see chapter 2), and as we will see in this and subsequent chapters, also uses a number of anti-realist techniques in her writing.

2. As I have already indicated, in some of Ernaux's works, particularly *La Place* and *Une femme*, the boundary between these two thematic strands and between autobiography and biography, is unclear (see preface and chapter 2, p. 30). Nancy K. Miller has also commented on the inevitable blurring of these boundaries in accounts of a parent's life: 'But when the biographical subject is a member of one's own family, the line between the genres blurs' (Miller, 1996, p. 2).

3. The *nouveau roman*: an experimental form of the novel developed in the 1950s and 1960s by writers such as Nathalie Sarraute, Alain Robbe-Grillet and Robert Pinget. Marguerite Duras is also sometimes included in this group. The *nouveau roman* questions conventional notions of realism, characterisation and narrative structure.

4. Both Garaud and Jones have commented on the circularity of *La Place* (see also notes 6 and 7 below). Garaud finds the circularity 'at first sight, depressing' (Garaud, 1994, p. 204). He also cites Ernaux's own comment: 'As for the circularity of *La Place*, it imposed itself as an internal necessity. All my books are closed worlds, alas! There is no way out' (Ernaux in interview with Jean-Jacques Gibert, 'Le Silence ou la Trahison', *Révolution*, 260, 22 February, 1985, cited in Garaud, 1994, p. 212, note 9).

5. The title of *Les Armoires vides* is taken from the quotation from Eluard's *La Rose publique* which is the epigraph to the novel:

   J'ai conservé de faux trésors dans des armoires vides
   Un navire inutile joint mon enfance à mon ennui
   Mes jeux à la fatigue

   (I have preserved false treasures in empty cupboards
   A useless vessel joins my childhood to my disillusionment
   My games to weariness)

6. This technique of bringing many voices into the text is an important feature of Ernaux's style and literary project (see note 8, below, chapter 3 p. 82 and chapter 4 p. 93). One is reminded of Bakhtin's notion of the polyphonic text, and of the contemporary discussion of relationality in auto/biographical writing (see Smith and Watson, eds, 1998; Bakhtin, 1981 cited in Lechte, 1994, pp. 9–10).

7. Garaud comments 'One realises that this account of a father's life, which was supposed to emerge from the collection of

"objective" signs, has become a kind of self-analysis' (Garaud, 1994, p. 202).

8. An interesting discussion of this technique is provided by Christian Garaud, who concludes that, despite her claims to the contrary, Ernaux's citation of words and phrases emanating from her culture of origin is far from objective. He argues that the context and placing of the citations in effect rehabilitates expressions which could appear clichéd or banal, lending them the status of meaningful aphorisms. He also contrasts this with the ironic treatment of bourgeois culture. For a discussion of the issue of objectivity in *La Place* see chapter 2 (Garaud, 1994, p. 211).

9. Tony Jones sees a parallel between the repetitive nature of the ex-pupil's work and the image of the boat 'going round and round' in the song. He also sees a link between the comparison of Ernaux's father with the ferryman and the song (Day and Jones, p. 30). One might add that the boat's movement in the song reflects the circularity of the whole text. In a sense, here, Ernaux has allowed herself a metaphor; significantly her source is popular culture, so that the reference to the song can be read as an attempt to make links between the two worlds, and a reinforcement of the positive nature of this part of the final section of *La Place*.

10. See Garaud, 1994, p. 204 on this point: 'The narrator finds no other solution in writing than to serve as an intermediary between the world she grew up in (. . .) and the world she has chosen (. . .)'.

11. Jones also provides a detailed analysis of the final pages of *La Place*. He arrives at the opposite conclusion, on the basis of his reading of some of Ernaux's comments, and the significance he attributes to the change of adverb to describe the mother's pronouncement of 'c'est fini' ('it's over') from 'd'une voix neutre' (in a neutral voice) at the beginning, to 'doucement' (gently) at the end: 'The shift is from negative to positive, from detachment to involvement, and from separation to union' (Day and Jones, 1990, p. 32). Garaud, on the other hand, comments on the final scene in the supermarket: 'The circle closes: there is no way out, for Ernaux or her former pupil' (Garaud, 1994, p. 204). However, this comment is followed by an analysis of the more positive elements of the final pages, specifically the description of the father taking his daughter to school.

Garaud finds a contradictory and ambiguous nostalgia in this image, which in his view undermines the pessimistic ending.

12. The inequality of manual and intellectual work is often represented by descriptions of the hands of those confined to the former (see particularly the description of the African worker's hands in *Journal du dehors*, p. 44, as well as *Journal du dehors*, p. 25 and *La Place*, p. 88).

13. Nancy K. Miller has also noted the similarity between Ernaux's text and Barthes's *Mythologies* (Miller, 1998). In this piece, entitled 'Autobiographical Others', she provides an interesting discussion of the 'others in the text' in relation to *Journal du dehors*.

14. The RER is the regional express train service which since the late 1980s has linked the centre of Paris with the Paris region. Galeries Lafayette is a department store and Auchan is a hypermarket.

15. For a full discussion of Ernaux's feelings of material insecurity, and of the significance of the material world in her writing, see chapter 3, pp. 55–57.

2

Ernaux's Auto/biographical Pact: The Author and the Reader in the Text

From Autobiographical Fiction to Auto/ biographical Pact

*P*hilippe Lejeune's *Le Pacte autobiographique,* published in 1975, still exerts a significant influence in discussions of autobiography, despite the fact that it has been subjected to numerous critiques, including those of Lejeune himself (Lejeune, 1986). For Sheringham, for instance, the publication of *Le Pacte autobiographique* is the beginning of 'serious attention to the genre' in France (Sheringham, 1993, p. 20). Definitions of autobiography, such as those proposed by Lejeune, are perhaps inevitably ill-fated at a moment in literary history characterised by attempts to question and subvert the conventions of genre. In this sense, Ernaux's work is in tune with the times. We do not find in her writing the characteristics associated with autobiography in its most classic form: the exemplary life, the momentous turning points, the cohesive sense of self, and the conclusion written with the benefit of hindsight. The identity described is more tentative, its textual presentation more fragmented than is the case for more conventional exponents of the genre, such as Beauvoir. Texts such as *Passion simple,* for example, deal with an aspect or episode of the author's life, rather than its totality (see Marrone, 1994, p. 78). In some of the texts the emphasis is not even on Ernaux's own life: *La Place* and *Une femme* focus respectively on her father's and mother's lives, and *Journal du dehors* on the author's experience of contemporary social reality, as it is embodied in chance encounters in the train and supermarket. As I have already indicated (preface, note 1), I have followed the spelling which Laura Marcus adopts in her recent book on theories of autobiography – *Auto/biographical Discourses* – in order to emphasise the lack of clear boundaries between biography and autobiography in Ernaux's writing from *La Place* onwards (Marcus, 1994). Here, this spelling may also serve to indicate that although Ernaux's work is indisputably auto biographical, deviations from the form, such as those mentioned above, prevent the texts from falling into the category of autobiography in the most classic, and narrow, sense of the term.

At this point, it is nonetheless useful to return to Lejeune: 'What defines autobiography, for the person reading it, is above all a contract regarding the author's identity, a contract which is sealed by the use of the real name' (Lejeune, 1975, p. 33). As this suggests, the defining feature of autobiography for Lejeune at the time of writing *Le Pacte autobiographique* was the coincidence of name and identity of the author-narrator-character, and the effect that this had on the reader, or mode of reading. In this sense it is possible to differentiate between Ernaux's first two novels, *Les Armoires vides* and *Ce qu'ils disent ou rien*, and the rest of her work. In these two texts narratorial and authorial voices do not coincide, despite the autobiographical material on which both are based. The narrator of *Les Armoires vides*, who is named as Denise Lesur, is a young woman of about twenty, and in *Ce qu'ils disent ou rien*, the heroine, Anne, is fifteen. There is a clear distance between these narrators and the author, who was in her early thirties at the time of writing. The fact that the narrators are named reinforces the reader's view of them as 'characters', and confirms the fictional nature of these works. Ernaux has commented that there were two decisive moments in her work: the initial choice to adhere to the novelistic form – 'le moment où je m'inscris dans une forme romanesque' – and the subsequent change to an openly auto/biographical 'I', with the writing of *La Place*: 'Ever since *La Place*, which is a real turning point in my writing (. . .) the "I" and the name on the cover, according to Lejeune's definition, are the same, without there really being an explicit pact. But in my opinion the pact is self-evident in the mode of writing itself' (IN). This view is, however, not universal among the critics of Ernaux's work. P. M. Wetherill's detailed account of the process of writing *La Place* over a period of years, from 1976 to 1982, leads him to the conclusion that 'the narrator is not to be confused with the author' (Wetherill, 1987, p. 34). Warren Motte, on the other hand, arrives at the opposite conclusion; for

him, the 'I' in *La Place* 'continually questions the theoretical dis-
sociation of narrator and author' (Motte, 1995, p. 55). For this
reason, Motte argues that the text is close to the discursive mode
of autobiography, which he sees as one of the boundaries of 'the
hybrid domain of autofiction'.

It may be useful at this point to clarify my own position. In
pointing to the difference between the 'I' of the first two texts and
the 'I' of *La Place* and subsequent work, I am far from denying the
nature of the auto/biographical 'I' as textual construct. Auto/
biography is clearly just as carefully constructed as any other
literary text; the gap between reality and its representation in
language is as much, if not more, in evidence here as in other
genres. In this sense Wetherill is quite right to point out the
difference between 'author' and 'narrator'. Nonetheless, auto/
biographical writing does have its own codes and conventions,
which in turn generate expectations and modes of reading
particular to the genre. It is largely thanks to Lejeune that the
concept of the reader has been introduced into the discussion, and
it is in part for this reason that his work is relevant here, given my
own interest in the reception of Ernaux's work (see chapter 5). My
aim at this point is to differentiate between different kinds of textual
construction of the 'I', and to point to the evolution of Ernaux's
texts from this point of view. Ernaux's own struggle with this issue
is a major focus of my analysis of her authorial interventions in
this chapter.

Ironically, as I have suggested, it is at the point when she turns
her attention away from her own life, to her father's, that Ernaux's
writing becomes overtly auto/biographical. As we have seen, it is
also at this point that there is a complete change of tone. The
fictional first-person narrator had allowed Ernaux to express her
feelings about her own past, and particularly about her change of
social class through education, in an extreme, at times violent, form:
'I needed the screen of the novel, doubtless it enabled me to take
as far as possible what I was researching at the time, that is, the
process of being wrenched from one's class of origin (*la déchirure
sociale*)' (IN). Because of her strong sense of responsibility for the
representation of her father's life and its reception, Ernaux adopts
a direct and unadorned mode of writing in an attempt to present
her position (*sa place*) clearly to the reader. The subject of *La Place* –
the life of a working-class man – means that this is by definition a
political choice:

But when it's about my father, the derisory mode of speaking is impossible, because of the danger of falling into miserabilism, or equally of writing from the standpoint of the dominant world, and of making a social judgement. Hence the questioning, as a result of which I concluded that the act of writing is a social commitment, not just in the content but also in the choice of form. (IN)

The move to auto/biography is thus accompanied in *La Place* by a more overtly political definition of her role as a writer, and by the adoption of an authorial voice characterised by the desire to specify rather than imply, by a sincere rather than ironic tone.

In an earlier interview, Ernaux described *La Femme gelée* as a transitional work in this move, a view which would seem to be supported by the fact that unlike the heroines of the first two novels, the narrator in this case is not named:

> With *La Femme gelée*, I begin to bid farewell to the novel. There really is no difference between the narrator and the character. From the outset the text does not present itself as a novelistic construction. The heroine, that is, the narrator, has no first name, no surname. The status of *La Femme gelée* is almost to declare itself as an autobiography. (Ernaux in Tondeur, 1995a, p. 38)

Again here the subject matter imposes a formal choice. *La Femme gelée* is an account of the narrator's history as a woman, emphasising the contrast between the reality of oppressive gender roles and the discourses of equality and liberation prevalent in the existentialist literature and middle-class intellectual milieu of the time. The anonymity of the narrator of *La Femme gelée* may, as Rita Felski has argued in relation to the feminist confessional, play a double role. Firstly, as Ernaux herself suggests, this is a step away from the novel and towards auto/biography, with its emphasis on the authenticity of personal experience. Secondly, like the heroine of Marie Cardinal's *Les Mots pour le dire (The Words to say it)*, published six years earlier, the narrator of *La Femme gelée* is perhaps anonymous because there is a desire to emphasise the representative nature of her experience as a woman (Felski, 1989, p. 94). *La Femme gelée* can thus also be seen as transitional in terms of the overt politicisation and *engagement* (commitment) which, as I have argued above, becomes a strong feature of Ernaux's work from *La Place* onwards. Finally, as P. M. Wetherill has shown, *La Femme gelée* was written during the long years of gestation of *La Place*, a fact which supports this view of it as a transitional text (Wetherill, 1987, pp. 30–5).

There are some reflections on the narrator's attempts to write in both *Ce qu'ils disent ou rien* and *La Femme gelée*, but it is from *La Place* onwards that the author's project and experience as a writer constitute a significant part of the text, and that the reader is $+$ addressed directly. In Lejeune's view, the coincidence of identity of the 'I' in the text and the name on the cover can be confirmed, even if the name itself is not repeated in the text proper, by 'an initial section of the text where the narrator makes commitments to the reader' (Lejeune, 1975, p. 27). This kind of intervention in the text – to discuss her intentions as a writer and her experience of the writing process – is one of the most striking characteristics of Ernaux's fiction, and an important aspect of its general evolution from autobiographical fiction to auto/biography. The change of genre, or perhaps more significantly, of voice, is associated with a dramatic increase in the amount of commentary on the aims of the text. In *Les Armoires vides* the narrator's intention to investigate and explain the chain of events which has led her to the crisis of abortion is the topic of a short passage, leading into the main flashback narrative. The theme of this passage is summarised in one sentence, an image which evokes the parents' early lives as factory workers: 'Trace it all back to then, call it all up, fit it all together, an assembly line, one thing after another' (*Les Armoires vides*, p. 17; trans. p. 11).

The textual space (around 600 words) occupied by this topic is at its greatest in the first three overtly auto/biographical works, *La Place*, *Une femme* and *Passion simple*. There is slightly less in *Journal du dehors* (around 500 words) and *La Honte* (around 400 words). In *'Je ne suis pas sortie de ma nuit'* there is a significant reduction of the textual space occupied by these reflections to around 200 words. The evolution of these interventions, their role in defining the auto/biographical enterprise undertaken, and the relationship between author, text and reader, are my concern in the sections which follow.

The Author in the Text

The Claim to 'Truth Value'

Laura Marcus has demonstrated how criticism of autobiography shows a consistent concern with the author's expressed intentions, which, even in relatively recent critical writing, are often crucial to the generic definition of the work. The *desire* to tell the truth becomes in itself a guarantor of the authenticity of the text, and thus resolves, for the critic, 'the intractable problem of 'referent-iality' – that is, the kind and degree of "truth" that can be expected from autobiographical writing' (Marcus, 1994, p. 3). Sheringham provides a more sophisticated interpretation than the critics referred to here by Marcus, by describing the obsessive expression of intentionality found in autobiographical writing as 'part of the discourse of autobiography' (Sheringham, 1993, p. 2). The analysis of the expression of intentionality in Ernaux's auto/biographical work is rendered complex by the duality of her own position. Ernaux's training as literary critic means that she is fully aware of the pitfalls and problems of any simple notion of truth or refer-entiality. Nonetheless, in her statements of her intentions, she often seems concerned to claim value for her texts in terms of their ability to represent social reality, rather than their literary qualities. As a result, her comments on her aims as a writer and relationship to the eventual reader of her texts are marked by tensions and contradictions. The quotation from Hegel on contradiction ('It is truly in the pain of living that it really exists') which introduces *Une femme* is equally relevant here, and could be amended to read 'in the pain of writing'. The discussion of Ernaux's expressions of authorial intentionality will of necessity involve the unravelling of these contradictions, as well as constituting a case-study of the discourse of intentionality identified by Sheringham.

One of the most frequently stated aims of Ernaux's texts is the search for truth. The quotation from *Les Armoires vides*, cited above (p. 33), along with the novel's flashback structure, indicates that a desire to go back to root causes underlies the writing. This type of structure is reminiscent of crime fiction in that it defines the text which follows as in some way explanatory of the disruption which initiates the narrative. The 'explanatory' or truth-seeking narrative is not present in every work, but it nonetheless persists throughout three decades of writing. The link between the search for truth and the narrative structure is supported by Ernaux's own comments, which suggest that it is precisely in a specific structure, or order, that the truth is to be found:

> At the beginning, I thought I would write quickly. In fact I spend a lot of time on the order of things to say, the choice and the placing of

words, as if an ideal order existed, the only one capable of expressing a truth about my mother – but I don't know what it consists of – and nothing else counts for me, at the moment of writing, except the discovery of that order. (*Une femme*, p. 43)

The primordial importance of the discovery of the correct order, or structure, indicated here, is matched by the sense that once the order has been found, it must not be tampered with. The writing becomes a kind of sacred object, since it is the outcome of the search for a truth about the author's own or her parents' past. Through the pain and struggle of the writing process the truth has been found, and all that remains is to preserve it, through publication. Thus in *Une femme*, Ernaux depicts herself as unable to rewrite the story of her father's death, since the definitive version, or more precisely order of words, has already been sought, and found, through the writing of *La Place*: 'I cannot describe those moments $+$ because I have already done so in another book, that is, another account, in other words, with a different ordering of sentences, will never be possible' (*Une femme*, p. 73).

Ernaux has also commented that she does not re-read her books, unless required to proof-read, for example for paperback publication (IN). This seems consistent with a notion of writing as production of a sacred object, which like the pots of pâté in the shop of the exclusive Parisian restaurant 'La Tour d'Argent', has a funereal, untouchable quality (*Journal du dehors*, p. 67).[1] I will return to this conception of writing later in my discussion. Here, it is sufficient to note that the authorial interventions in the text emphasise the important contribution made to the search for authenticity by the structure of the writing, and that these interventions are in this sense in harmony with the choice of a narrative structure based on the desire for knowledge.

Unlike great writers of the French canon such as Marcel Proust, for whom the discovery of truth through writing involved a turning inwards, a focusing on the inner life, the truth sought by Ernaux is $+$ primarily social. Like the detective figure in a crime novel, Ernaux depicts herself as a searcher for a truth which is difficult to attain (Neale, 1980). In *La Femme gelée*, Ernaux describes her aim to cut through the tangled undergrowth of the path of her social development as a woman – 'débroussailler mon chemin de femme' (*La Femme gelée*, p. 63). In *La Place*, she uses verbs such as 'révéler' (to reveal), 'ramener au jour' and 'mettre au jour' (to bring to light), and the noun 'le déchiffrement' (decoding) to describe her task in writing about her father. Fifteen years later, in *La Honte*, Ernaux still describes her literary project as a search for a particular personal and social truth; she again uses phrases such as 'mettre au jour' (bring to light), 'retrouver les mots' (find the words again), 'atteindre ma réalité' (grasp my reality), and warns against the danger of inventing, rather than seeking, the reality of her life as it was in 1952 (*La Honte*, p. 37). Alongside the descriptions of writing as an almost archaeological process of unearthing and decoding buried social truths, Ernaux at times claims to be merely presenting reality. In one of her earliest statements of her intentions as a writer, in *La Place*, Ernaux describes herself as the collector of the facts of her father's life: 'I will collect my father's words, gestures and tastes, the important events of his life, all the objective signs of an existence which I also shared' (*La Place*, p. 24). Thus Ernaux uses fragments of reality in her writing: encounters in the metro or supermarket in *Journal du dehors*, descriptions of photographs in *La Place*, *Une femme* and *La Honte*, and perhaps most significantly, examples of the vocabulary and idioms of the working-class speech of her childhood, particularly in the latter three works (see chapter 1, note 8).

The complexities of the presentation of this kind of data are a significant theme of the authorial interventions in the text; they are analysed in more detail later in this chapter and in the discussion of Ernaux's representation of social difference as it is inscribed in language in chapter 3 (p. 81). Ernaux argues repeatedly for their inclusion, on the grounds that they are a more reliable way of approaching objective reality than memory, imbued as it is with subjective interpretation and emotion. In *Une femme*, Ernaux describes herself as the archivist of the way of life of previous generations of her family, and her aim to capture the social rather than private reality of her mother's life: 'I would like to capture the woman who existed independently of me, the real woman, born in the rural district of a small Normandy town, who died in a geriatric hospital in the Paris region' (*Une femme*, p. 21). This emphasis on the portrayal of her mother within a social context is described later, albeit in a cautious and guarded phrase, as a way of being more truthful: 'this way of writing, which seems to go in the direction of the truth' (*Une femme*, p. 52). The desire to go beyond her own feelings about her mother, in order to present a fuller picture of her and the social context which formed her, may perhaps explain the title of the work – *Une femme* – rather than a title containing the relationship word, 'mère' (see chapter 1, p. 17). In *La Place*, with perhaps a veiled reference to Proust, Ernaux similarly rejects subjective memory, which she regards as a distraction, an invitation to self-indulgent reminiscence, in favour of observation of contemporary social reality: 'I could not count on reminiscence; in the grating sound of the door-bell of an old shop, the smell of over-ripe melon, I only find myself, my summer holidays in Y. . . . The colour of the sky, the reflections of the poplars in the nearby river Oise, had nothing to teach me' (*La Place*, p. 100). In *La Honte*, this distrust of memory has crystallised to become a short, succinct phrase: 'There is no real memory of the self' (p. 37). Similarly, in an edition of *Bouillon de Culture*, broadcast after the publication of *La Honte* and *'Je ne suis pas sortie de ma nuit'*, in January 1997, Ernaux suggested that it would be easier to feel close to any little girl of twelve of the 1990s, than to her twelve-year-old self, because of the shared social reality which the writer in her fifties and the girl of twelve inhabit.

The questioning of memory as a source of artistic inspiration is accompanied by a distrust of literature itself. At times Ernaux presents her writing as an academic, almost scientific, activity: 'I have always considered writing to be a form of research' (IN). In *Journal du dehors*, her subject is the social world of the late 1980s and early 1990s, and in one of the direct comments on the nature of the work, she describes it as an 'ethnotext' (*Journal du dehors*, p. 63). Similarly in *La Honte*, Ernaux describes herself as an 'ethnologist of the self' (*La Honte*, p. 37). The use of these terms is suggestive of Ernaux's positive links with some aspects of academia, and of the questioning of traditional definitions of literature, which, for Ernaux, is a crucial aspect of the politics of writing. This rejection of literature and its association with self-indulgence and luxury is a constant theme of Ernaux's authorial interventions. In *La Place*, she declares: 'Recently I have become aware that it is impossible for me to write a novel. In giving an account of a life which was subjected to the struggle to survive, I have no right to place myself on the side of art, or to try to do something "exciting" or "moving"' (*La Place*, p. 24). The phrase 'I have no right' is significant here, in that it indicates the moral dimension of the act of writing for Ernaux. Writing is a duty, and it is contained within moral parameters associated with Ernaux's guilt in relation to her change of class. She is in a sense refusing to belong fully to the bourgeoisie by deploying all of the literary devices which as a result of her education she nonetheless has at her disposal. Hence, later in the same passage in *La Place*, she declares her intention to restrict herself to 'l'écriture plate', the simple, factual tone of her letters to her parents. This style has been maintained ever since its first expression in *La Place*, and in *La Honte* we find a similar rejection of the overtly literary: 'I will never know the delights of metaphor, the joys of style' (*La Honte*, p. 70). Ernaux states her aim in *Une femme* to remain 'beneath literature' (p. 22), and later defines the work as neither biography nor a novel, but 'something between literature, sociology and history' (p. 106). Just as the subject matter of Ernaux's work exposes the cultural inequalities resulting from a social hierarchy based on exclusion, the form of her writing, and more pertinently here, her discussion of that form, question the conventions and nature of literature itself. Ernaux's 'écriture plate' is designed to resist the conventional signs of the literary, and to cross the artificial boundaries constructed between different areas of intellectual activity, just as she herself has crossed the social boundaries between the classes.

Ernaux thus presents her writing as a search for truth, which is primarily social in nature and therefore of wider relevance than the merely personal. Even the structure of many of her works supports this version of the role of literature, and the struggle to find the correct order is one of the preoccupations which Ernaux discusses in the texts. She also presents herself as bound by a moral and political sense of duty to avoid the pleasures of style for its own sake. Literature, or literary devices, along with emotion and memory, are to be distrusted, as potentially distracting the writer from her task of bearing witness. However, Ernaux's interventions in the texts do not merely present writing as the seamless and unproblematic depiction of reality which the above might suggest; it is to her problematisation of the process of writing, and particularly of writing auto/biography, that I will turn in the section which follows.

Auto/biographical Truth as Textual Construct

One of the many tensions in Ernaux's presentation of her task as a writer stems from her awareness of the constructed nature, not only of society, but also of her own texts. Very early in her career as a writer, in *La Femme gelée*, she comments on her power as author of

the text: 'I am writing myself, I can make what I want of myself, –
turn in any direction, recant at will' (*La Femme gelée*, p. 63). Ernaux
is here reminding herself, and her reader, of her moral duty as a
writer to remain truthful, and to include even the less attractive
aspects of her past self in her auto/biographical exploration. In
Une femme, in the passage quoted earlier, we find a similar balancing of the awareness of the possibility of alternative versions and
attachment to the notion that there is nonetheless a true story. She
describes herself as passionately seeking a particular narrative
order *as if* an ideal order existed; the 'comme si' indicates an
awareness that this is not the case, that she is in fact choosing one
of several possible versions. Despite the resistance to literature
already referred to, in *Une femme* Ernaux does recognise the literary
nature of her project in writing about her mother: 'it's a question
of seeking a truth about my mother which can only be arrived at
through words' (*Une femme*, p. 22). As I have suggested earlier, it
is in *La Place* that Ernaux confronts the difficulty of representing
an oppressed group which she no longer belongs to. The problem
here is particularly acute because of her father's rejection of literary
culture, and the distance between his limited linguistic repertoire
and her own. Again, Ernaux reveals her awareness of the writing
process as a series of choices, in this case all loaded with political
implications and meaning:

> Writing is about steering a difficult course between the rehabilitation
> of a world considered inferior, and the denunciation of the alienation
> which is part of it. Because those ways of life were ours, and even a
> source of happiness, but also the humiliating limitations of our
> condition (the awareness that 'our place is not good enough'), I would
> like to express both the happiness and the alienation. In fact, I have
> the impression that I lurch from one side to the other of this
> contradiction. (*La Place*, p. 54)

Whereas in the first two works, which are more fictional in
character, vitriolic rejection of working-class culture predominates,
from *La Femme gelée* onwards, more positive representations
become possible, or even imperative, as the auto/biographical
nature of the writing is fully declared. At the same time, the desire
to reclaim her past as a member of an oppressed group, and to
represent that group and its culture positively, carries with it
the danger of romanticisation. The need to balance the positive

'owning' of the culture of her childhood with an honest depiction
of its considerable constraints and limitations leads Ernaux to the
kind of discussion cited above, where it is clear that trying to 'go
in the direction of the truth' is not a straightforward process (*Une
femme*, p. 52).

A further problem, discussed in both *La Place* and *Une femme*, is
the struggle to be objective about deeply personal and emotionally
charged subjects such as childhood experiences. If, as I have already
shown, this is the stated aim of Ernaux's writing in these two texts,
the author's comments do not attempt to conceal the difficulties
involved, or the power of subjective memory:

> I write slowly. In forcing myself to reveal the significant threads of a
> life in a series of facts and choices, I have the impression that I am
> gradually losing touch with my father as an individual. The blueprint,
> the idea, seems to take over. If, on the contrary, I allow the memories
> to flow, I see him as he was, his laugh, his way of walking; he takes
> me by the hand to the fair and the roundabouts terrify me, all the signs
> of a condition shared with others become indifferent to me. Each time,
> I tear myself out of the trap of the individual. (*La Place*, p. 45)

This passage seems to suggest the opposite of Ernaux's 'policy' in
La Place; her most vivid images of her father are the childhood
memories which she has rejected as unreliable. She concludes the
passage by reaffirming her decision to resist the temptation of the
subjective, and the violent language of the last line conveys the
intensity of this struggle: she must *tear* herself from the *trap* of the
personal. In *Une femme*, she describes a similar battle for objectivity:
'But I feel that something in me resists, would like to preserve
purely emotional images of my mother, warmth, tears, without
giving them any meaning' (*Une femme*, p. 52). Here, Ernaux describes the same struggle with the subjective which she refers to in
La Place, and a similar desire to emphasise the parent's social
persona. It is significant that the concluding phrase in this passage
is a return to her emotional resistance to this undertaking; the image
of the author bravely tearing herself away from her subjective
experience of the parent figure is replaced by a picture of the author
as a small and vulnerable child and the mother as the all-powerful
provider of warmth, if also of sorrow. The passages describing the
struggle for objectivity in *Une femme* often end, in this way, with a
reaffirmation of the power of subjective memories, whilst in *La
Place*, the conclusion is generally the kind of 'return to order' quoted

above. The greater intimacy between mother and daughter, and the visceral bond between them, may explain this phenomenon (see the discussion of the mother–daughter relationship in chapter 4).

This process of claiming and then questioning objectivity becomes in some ways even more intense in the more recent works, as a result of either their subject matter or of the nature of the authorial comments. In *La Honte*, published in 1997, Ernaux returns to the topic of her childhood, to the year of her twelfth birthday, 1952, to be precise. The very fact of returning to some of the ground already covered, fictionally in *Les Armoires vides* and auto/biographically in *La Femme gelée*, *La Place* and *Une femme*, seems to confirm that she has finally abandoned the notion that only one version of the past is possible. In her statements of intent in *La Honte*, there seems to be the same recognition; the claim for truth and authenticity is perhaps more mitigated than in *La Place* or even *Une femme*, and some of the earlier contradictions have perhaps been worked through. In *La Honte*, whilst reiterating the distrust of narrativisation and of 'pure' memory expressed in the earlier works, Ernaux seems to arrive at a working compromise. As well as basing her text on a historical investigation of the social context of the time, Ernaux is prepared to use her memories, but intends to submit them to a variety of approaches. She has moved from the almost total rejection of memory found in the earlier works to an acceptance of its limitations, and a notion of its relevance, when treated as a resource rather than absolute truth, and combined with other types of material: 'Nor will I merely unearth and transcribe images from memory – rather, I will treat the latter as documents, which can be illuminated (qui s'éclaireront) by submitting them to a variety of approaches' (*La Honte*, p. 38). The text in which the repressed is in this way given permission to return is perhaps ironically the place where the author is most in control of her material. *La Honte* trawls systematically through the layers of that twelve-year-old reality which is its subject. The events described in the opening pages may have been excruciatingly painful, but the pain is not visible on the page, as it is in the ruptures and fragmentations of *La Place*, *Une femme* or *'Je ne suis pas sortie de ma nuit'*. A line of development can be traced in the texts dealing with the lives of Ernaux's parents, arriving at some kind of resolution of the problem of realism in *La Honte*, which makes its peace with alternative versions, whilst retaining the notion of a deeper, more illuminating understanding,

Annie Ernaux

enshrined in the verb 's'éclairer'. A parallel line could be traced in
the texts dealing more overtly with Ernaux's own life, and particularly sexuality, in that they seem to contain, in the end, the most
profound challenge to the reader. With its rebellious and angry tone,
Les Armoires vides disturbs and confronts the reader, just as *Passion
simple* and to a lesser extent *Journal du dehors* challenge the reader
to take seriously an author/narrator who reads horoscopes, and
writes about both her everyday life and erotic experiences (see
p. 51 below).

The Pact with the Self

Having examined the contradictory and many-layered public voice
of the author, I would now like to turn to the relationship between
writing and emotional life, the private face of the writer, by drawing
attention to those moments in the texts when Ernaux's theorisation
of her intentions and aims as a writer allows the affective dimension
of the act of writing to emerge. At these points the prevalent sense
of public and political duty is subordinated to discussion of the
personal and private need to write. The distinction is in some
ways artificial, since it seems likely that in bringing her parents'
oppressed culture into literature, for example, Ernaux is also
working through the feelings of shame, guilt and anger caused
by the experience of changing social class. In *La Honte* Ernaux
expresses her horror of the word 'private', stemming from her
experience of a Catholic private school, and declares: 'Writing is a
public thing' (*La Honte*, p. 86). Nonetheless, she does distinguish
between the public and private aspects of the act of writing.
Significantly, given the subject matter, it is in *Passion simple* that
she develops this discussion, emphasising in two passages (p. 42
and p. 70) the crucial importance of the time-lapse between writing
and publication. The privacy of the moment of writing itself, even
if it depends on denial of the eventual reality of publication,
provides Ernaux with the space she needs in order to write, just as
the choice of living in Cergy-Pontoise, rather than the sixth arrond-
issement, places geographical and cultural space between Ernaux
and the Parisian intelligentsia: 'It's because of this time-lapse that
I am able to write at present, just as at sixteen I would lie in the
burning sun all day, and at twenty make love without contra-
ceptives: without thinking of the consequences' (*Passion simple*,
p. 42). In the second passage on this theme in *Passion simple*, Ernaux

{ 42 }

notes the visual distinction between the pages written in her own handwriting, whose limited legibility enables her to believe that her writing is 'something private', and the typewritten text which she will eventually produce: 'the public characters'. At that point the illusory privacy will come to an end and 'my innocence will be over' (p. 70).

This notion of a period of innocence suggests that, at least initially, writing is a private business; Ernaux makes a number of comments, throughout her works, on the role of writing in her own life. In *Une femme*, we are aware of both the terror and necessity of writing about her mother's life and death: 'Only the day before yesterday I overcame the terror of writing at the top of a blank page, as if starting a book, rather than a letter to someone, "my mother has died"' (*Une femme*, p. 21). In the opening pages of *La Honte*, again, there is a strong sense of the terror inspired by the prospect of writing about traumatic experiences, but at the same time Ernaux suggests that overcoming this terror can play a therapeutic role. Firstly, subjecting disordered experience to the demands of structured narrative can in some sense neutralise or normalise that experience: 'Moreover, since I have managed to produce this account, I have the impression that it's just an ordinary event, more common in families than I had imagined. Perhaps a narrative, all narrative, has the effect of normalising any act, including the most dramatic' (*La Honte*, p. 16). Secondly, writing may be a way of working through, as well as working on, difficult experiences or emotions, so that they lose their time-honoured and powerful place in psychic life: 'This scene which has been static for years – I want to make it move, to take away from it its sacred quality as icon of my inner life (which is expressed in the belief that this scene made me write, was the source of all my books)' (*La Honte*, p. 30). These comments in *La Honte* are more overt in their recognition of the emotional value of writing than earlier texts, such as *Une femme* and *La Place*. In the latter case, although, as I have shown above, references to the power of subjective memory abound, the author/narrator seems more concerned to emphasise the struggle for objectivity than the emotional satisfaction of writing. Perhaps there is a sense in which success as a writer, and the fact that she has established herself as a 'trustworthy' voice, now allow Ernaux to reveal more of herself, or to question the polarisation of public and private, objective and subjective which is a strong feature of the earlier work.

The subject matter of *Passion simple* would seem to support this
view, since it is clearly less 'respectable' than the works written in
homage to a beloved mother and father, however contradictory
the child–parent relationship may have become (see pp. 50–51
below). *'Je ne suis pas sortie de ma nuit'* is, however, an even more
daring experiment. Here, Ernaux completely drops any claim to
objectivity. She makes it clear that the text she is publishing was
written 'in the heat of the moment' and that these pages have not
been subjected to the form of authorial control, almost censorship,
which she describes in the earlier texts: "I offer them as they were
written, in the shock and upheaval which I felt at the time. I have
not wanted to change anything in the transcription of these
moments when I was close to her, outside time – or in the time of a
return to early childhood – devoid of all thoughts except "she's
my mother"' (*'Je ne suis pas sortie de ma nuit'*, p. 13). Writing the
notes which will eventually be published as *'Je ne suis pas sortie de
ma nuit'* is described as an emotional necessity, almost an expurg-
ation of violent and negative emotions through the use of language
which hides none of the horror of the experience: 'Later, when I
returned from seeing her at the hospital in Pontoise, I was
compelled to write about her, her words, her body which was closer
and closer to me. I wrote very quickly, amidst the violence of the
sensations, without thinking or seeking an order' (*'Je ne suis pas
sortie de ma nuit'*, p. 11). With the publication of this work, Ernaux's
writing has thus turned full circle; the painful search for the precise
and perfect structure of *Une femme* is here replaced by a commitment to reproducing the disorder of a personal journal, written in
the midst of the events described – her mother's final years and
death – rather than with the advantage and distance of hindsight.
The desire to write objectively about the mother as a social being
is here abandoned, and the perfect mother/child dyad which
haunts *Une femme* can here be openly reclaimed. The text is declared
to be the space into which the excess of pain has been channelled:
'the remaining traces of the pain' (p. 13). The notion of the
completed text as the final truth on a particular subject is also called
into question by the publication of *'Je ne suis pas sortie de ma nuit'*,
which provides a different version of the period of time covered
in the final pages of *Une femme*. This seems to be the culmination
of the many suggestions in the earlier work that writing implies
the choice of a particular version, and that writing about the self
renders this choice particularly complex. Here Ernaux frees herself

from the constraints of a self-imposed objectivity, and recognises the profoundly intertextual nature of her work. Her books can be, and are, read in isolation, but they can also be read in dialogue with each other, as a continuous process of posing questions, and providing inevitably limited responses, in areas such as the lived experience of class and gender, the politics of writing and the nature of identity.

The relationship between writing and the search for identity is a significant aspect of Ernaux's comments on her personal motivation to write. The theme of identity generally is omnipresent + ?
in Ernaux's writing, and will be discussed in more detail in chapters 4 and 7. Here, however, it is relevant to note that writing is often presented as a solution to the problem of an uncertain or frag- +
mented identity. In *Une femme*, the textual inclusion of her mother in her own educated and literary world enables Ernaux to feel 'less alone and artificial' (*Une femme*, p. 106). The choice of the adjective 'artificial' ('factice') is significant, since it indicates that the struggle for authenticity discussed earlier and the search for identity are intimately linked (see chapter 7, pp. 169–70). Ernaux describes herself as earnestly seeking authenticity in the narration of her own or her parents' life. At different stages in her evolution as a writer this authenticity is seen to be obtainable by rejecting emotion and seeking the true order of events, or by submitting memories to a range of approaches, or, finally, simply by presenting unstructured experience without any claim to a generalisable, objective truth. Despite these changes in approach, the search for an authentic voice or writerly identity is consistent. The search for the lost or frag- mented self through the production of written texts is, for Ernaux, part of a more general, almost existential, project. Writing seems to offer the only possible protection against the losses imposed by time, the limitations of memory and ultimately death (see chapter 4, p. 100). Unsurprisingly, it is in the description of a relationship based on absence, and on the rehearsal and finally the realisation of the threat of total loss, that Ernaux discusses in most detail the role of writing as a means of preserving the past. At times, the sense of loss dominates and the attempt to preserve through writing seems doomed to failure:

> Often, I would write on a piece of paper the date, the time and 'he's coming' with other phrases, fears that he would not come, that he would desire me less. In the evening I would go back to that piece of

paper, noting 'he came' and a disordered account of the details of our encounter. Then, in a daze, I would look at the scribbled page, the two paragraphs written before and after, which later could be read without a break. Between the two there had been words, gestures, which made everything else, including the writing I was trying to capture them with, derisory. (*Passion simple*, pp. 18–19)

The page covered in scribble may have its own reality, but it is not equivalent to the words and gestures of a relationship, nor is it capable of conveying the experience of time passing, and the loss of the present. Nonetheless, at other points, Ernaux comments that writing may be a way of coping with absence and loss, like the wishes and superstitions of popular culture (p. 61). Writing perhaps becomes a substitute for the lost object, acquiring the fetishistic quality discussed earlier: 'Even now, re-reading these pages is as painful as touching the towelling bathrobe he wore at my place, and took off at the moment of getting dressed in order to leave. The difference: these pages will always have a meaning for me, perhaps for others' (*Passion simple*, p. 61). In '*Je ne suis pas sortie de ma nuit*', in a characteristically succinct phrase, Ernaux seems to arrive at an understanding of her personal and political motivation to write. On the one hand, writing is the preservation of lives, identities and experiences. This is both an existential and personal struggle against time, death and loss, and since Ernaux's writing often focuses on lives and areas of experience which are conventionally excluded from culture, it also becomes a political project. On the other hand, writing is an attempt to understand the self and others as social beings, and a way of exploring the impact of a particular social context on the self, whether in terms of psychic and emotional life, or of identity: 'I can see the difference between this and the other books I have done, or rather, there is no difference, for I don't know how to write books which are anything other than this desire to save, to understand, but above all to save' ('*Je ne suis pas sortie de ma nuit*', p. 103).

The Reader in the Text

In adopting a stance towards the reader autobiographers choose their tone and decide where they stand; but they do so in the dark: the reader is the Other and remains so to the end. (Sheringham, 1993, p. ix)

In his chapter on the reader–writer relationship ('Dealing with the Reader', pp. 137–64) Sheringham argues that the reader's relationship to autobiographical and fictional narrators is qualitatively different, since in the case of the former there is an imagined relationship with a real human being. Following Lejeune, he suggests that the presence of the proper name on the cover of the work lends an 'uncanny palpability' to both the writer and the reader, and that both enter a border zone between fiction and reality which is distinguishable from the domain of fiction proper (Sheringham, 1993, p. 138). The French word *témoignage* (testimony), often used in discussions of life-writing, is suggestive of the close relationship between autobiographer and reader, for if the former is to bear witness to her or his experience, this activity becomes pointless in the void: the 'eye-witness account' requires the presence of the jury. As Sheringham suggests, among the many and varied motivations for writing autobiography is the inescapably public nature of the act; like any other narrative of life-history, autobiography depends for its existence on the notion that somewhere, somehow it will be received by an audience. The parallel between the role of the reader of autobiography and the confidant listening to the close friend's narrative of their recent past is an important dimension of the distinction between the implied readers of autobiography and fiction. The autobiographer is involved in 'an engagement, an imaginary negotiation, not only with the conventions of a particular kind of discourse, but with an imaginary Other, an interpolated subjectivity which receives and responds to their utterances' (Sheringham, 1993, p. 137).

Sheringham goes on to distinguish between, firstly, the implied reader of the autobiographical text as a symbolisation of the splitting of the self involved in the process: the reader can be seen as that part of the self which observes and records – 'the Other who inhabits all acts of self-scrutiny' (Sheringham, 1993, p. 139). Alternatively, the implied reader is the textual reflection, or internalisation, of the external reality of social codes and conventions. In either case, Sheringham observes an ambivalent relationship between the autobiographer and the textually constructed reader, an oscillation between the desire to seduce the reader ('ingratiation') and the rejection of the laws and norms which the latter seems to embody ('repudiation'). The amount of textual space which Ernaux devotes to direct address to the reader suggests a particularly anxious approach to a genre which Sheringham sees as in general fraught with tensions. All of the passages from Ernaux's works discussed in the first part of this chapter are not only setting out her intentions and strategies as a writer, but constructing implied readers and a relationship with them. Here, I will argue that Sheringham's two poles in this relationship are relevant in the discussion of Ernaux, and that his notion of the simultaneously public and private nature of autobiography is very much a feature of Ernaux's own deliberations.

The Challenge to the Reader

In *Journal du dehors* Ernaux is reminded of the tension between writing as a private and personal experience and the eventual offering of this private world to the public, by the sight of two young lovers: 'In the metro, a boy and a girl alternatively speak to each other violently and caress, as if there was no one else present. But this is wrong: from time to time they cast a defiant glance at the other passengers. A terrifying thought. This is my relationship to literature' (*Journal du dehors*, p. 91). This sense of casting the occasional defiant glance over her shoulder to the reader is an interesting commentary on Ernaux's writing. The word 'défi' (challenge) is particularly significant, for in some of the passages where the reader is addressed directly, it does seem that the author is challenging the reader, or at least making a strong statement about the ways in which her works should be read. In a talk on writing in the first person, Ernaux described how the reader is implicated and interpellated by the use of the first person. She also described the use of the first person as 'an invasion of the text by the author' (Ernaux, King's College, London, 8 March 1994). The direct authorial comments could be seen as an extension of the first person, a further intensification of the author's presence in the text, and a desire, if not to repudiate, at least to challenge and in some sense dominate the reader (see chapter 6, pp. 156–161).

In some ways an extreme example of this kind of assertion can be found in a significant passage in *La Place*. I have already discussed the political difficulties which Ernaux faced in the representation of a life governed by the struggle to survive and to emerge from poverty. It is in this area that Ernaux's 'messages' to her reader are most clear. In *La Place*, we find a stern warning to the reader, and an awareness of the risk taken in presenting fragments of working-class speech:

Naturally, there is no pleasure in writing, in this undertaking in which I keep as closely as possible to the words and phrases I heard, at times marking them with italics. Not in order to indicate a double meaning to the reader and offer him the pleasure of a complicity which I refuse in all its forms, nostalgia, pathos or derision. But simply because these words and phrases express the limits and the colour of the world my father lived in, and which I also inhabited. And in that world, one word was never mistaken for another. (*La Place*, p. 46)

The refusal of an ironic or patronising complicity with the reader could not be expressed more strongly. The last sentence of this passage also seems to act as a kind of warning to the reader; just as words were carefully and precisely chosen in her father's culture, the reader should take care to avoid misinterpretation, and to respect the author's approach to the undervalued culture which she is representing. The author's extreme anxiety about this representation thus extends beyond her own choices as a writer to the eventual reading of the texts, and leads her to attempt an uncharacteristic closure. Here Sheringham's notion of the reader as the Other within the writing self seems most appropriate. Ernaux's guilt in relation to her father, resulting from her own abandonment of his culture, leads to an element of self-castigation in her depiction of the writing process; she cannot allow herself to enjoy happiness or satisfaction in her work, as this would be the final act of betrayal of a man whose life permitted him no such luxuries. The reader, or the observing and writing part of the self which s/he represents, must also be punished – the pleasure of complicity is refused in all its forms. It is possible to note an almost sado-masochistic element in the construction of the reader–writer relationship. The reader too, as symbol and companion of the part of the writer's self which has emigrated to the dominant class, is to be punished for this act of betrayal. Ironically, at the point when the desire to control the reader and the mode of reading is at its most intense, the futility of the gesture is also evident. The author may refuse complicity, but the reader is free to ignore her refusal or denial.

However, the controlling author is a less dominant mode of engagement with the reader in Ernaux's texts than the questioning or challenging role. The implied reader can generally be seen as a projection of part of the writing self more in terms of self-doubt than self-castigation. The 'repudiation' of the reader, to use

Sheringham's term, is more frequently associated with the questioning of expectations, and with a desire to unsettle, rather than
control. Ernaux's comments on the writing process, whether
implying awareness of the constructed nature of all texts, or the
problems of representation of an oppressed group, or finally,
commenting on the author's struggle with her own feelings, could
be seen to undermine or contradict the claim for the 'truth value'
of the texts. If the author herself is aware that she is choosing
a particular version of her own life, why should the reader be
convinced of the authenticity or value of this version? The differ-
entiation between fiction and auto/biography would seem to be
questioned, and the appropriate mode of reading uncertain: at
times Ernaux seems to be encouraging the reader to read the texts
as *témoignage*, at other moments almost as literary analysis. If in
Une femme the text is defined as something in between literature,
sociology and history, in *Passion simple* the definition even of this
generic *mélange* is impossible: 'Throughout this time I had the
impression I was living my passion in a novelistic way, but now I
don't know what mode I am writing it in, whether as a testimony,
or confession, as it is practised in women's magazines, or in the
manner of the manifesto, the official report or even literary
commentary' (*Passion simple*, p. 30). The reader of Ernaux's work
must operate outside the reassuring structures provided by generic
conventions, uncertain whether the text is popular or high culture,
romance or *témoignage*, or in the end even literature at all. The
disarray which this produces in the critical world will be one of
the topics of chapter 6. I would argue that the questioning of the
authenticity of the text provoked by the authorial interventions is
balanced by the representation of the author's struggle with these
issues, which gives the impression of sincerity and openness. There
may be a sense in which the more Ernaux declares the difficulties
of bearing witness to the experience of an excluded group, the more
we as readers are inclined to trust her. In this sense, the direct
address to the reader, even when raising issues about realism
and representation, may not only challenge the reader, as Ernaux
herself has suggested, but also reinforce the illusion of being the
author's friend, or confidant. This is a question I will return to in
chapter 5.

Here, however, an evolution in Ernaux's writing can be noted.
As the quotation above suggests, a text such as *Passion simple* seems
to question the authority of the 'I' more than the works dealing

mainly with earlier phases of Ernaux's life. This is partly the result of the increased level of uncertainty and questioning in the authorial interventions which I have indicated, but also seems to emanate from the subject matter itself: a description of a woman in her late forties in an erotic liaison with a married man is a daring topic for an auto/biographical work, even in the 1990s. The fact that Ernaux describes herself living this passion 'sur le mode romanesque' – consulting horoscopes, making wishes and so on – makes the text even more daring. A passage in *Journal du dehors* discusses this issue:

> I bought *Marie-Claire* at the station of the New Town. The horoscope of the month: 'You will meet a wonderful man'. Several times during the day I wondered if the man I was talking to was the one.
>
> (In writing this in the first person, I am exposing myself to all sorts of comments, which would not be provoked by 'she wondered if the man she was talking to was the one'). (p. 18)

Can a woman who reads the horoscope write literature? Can her auto/biography be taken seriously? Here Ernaux is attacking the fundamental sexism of the boundaries of high culture, particularly in France. If in her earlier texts she is bringing her parents and their dominated culture into literature, in these later texts she is bringing the equally unacceptable culture of femininity into her work.[2] In so doing, she is perhaps straining her auto/biographical pact to its limits, and undermining the trust placed in the sincere and struggling authorial voice of the earlier texts. Ernaux's challenge to the reader seems to operate on many levels, but it is perhaps in this latter sense that it is at its most intense. It would be unwise to underestimate the difficulties and complexities of attempting to represent working-class culture and speech in literature, and Ernaux's own sense of these difficulties leads to one of her most aggressive moments of *défi*, as I have shown above. Nonetheless, the images of the grandmother keeping the skin of the milk and the stale bread, or the father's shame over his misspelling of 'lu et approuvé' are more acceptable to existing literary traditions than the author who reads *Marie-Claire*. Even if Ernaux eschews it, a heroic version of poverty does exist in high culture, whereas popular femininity arguably has no place (see chapter 6, pp. 152–154).

Annie Ernaux

The Reader as Object of Desire

As I have demonstrated above, Ernaux's interventions in her texts simultaneously reaffirm and question the authority of the 'I', and the reader's trust in that voice, or persona. As well as challenging the reader, Ernaux's desire seems to be to convince him/her of the reality of her own existence and identity, and of the authenticity and trustworthiness of her voice. Again in this sense the reader constructed in the text can be seen as an externalisation of an inner need or dynamic (see chapter 4). Although theoretically at the opposite pole, the overt struggle for objectivity of *La Place* or *Une femme* may, in this respect, have the same function as the unashamed subjectivity of *'Je ne suis pas sortie de ma nuit'*, particularly since the less guarded presentation of the latter text is founded on three decades of successful auto/biographical publications. It is appropriate that in a text a dealing with the alienation of modern urban life, Ernaux expresses the link between the search for the self and the desire for intimacy, or at least recognition, from others: 'Why am I recounting this scene, and the many others which figure in these pages? (. . .) Perhaps I am seeking something about myself in them, their posture, their conversations' (*Journal du dehors*, p. 36). Exploration of the self through writing may in this way be closely linked to the desire to enter, or indeed create, a community of readers, just as the desire to write about strangers in the metro may be both a search for her own identity and a desire to be closer to other human beings, and thus both 'less alone' and 'less artificial'. Sheringham's term 'ingratiation' has, unfortunately, rather negative connotations, suggesting that the author is seeking to obtain something – approval, attention, admiration – from the reader. This may be inevitable, but Ernaux's version of the auto/biographical pact with the reader suggests a more positive formulation. She repeats the same question, almost word for word, at the end of *Une femme*, published in 1988, and in *'Je ne suis pas sortie de ma nuit'*, published almost ten years later: 'Isn't writing, and what I write, a way of giving?' (*'Je ne suis pas sortie de ma nuit'*, p. 79). The repetition of the phrase suggests both that the notes which came to constitute *'Je ne suis pas sortie de ma nuit'* were used in the writing of *Une femme*, and that the idea of the gift is highly significant. In the end, the challenges to the reader and attempts to assert a particular mode of reading are futile. The reader remains supremely 'other' – unknown, invisible, yet omnipresent in the auto/biographical text.

Ernaux's recognition of this state of affairs is encapsulated in this question, in which, however tentatively, she offers her writing as a gift, and frees the reader to make of it what s/he will. The reception of Ernaux's gift will be my topic in part 2, particularly chapter 5; before this turn from textually constructed to real readers, chapters 3 and 4 will provide a greater understanding of the nature of the gift through a detailed discussion of the themes of Ernaux's writing.

Notes

1. This conception of writing is not, however Ernaux's only, or final, view on the subject. At other times, she links writing with the erotic (see the translation of 'Fragments autour de Philippe V.', appendix 1, p. 177).
2. Siobhán McIlvanney provides a useful discussion of Ernaux's relationship to aspects of feminine popular culture in her article 'Recuperating Romance: Literary Paradigms in the Works of Annie Ernaux' (McIlvanney, 1996). Drawing on *Passion simple* and on an article written by Ernaux for *l'Autre Journal* in 1993 – 'Annie aime les romans à l'eau de rose' ('Annie likes Mills and Boon') – she reads Ernaux's defence of romantic fiction as a feminist 'recuperation' of the genre. See chapter 3, p. 71, and for a discussion of the impact of this on the reception of Ernaux's work, chapter 6, pp. 152–154.

3

Gender, Sexuality and Class

Introduction

*T*here has been some discussion in academic circles of the relative importance in Ernaux's writing of class and gender. I provide a brief account of this discussion in chapter 6 (pp. 141–2), but find it more useful here to emphasise the links between these areas of social inequality and oppression, as they are represented in Ernaux's writing. Like Loraine Day in her analysis of *Les Armoires vides*, I would argue that Ernaux's texts demonstrate the relationship between class and gender oppression, which become 'cumulative and mutually reinforcing' (Day, 1990, p. 53). As a result, in the analysis of the representations of gender, class and sexuality in the texts I have found it almost impossible to separate the three areas. It is no coincidence that one of the keywords in Ernaux's writing is 'lien' (link), and that making connections is presented as the first step towards both political understanding and emotional recovery from the traumas imposed by an unequal society.

This combination of the political and the personal is perhaps in part responsible for the different modes of writing about oppression in Ernaux's work – broadly speaking, emotional denunciation, analysis and description *sans commentaire*. A related issue is the difference between representations in the earlier works, particularly *Les Armoires vides* and *Ce qu'ils disent ou rien*, which often seem to be written from within the experience of oppression, and the writing since *La Place*, with its adoption of a more 'objective' style. If the first three novels combine analysis of oppression with a vivid and immediate sense of its lived experience, from *La Place* onwards, the denunciatory, angry tone of the early texts is replaced by a more distanced position. This is not to say that the personal experience of oppression is excluded from the later works, in fact on the contrary, in *La Honte* Ernaux reveals hitherto concealed aspects of the effects on her emotional development of the change of class. However, the place from which she speaks is increasingly that of observer, rather than victim of oppression, whether she is observing and analysing her own past, as in *La Honte*, or contemporary social reality in *Journal du dehors*.

Despite these differences, Ernaux's works demonstrate a very high degree of continuity, and can be read intertextually, as one text seems to comment on, or respond to, another. A very clear example of this – *Une femme* and *'Je ne suis pas sortie de ma nuit'* – was discussed in chapters 1 (p. 24) and 2 (p. 44). The auto/biographical nature of the writing ties the works together, so that they can be read as a continuing narrative of Ernaux's life, each introducing a new perspective or theme. Like the physical sensations experienced by Denise as a child in *Les Armoires vides*, the texts are 'held together by a strong, slender, talkative thread that was me' (p. 47; trans. p. 31). Here, I am concerned both to trace the development of Ernaux's representations of class, sexuality and gender, and also to explore the intertextual dialogues and relationships she has created, paying particular attention to the process of questioning earlier certainties which seems to be characteristic of Ernaux's work. As a result of this process, a series of turning points, or reversals, in the represention of these three areas, and of the life as a whole, can be identified, both within and across the texts.

The Material Locations of Social Difference

Money

> The social distribution of material things has more meaning than their existence. (*La Honte*, p. 36)

In her representations of gender and class, Ernaux is particularly concerned to demonstrate the material basis of inequality. This is in part related to her rejection of the abstractions of middle-class culture (see p. 80) and leads logically to the choice of realism as the most appropriate mode of writing about people such as her parents, whose concerns and conversation were predominantly practical. The interest in the description of the material world also results from Ernaux's political position, the strong belief in the socially constructed nature of class and gender difference, and the links between this construction and its material or economic base. This is an element of the position of hindsight from which *Les Armoires vides* is narrated; in the present time of the narration, Denise is able to make the connections which eluded her in the past, and thus the angry denunciations of *Les Armoires vides* are combined with glimpses of a political understanding: 'It never occurred to me that money might be at the root of these differences, I thought one was born clean or dirty, orderly or slovenly' (*Les Armoires vides*, p. 97; trans.p. 64).

In the later work, there is a constant awareness of the impact of material security on the cultural and even emotional opportunities available to an individual. At this point Ernaux's position has of course changed, as is suggested by the observer role noted above: she now enjoys the economic advantages which previously were denied to her, and her parents. The past, however, is never forgotten. Thus, in *Passion simple* Ernaux rejects psychoanalytical explanations of her passion, commenting instead on the material privileges which have made it possible: 'the only relevant information would be of a material nature, the time and freedom I had at my disposal to experience this' (*Passion simple*, p. 32). In *Journal du dehors*, Ernaux's observation of others in shops and trains is marked by a particular awareness of those who are economically and culturally marginalised (see chapter 1, p. 20). In *La Place* Ernaux described her parents' increased economic prosperity as constantly undercut by anxiety and tension; they were too close to poverty to feel secure (*La Place*, p. 58). The parents' need to hold on to the new social status they have acquired in becoming shopkeepers ('tenir sa place', *La Place*, p. 45) leads to great fear of being unable to pay their way. This experience conditions Ernaux's adult view of the world, and her representation of it in her writing: thus she interprets a supermarket customer's anxious checking of the contents of his trolley as perhaps resulting from the terror of not having enough money to pay (*Journal du dehors*, p. 13). When an automatic cash-machine rejects her card, Ernaux is plunged into the feelings of anxiety and shame acquired in childhood. Interestingly, they are expressed in religious terms, emphasising the role of the church, and in Ernaux's case her private Catholic school, in maintaining social hierarchies. The cash-machine is compared to 'a confessional without curtains' and the illegible card message leaves Ernaux feeling that she has been 'accused of a reprehensible act, the exact nature of which is a mystery to me' (*Journal du dehors*, p. 28). Money and material possessions are thus seen to be a buffer, a protection against social humiliation and anxiety. The impact of their possession or absence on individuals is omnipresent in Ernaux's descriptions of social reality, where economic and cultural capital are more significant than psychoanalytical explanations of behaviour. Having a place in society and maintaining it, one of the connotations of the title of *La Place*, is of prime importance, and money, though in itself insufficient to guarantee such a place, is nonetheless the first requirement.

As I have already suggested, this emphasis on the material basis of oppression seems in many ways to be at the root of Ernaux's espousal of a realist mode of writing. However, unlike the realist novel of the nineteenth century, exemplified by Balzac's *La Comédie humaine*, Ernaux's technique, particularly from *La Place* onwards, consists of selecting a few resonant and significant details, rather than providing a comprehensive description. In this way emotional states and nuances are invoked through the depiction of aspects of the material world, rather than by direct description. This technique has often led to comments on the euphemistic and restrained style of Ernaux's descriptions of emotional trauma; it has also probably saved her from the accusation of writing 'purple prose' which is often reserved for women writers (see chapter 6). In *Passion simple*, for example, descriptions of objects convey the intensity of the time spent with A.; a tiny detail becomes symbolic of a particular encounter between the lovers: [1] 'One afternoon, when he was there, I burnt the living-room carpet down to the weft by putting a boiling coffee-pot on it. I didn't mind. In fact, each time I noticed this mark, the memory of that afternoon with him made me feel happy' (*Passion simple*, p. 29). In this way apparently insignificant details can carry profound levels of meaning. In *La Place*, the father's attempt to take an interest in the fact that a mattress has recently been re-covered is associated with his physical decline, and the approach of death: 'In remembering this moment, I still believe that all is not lost, but these words are meant to prove to me that he is not very ill, when in reality this effort to cling to the world means precisely that he was leaving it' (*La Place*, pp. 107–8).

In these two examples Ernaux has provided both the description and its interpretation; at other times, these glimpses of material reality are allowed to speak for themselves. In a short story which

Ernaux wrote describing her final visit to her mother, whilst the latter was still living independently in a studio flat, the lack of purpose and loneliness in her mother's life are expressed by her preoccupation with material details: '"Paulette brought me some gooseberries. Look at how lovely they are. It's true that it's the time of year for them. Remind me to give you some before you leave"' ('Retours', 1985, p. 71). At the end of the story, Ernaux returns to her mother's flat a month later, after the mother has been admitted to hospital: 'In the vegetable rack of the fridge I found the gooseberries which I had forgotten to take the last time, all ready in a plastic bag knotted at the top, they had turned into a brown, liquid heap' ('Retours', 1985, p. 71). At this point there is no commentary or analysis; this tiny detail of domestic deterioration has a number of connotations which the reader is able to deduce from the rest of the story: the mother's decline, the passing of time, the difficulties of communication between mother and daughter. The mother's desire to nurture and to be nurtured by her daughter, her 'greedy tenderness', is expressed by the gift of the fruit, which the daughter significantly forgets to take back with her to her full life, in which the mother plays no part. The failed gift also encapsulates the social and cultural difference between mother and daughter, particularly as a parallel, equally inappropriate gift from daughter to mother is described earlier in the story: 'She accepted the gladioli with embarrassment, thanking me in an artificial tone. I had forgotten: when I gave her bought flowers she thought of it as an affectation, something that posh people would do, and that irritated her' (p. 70). There is no need for psychoanalytical or sociological analysis: the image of the bright gladioli and the abandoned gooseberries, the two failed gifts, is evocative of the attempts to cross the abyss separating classes and generations.[2]

Space

The word *place* (space, room or place) in Ernaux's writing often has negative connotations: the inferior place, or space which is assigned or imposed by the social hierarchy. Thus being 'déplacé', in the wrong place or a place to which one is not entitled, such as a first-class compartment on a train, is a constant fear for Ernaux's father in *La Place* (p. 59). The fact that *place* in French can refer both to a symbolic status or place, as well as space or room, renders Ernaux's use of the word particularly appropriate; she is concerned both with real differences between the classes and genders in their relation to public and private space, and with space as a symbol of opportunities and freedom, or their absence.

The social value attributed to different spaces, and the internalisation of that value system, as evidenced by the father's fears in *La Place*, are significant themes of Ernaux's representations of class and gender. In *Les Armoires vides*, there is a description of Denise as a child walking back from church with her mother, through the quiet, empty middle-class areas near the centre to the noise and bustle of the rue Clopart[3] where they live. The perspective of the child is adopted, so that the hierarchical value attributed to these different areas of urban space is as yet unclear. The bourgeois houses are simply seen by Denise as sad and empty: 'We come to rue de la République, a quiet area with large houses and tidy lawns. Dismal. No one we know' (*Les Armoires vides*, p. 38; trans. p. 25). In *La Honte*, however, writing from the perspective of someone who has left her class and acquired a political analysis, Ernaux carefully reviews the social inequalities inscribed in the topography of her native town, Yvetot:

> From the rue de la République to the pathways of the Champ-de-Courses, in less than three hundred metres you go from opulent wealth to poverty, from the urban to the rural, from space to proximity. From protected people, about whom nothing is known, to those about whom everything is public knowledge, including how much social security they get, what they eat and drink, when they go to bed. (*La Honte*, p. 48)

The series of oppositions in this description are fundamental to Ernaux's depiction of the spatial expression of inequality. In general, working-class culture, the culture of origin, is associated with proximity and lack of space, and middle-class culture with distance and the luxury of privacy. There are, however two sides to this coin: in the depiction of Denise's childhood in *Les Armoires vides*, physical closeness to her parents and their customers is associated with intimacy and pleasure (see p. 94). At adolescence, on the contrary, the lack of privacy afforded by the *épicerie-café* has become problematic. The parents' home seems crowded, untidy and dirty, and lack of suitable space and amenities makes it impossible to invite friends home: 'What bothered me the most was that we had no hall or dining-room, the only place to invite people in was the kitchen wedged between the store and the café, worse than useless' (*Les Armoires vides*, p. 109; trans. p. 72). The culture which once contained and nourished in a positive way, now stifles and invades, like the customers of the café: 'They invade us, swarm all over us, ten times worse than anything in Balzac or Maupassant' (*Les Armoires vides*, p. 111; trans. p. 74). As this literary reference indicates, comparisons with the works of literature she is studying at school, with their descriptions of 'drawing-rooms, parks and the old auntie who asks you for tea and cakes', deepen Denise's sense of the inferiority of her home and parents (*Les Armoires vides*, p. 100; trans. p. 67).[4]

Middle-class culture, acquired through education, becomes an escape from claustrophobic proximity, and provides Denise with intellectual, if not, as yet, physical space: the next lesson in her school-books becomes 'a foreign country which must not be explored alone, but which will come to life, with the teacher's help, at the right time' (*Les Armoires vides*, p. 93). Later, as a student in Rouen, Denise describes how the privileged space of the library, redolent of past tradition, becomes, like the church during childhood, a fairy-tale image of a more hygienic and aesthetic way of life: 'I go up the stone steps, I walk across the faded carpets, it's Sleeping Beauty's castle' (*Les Armoires vides*, p. 166; trans. p. 112). Here intellectual and physical space are at last combined; the comparison with a fairy-tale emphasises the contrast between this and the crowded, disordered home, as if Denise has been transported by magic into her new culture (see chapter 7, p. 170). In the description of the narrator's student days in *La Femme gelée*, there is also a strong sense of space and expansiveness: the freedom to wander anonymously in city streets is associated with the intellectual exploration which the narrator enjoys at this stage in her life: 'A time when you could have a yoghurt for dinner, pack in half an hour for an impromptu weekend, talk through the night. Read in bed all day on a Sunday. Languish in a café, watch people go in and out, imagine oneself floating among these anonymous existences' (*La Femme gelée*, p. 109). Like the claustrophobic proximity of the culture of origin, the anonymity and space of a middle-class urban existence also have a negative side; the narrator of *La Femme gelée* experiences the pleasure of her freedom, but in the end is frightened by it, her existence seems devoid of meaning, uprooted: 'Staying up all night, onion soup at dawn on the quays of the Seine, baby-sitting and youth-hostels, life far removed from order, it's all wonderful. But also the impression that this availability is a kind of emptiness' (*La Femme gelée*, p. 117). The floating sensation described positively at first becomes negative, a sense that life is pointless, unreal. At the end of this section of *La Femme gelée* the narrator concludes that the solution to this problem would be 'a man at my side' who would witness and give importance to the most trivial details of everyday life (p. 118). As we will see, the consequences of this view prove to be disastrous.

The physical separation of the social classes is paralleled by a similar separation on the basis of gender: in *Les Armoires vides*, Denise describes with disgust the old men who get drunk in her father's café, whilst her mother's shop seems to be the archetypal female space, combining the nurturing aspect of femininity, in its plentiful supplies of basic foodstuffs, with the whispered conversations about 'bad women' and 'women's troubles' which are overheard by the child (*Les Armoires vides*, p. 29). Again, *La Honte* provides the analysis of this division, with the café described as 'the masculine side' and the shop 'the feminine side' of Ernaux's childhood home (*La Honte*, p. 52). Nonetheless, as *La Femme gelée* makes clear, Ernaux consistently depicts her parents' relationship as less oppressive than the bourgeois marriage she first observed, and then experienced. The shop at least provides an independent sphere of activity and contact with the outside world for the mother, whilst the father often combines the preparation of family meals with his work in the café. In *La Femme gelée*, women are prisoners in a domestic space, which is entirely devoted to the servicing of men and children. Whilst the female narrator's universe is narrowed down, and focused on the small but tastefully furnished flat, the husband still has access to public space: 'He alone will enjoy the cold air of the street, the smell of the shops opening' (*La Femme gelée*, p. 154). For the woman, on the other hand, both space and time acquire a new and oppressive dimension, as the home becomes a leisure site for the husband, and a constant round of chores for her: 'In this cosy interior, what difficulties, what triumphs, not curdling the mayonnaise, making the baby laugh when he cries. I began to live in another time' (*La Femme gelée*, p. 154).

In the later works, Ernaux's representation of space acquires a new dimension: the possibility of escape from both the claustrophobic elements of her culture of origin and the confinement to the home associated with conventional femininity. In *La Honte* she reflects on the effect of returning to her home town, which, because it once represented the limits of her existence, has an emotional significance only tenuously linked to its contemporary geographical and social reality:

> Naming this town, as I have elsewhere, is impossible for me here, where it is not the geographical place indicated on a map, or crossed on the way from Rouen to Le Havre, by train or by car on the *route nationale* 15. It is the place of origin, without a name, where, when I go back, I am immediately seized by apathy, incapable of thought, almost of any precise memory, as if the place might engulf me again. (*La Honte*, p. 44)

During the years of childhood and adolescence the boundaries and divided spaces of the town were internalised, along with the restrictive codes and conventions of the social milieu and school. It is not surprising that the resulting feelings of passivity and hopelessness, the fear of being engulfed, persist into adulthood, and that the memories of the hierarchical division of urban space remain vivid. Cergy-Pontoise, the new town where Ernaux has lived since 1975, is described in *Une femme* as 'a vague, expressionless place, where one seemed to float, deprived of feelings and thoughts' (*Une femme*, p. 81). The theme is taken up again in *Journal du dehors* : 'The new town in the March sunshine. No depth, just shadows and light, car-parks darker than ever, dazzling concrete. A place with a single dimension' (*Journal du dehors*, p. 47). Cergy is represented as a new and relatively neutral space, which offers an escape from the weight of memory, the connotations of personal and social history, associated with Yvetot. Unlike Proust's Combray, Yvetot seems to deaden and stifle creativity, whilst Cergy provides the possibility of a return to the free-floating, anonymous student existence described in *La Femme gelée*. There are hints of the old fears of loneliness and isolation which drove the student narrator into marriage: on arriving in the new town, Ernaux would often get lost, driving around in a state of anxiety, whilst the subterranean car-parks inspire fears of rape (*Journal du dehors*, p. 29). The price paid for anonymity is the new town's physical and symbolic lack of landmarks, of comforting familiarity, which perhaps leads to the attempt to make connections with others recorded in *Journal du dehors*. The acquired freedom and space symbolised by the new town are represented with typically Ernausian ambivalence; the only certainty is that unlike the traditional backdrop for the literary élite – the boulevards and cafés of central Paris, or the provincial settings of the past – Cergy can provide a home, and a space in which to write. Despite the omnipresent and probably inevitable ambivalence, claustrophobia has been replaced by expansiveness, limitations by possibilities: 'I am filled with a feeling of intense satisfaction when I recognise the signs of the Parisian suburbs. The same feeling I have as I arrive on the A15 motorway, on the viaduct at Gennevilliers when the immense panorama of factories, tower-blocks, pre-war houses suddenly opens up before me, with as its backdrop *la Défense* and Paris' (*Journal du dehors*, p. 105).

The Body

The discussion of space as a location of social difference must lead to consideration of a still more fundamental set of boundaries, those of the body. Here an even more complex and contradictory trajectory than that analysed above can be traced. In *Les Armoires vides*, there is a powerful evocation of a childhood characterised by physical freedom and sensuous exploration of the world. As indicated in chapter 1, the senses of touch, sight and smell are all referred to in the description of the bright colours, sticky sweets and salacious stories of Denise's early years, remembered as a profusion of intense physical sensations, which includes, but is not subsumed by, the sexual:

> Ninise Lesur, who grew up among the smoke, the tomatoes put to ripen under the shutters keeping out the sun . . . like a kitten blissfully opening its eyes and looking, everything there for the taking. I don't want to remind myself of what I used to like and admire. But the world was mine, made up of a thousand pieces to hunger after, to thirst after, to touch and to tear, held together by a strong, slender, talkative thread that was me, Denise Lesur, me. (*Les Armoires vides*, pp. 46–7; trans. p. 31)

There is no equivalent to the intensity of this description of bodily pleasure and *joie de vivre* elsewhere in Ernaux's work, and it is significant that it is such a striking feature of the text which devotes most attention to early childhood (see p. 65 of this chapter).

It is only when she goes to school that Denise learns that her physical well-being and pleasure are irrelevant and even unacceptable in her new surroundings, and that on the contrary the body is to be controlled and subordinated to a culture of arid abstraction. The uncomfortable environment and the discipline of long hours of classes are the physical expression of the cultural lessons to be learnt: the primacy of the intellectual over the physical, as well as formality and 'refinement' of language and tastes. The school's 'huge, cold yard bordered by lime trees' is contrasted with the small yard at home, with its 'crates and boxes smelling of what was in them, yellow, acid-tasting jars from the shop window' (*Les Armoires vides*, p. 57; trans. p. 38). The serried ranks of lime trees, typical of the French urban environment, seem here to symbolise cold rationality, in contrast with the vivid smells and colours associated with the physical and emotional intimacy of home. Here, the contrasting value systems of the home and school, and the value attributed by the latter to intellectual achievement and moral virtue, are mainly conveyed by vivid evocations of place and sensations. In *La Honte*, Ernaux provides a more consistently analytical account of the school-rules and ethos, and of the contrast between the school's denial and repression of the body, and the pupils' own obsession with their physical development. Her participation in the many stage performances and religious festivals put on by the school, as a marker of its superiority to the town's lay, state school, is an instance of the attempt to control and discipline the resistant and recalcitrant body:

> In April 1952, at the festival 'des Anciennes', my role was to bring offerings to the dead, in a Greek tableau. My body was bent, resting on one leg held out in front of me, my arms outstretched. A memory of torture, the terror of collapsing on stage. Two static roles, doubtless because of the lack of grace witnessed by the photos. (*La Honte*, p. 83)

The image of torture which Ernaux uses in this passage indicates the intense way in which the school's ethos denied and punished the flesh. At this stage, as I suggested earlier, the home environment represents physical freedom, so that in her representations of her childhood home and school Ernaux both reproduces and comments on the traditional association of the body with working-class and the mind with middle-class, culture. Similarly, in his discussion of middle-class taste, in this case in art, Bourdieu has noted the rejection of the physical and of sensual pleasure which it involves: 'Rejecting the "human" clearly means rejecting what is *generic*, i.e., *common*, easy and immediately accessible, starting with everything that reduces the aesthetic animal to pure and simple animality, to palpable pleasure or sensual desire' (Bourdieu, [1979] 1984, p. 32).

If the role of the school, and by extension education, seems precisely to be the repression of the 'pure and simple animality' associated by Ernaux with early childhood and with working-class culture, the introduction of religion into the discussion complicates this picture, through the focus on the sexual body, and specifically on female sexuality. Loraine Day has commented on the signific-ance of religious imagery in *Les Armoires vides* (Day, 1990, p. 46). The cash-machine passage in *Journal du dehors* analysed earlier in this chapter suggests that Catholicism continues to be an important influence, providing some of the rare metaphors in Ernaux's writing; as Ernaux herself comments in *La Honte*: 'nothing can change the fact that up until adolescence God for me was the only normality, and the Catholic faith the only truth' (*La Honte*, p. 80).[5] In her article Day speaks of the 'original sin' of a working-class background and the 'grace' of middle-class culture, suggesting that Denise is released from her sinful, original state to purification by education. I would agree that this is a significant aspect of Denise's trajectory, and will pursue this idea in the discussion of the representation of adolescent sexuality which follows. However, the reverse would seem to be equally true; on another, perhaps more subversive level, it would be possible to compare the utopian state of early childhood to Eden before the fall, which in this case, as in the original story, is the outcome of knowledge, here provided by the priest and the Catholic school. At her first confession, Denise discovers that her sexuality is the only sin the priest is interested in; she emerges convinced of her indelible wickedness, and of its link with her social background: 'Something unclean and impure will stick to me forever because I come from a different background. I can pray for forgiveness all I like. I must be punished' (*Les Armoires vides*, p. 67, trans. p. 44). As this passage demonstrates, it is certainly the case that Denise's working-class origins become associated with what she comes to regard as the sinfulness of her bodily pleasures and desires, but it is middle-class, Catholic education which plays the role of the serpent. It is significant that Ernaux expresses her deep ambivalence in relation to middle-class, educated culture by representing it here as the source of both redemption and loss of innocence. In this scenario, early childhood, with its innocent but intense physical pleasures, can be seen as a lost state of grace, whose very ephemerality ensures its symbolic significance in Ernaux's narratives of her life.

At adolescence, a further series of reversals takes place. In both *Les Armoires vides* and *Ce qu'ils disent ou rien*, the discovery, or rediscovery, of sexual pleasure is depicted as a return to the positive experience of the body associated with early childhood, and, significantly, to the state of grace: 'I didn't wash for two days, so as not to rub anything away. I felt full of grace, the café was a low background murmur' (*Les Armoires vides*, p. 138; trans. p. 93). At this point, working-class culture seems to be the source of repression, the whispered stories about 'fallen women' overheard by Denise as a child have prepared the ground for the policing of female sexuality which her culture of origin now seems to represent, or at least to participate in. In this, the mother plays a central role: in *Une femme*, in one of the most striking and violent images of Ernaux's writing, she is compared to 'those African mothers who hold their little girl's arms behind her back while the midwife cuts out the clitoris' (*Une femme*, p. 62). The disturbing nature of this image and the way it stands out from the rest of the text have been commented on by Laurence Mall (Mall, 1995, p. 48). The body, which was represented as a site of pleasure in early childhood, has been subjected to a concerted attack, which has both physical and psychological dimensions and which is enacted by the forces of religion, social convention and the school, with the mother at their helm. The mother is 'the representative of the religious law and regulations of the school' (*La Honte*, p. 100). Her participation in the attempt to control her daughter's sexuality is analysed in *Une femme* as resulting from her fear of an unwanted pregnancy, and the loss of social status which it would entail (*Une femme*, p. 61). I will return to the question of the mother–daughter relationship later in this chapter (pp. 74–5 and pp. 84–5) and in chapter 4; here the significant points are that the mother represents the repressive aspects of working-class culture, and that it is specifically in relation to female sexuality that these aspects emerge.

The middle-class boys who accompany Denise down the 'primrose path' are, on the other hand, at this point capable of 'purifying' even her sexual desires. Classical music and educated conversation temporarily remove the shame associated with physical pleasure: 'It doesn't occur to me to worry that I might get punished for what I'm doing as we nestle on the deerskin, listening to the *Saint John Passion*. My parents could not imagine me in this setting. Nor could they understand that I feel there's nothing wrong with showing my "privates" here' (*Les Armoires vides*, p. 173; trans.117). However, as this quotation suggests, punishment, or the threat of being punished, is at the very least always lurking in the background in *Les Armoires vides*. In *Ce qu'ils disent ou rien*, similarly, the liberation of sexual expression turns out to be short-lived, as Anne discovers the sexual double standard: 'Could the same thing happen to a boy, relentless girls who would drive him mad with humiliation, I couldn't imagine it. I began to think that what I had been lacking was a code, rules, not those of my parents or school, rules about what to do with my body' (*Ce qu'ils disent ou rien*, p. 123). *La Femme gelée* also makes clear that the feelings of liberation experienced at adolescence as a result of the combination of sexual experiences and the move into middle-class social circles are illusory. Sexual self-expression may be permitted, but even for middle-class women there are clear boundaries which must not be crossed. In the end, monogamous marriage is the bourgeois norm, and it is seen to be far more beneficial to men than women. It may be possible to listen to Bach lying naked on a rug, but the body which is thus exposed must conform to the ideal of female beauty which Ernaux associates more with bourgeois than with working-class culture. Encounters with middle-class women, the mothers of school-friends, confirm the differences between them and her mother, in terms of domestic environment and skills, and importantly, physical appearance: 'A slim woman, in a pink overall, gliding between the sink and the table. . . . A sleek woman, happy I thought because everything around her seemed pretty' (*La Femme gelée*, p. 61). The acquisition of middle-class culture has merely added a further set of codes, a still more oppressive role-model to those of the education system, religion and the culture of origin. In Ernaux's writing about her own development, particularly in the first three novels and *La Honte*, but also in the relevant passages of *Une femme* and *La Place*, there is thus a very strong sense of the importance of sensuality in the widest sense, and of the social forces which combine to constrain and confine the female body and sexuality. My final question in this section concerns the representation of the body in the works concerned with the more recent past, the writer's adult persona: is the same cycle of sensual pleasure and its repression by oppressive social conventions repeated in *Passion simple* and *Journal du dehors*?

Passion simple begins by measuring the cultural revolution which has taken place in Ernaux's lifetime. She describes a pornographic film, seen on satellite television; the image is fuzzy because Ernaux does not own a decoder, but the (hetero)sexual act is nonetheless clearly visible. Ernaux comments that: 'what could not be watched without almost dying is now as easily visible as a handshake' (*Passion simple*, p. 12). After this initial section, the body is relegated to the background of *Passion simple*, which focuses on the psychological manifestations of passion. It is as if the reader is required to insert the television image into the gaps in the text, between the arrival of the lover, 'A.', and his departure. The lack of any description of the specificities of this sexual relationship, and the possibility of the transposition of the filmic representation in this way, succeed in emphasising the ordinariness of the passion, the shared nature of the experience: 'Without knowing it, he made me feel closer to other people' (*Passion simple*, p. 76). In at least one instance, however, the sexual pleasure of the relationship with A. is positively represented, albeit in fantasy: 'At the very second when I lapsed into this state, my mind seemed to experience a spasm of well-being. I felt as if I was abandoning myself to a physical pleasure, as if through the repetition of the same images, the same desires, the brain could experience orgasm, as if it were a sexual organ like the others' (*Passion simple*, pp. 41–2). Here, as in the opening section, Ernaux describes herself in the role of spectator, deriving pleasure from the image, rather than the experience itself, just as throughout *Passion simple* she is concerned to observe and record her own reactions, adopting the more distanced perspective of the later texts. The difficulty of finding a positive way of representing female desire may also be at the root of this distancing technique, and the significant absence of the body in this text. Unlike *Les Armoires vides* or *Ce qu'ils disent ou rien*, *Passion simple* is not a work of fiction; the narrating 'I' is clearly identified with the author herself, and the sexual experience in question is in the recent rather than distant past; all of this may compound the difficulty. Is the adoption of the 'spectator' role merely a case of stepping into a masculine subject position, which, as Laura Mulvey (1975) has argued, is all that is available in patriarchal culture? As Anne, the narrator of *Ce qu'ils disent ou rien*, was aware, the language to describe sexual experience is woefully inadequate, replete with negative and oppressive versions of the female body and sexuality: 'I didn't like all this vocabulary, it made me sad. I think it's better not to name things, or to invent words' (*Ce qu'ils disent ou rien*,

p. 95). Perhaps in *Passion simple* Ernaux has adopted the former policy; the image must of necessity remain unclear, as the decoder which could translate female sexual experience into a language free of misogyny and oppressive connotations has not yet been invented.

Despite this difficulty, which like the body is not an overt subject in the text, Ernaux is at pains to represent the experience of passion positively, commenting after a description of her obsession with A., and his suspected indifference, that 'In a sense, I was luckier than him' (*Passion simple*, p. 40). The desire to suture this positive reading into the text leads logically to the closure, where the experience of passion is defined as a gift: 'When I was a child, luxury was fur coats, long dresses and villas by the sea. Later I thought it was leading the life of an intellectual. It seems to me now that it is also the possibility of living to the full a passion for a man or woman' (*Passion simple*, p. 75). Although this clearly presents the experience in a positive light, the emphasis on pain rather than pleasure in the text as a whole creates a tension between positive and negative interpretations.[6] A reading of the text where the psychological sufferings described are a punishment for the physical pleasure (implied), a self-imposed continuation of the repressive upbringing described in earlier texts, does suggest itself. This reading would follow on logically from Loraine Day's discussion of masochism in *Les Armoires vides*, where, despite the psychoanalytical origins and connotations of the term, masochism in Ernaux's representations of female sexuality is interpreted as the result of 'internalised class and gender oppression' (Day, 1990, p. 52). In *Passion simple*, the religious connotations of the word 'passion' would support this interpretation, along with the description of the suffering body and the fantasy of dying for love which occurs after A.'s departure: 'My whole body was hurting. I would have liked to tear out the pain, but it was everwhere. I wanted a burglar to come into my bedroom and kill me' (*Passion simple*, p. 52).[7]

Glimpses of the sensuality described in the earlier works nonetheless emerge. Consistently in Ernaux's works, the male body is represented as object of desire, suggesting that Ernaux's writing, like the avant-garde approach to film recommended by Mulvey, can challenge the representational limitations which Mulvey sees in conventional Hollywood film. There are, in fact, already examples of this in the text published one year before the Mulvey article, *Les Armoires vides*: 'One thing follows another, discovering teeth, corners, rough cheeks, I can feel each finger separately on my back, a celebration of touch' (*Les Armoires vides*, p. 137; trans. p. 92). In *Passion simple*, Ernaux describes the attempt to remember every detail of A.'s body: 'I could feel his teeth, the inside of his mouth, the shape of his thighs, the texture of his skin' (*Passion simple*, p. 54). The emphasis on touch and on a sensual relationship to the whole body here are clearly reminiscent of the earlier text's description of Denise's sexual awakening, and in contrast to the spectator role discussed earlier. However, the negative context of loss and pain reasserts itself in the next sentence: 'I thought that there was very little difference between this reconstitution and a hallucination, between memory and madness' (p. 54). The oppressive force of social conventions remains more marginal in *Passion simple* than in most of Ernaux's texts; nonetheless the fear of social opprobrium, so strongly inculcated in early life, is still present. Ernaux observes, at the hairdresser's, how a woman's announcement that she is 'suffering with her nerves' places her into the category of the abnormal, subtly changing the way she is treated by the staff. This experience encourages Ernaux to remain silent about her passion: 'I too was afraid of appearing abnormal, if I had said "I am passionately involved with someone"' (*Passion simple*, p. 24).

The linking of female sexuality with madness, perhaps the result of the internalisation of oppression, is, however, not the end of the story for Ernaux. *Journal du dehors* contains several passages where there is a strong sense of delighting in the world, and deriving sensual pleasure from its sights and sounds, as if there has been a return to the certainty that 'the world was made for us to throw ourselves into it, and enjoy it', which, significantly, the narrator of *La Femme gelée* claims to have inherited from her mother (p. 30). In particular there is a long description of a shop in Paris selling silk underwear, where the pleasure of colour, to a great extent absent from the writing since *Les Armoires vides*, returns:[8] 'Rue des Saints-Pères, on this cold February evening. The *Sabbia Rosa* lingerie boutique: everywhere silk in the colours of sweets, sunrise on the Indian ocean, flowers from Monet's garden. Absent or subdued eroticism, only beauty, fragility, lightness (the whole shop could be packed into a trunk)' (*Journal du dehors*, p. 95). The passage closes with a positive representation of female desire for the male body: 'Men should wear silk underwear to give us the pleasure of touching such softness and fragility on their bodies' (*Journal du dehors*, p. 96). This passage, along with others in *Journal du dehors*, perhaps provides a key to a possible reading of *Passion simple*, where submission to patriarchal control is not the only possibility for women. In this light the text can be read as the first step towards a rehabilitation of femininity and feminine culture, which becomes still more pronounced, and indeed defiant, in *Journal du dehors*.[9] In *Passion simple*, as I argued in chapter 2, Ernaux brings into literature aspects of feminine culture such as women's magazines and horoscopes, which would be anathema to the bourgeois aesthetics discussed by Bourdieu (Bourdieu, [1979] 1984). Like the feminist theorists of the 'object relations' school of psychoanalysis, Ernaux would seem to be arguing against the conventional view of the feminine prioritisation of relationships as pathology (see chapter 4, p. 92).[10] A., who, unlike Ernaux, sees their afternoons spent making love as no more than that, is perhaps, as she suggests, the more impoverished of the two (*Passion simple*, p. 35). The material base, as argued earlier in this chapter, is of course crucial. Ernaux is speaking from a position of strength; the social disapproval encountered at the hairdresser's no longer has the power it held for the adolescent heroines of the earlier texts, and the narrator of *Passion simple* is free to pursue her own desires. Their apparently masochistic tendency may in part be a reaction against the rational, masculine culture which as a successful product of the French education system Ernaux is well acquainted with. She is at last able to think 'with a profound satisfaction' about the working-class women of her childhood who braved the gossip and spent their afternoons with a man, rather than cleaning their windows (*Passion simple*, p. 30). Like the women whose children expressed their disapproval of their mothers' liaisons in the magazine *Marie-Claire*, here Ernaux finally gives up the struggle to be a good pupil, and allows herself to dream (*Passion simple*, p. 26).

A. remains a shadowy figure in *Passion simple*, and with the notable exception of the description of his body quoted above, there are only sketches of his physical appearance and taste in clothes, television programmes and cars. Even if *Passion simple* is read as a rehabilitation of femininity, the *desiring* female subject of the *Sabbia Rosa* extract from *Journal du dehors* is still not fully expressed. In 1996 Ernaux published a short piece, 'Fragments autour de Philippe V.', which seems to cross this final barrier, to present the decoded image. Here, any trace of masochism is banished, as the text celebrates her power as a woman and as a writer: 'For a woman, the freedom to write without shame is connected to that of being the first to touch a man's body with desire.'[11]

The Gaze

As this discussion of the role of the body in Ernaux's represent-ations of gender, class and sexuality has suggested, positioning oneself as the subject, or being positioned as the object of the gaze, is a significant element of the oppressive social system which Ernaux describes. In her works, the separate spaces allocated to middle class and working class, men and women, are traversed by a network of gazes which police, censor and assess. My aim here is to look at Ernaux's examination of the role of these gazes in attributing social meanings and values to gender and class differ-ence. If, as the title of *La Place* and the recurrence of expressions such as *déplacé* (out of place) or *à sa place* (in one's rightful place, at home) suggest, Ernaux is particularly concerned with positions both assumed and socially imposed, the gaze seems to be one of the mechanisms which facilitates the constant process of placing others and being placed by them. Because we are concerned here both with the physical reality of the look and with its psychic and cultural effects, this section thus forms a link between the analysis of the material and cultural locations of social difference in this chapter.

Perhaps the fullest analysis of the power of the gaze to make one feel at home or completely out of place is provided in *La Honte*. Initially, Ernaux draws attention to the self-imposed surveillance of working-class culture:

> People's main leisure pursuit was watching each other. We would go to watch people coming out of cinemas, or the arrival of trains at the station in the evening. The fact that people were gathered together seemed to be a sufficient reason to join them. A torchlight procession, a cycle race were an opportunity to enjoy the sight of the people who were there as much as the spectacle itself, to go home saying who had been there too, and who they were with. (*La Honte*, p. 62)

This aspect of the culture of origin is represented as particularly oppressive, since the lack of private space in a home which is also shop and café means that the family is constantly exposed to the public gaze: 'The clients see us eat, go to mass, to school, hear us wash in a corner in the kitchen, piss in the bucket. A constant exhibition' (*La Honte*, p. 67). It is not surprising, in the light of this, that Ernaux describes 'avoiding the critical gaze of others' as a rule of her father's existence in *La Place* (p. 61). This rule is general, since the parents are equally suspicious of those of the same social milieu and those outside it. In relation to the former there is a thin dividing line between maintaining the hard-won image of respectability and being accused of snobbishness or showing off. Ernaux's academic success is in this context a social embarrassment, 'almost shame', which has to be justified: 'We never pushed her, she had it in her' (*La Place* , p. 81).

However, Ernaux depicts the self-policing of the working-class community very much as an effect of the social hierarchy as a whole, and the critical middle-class gaze is represented as the most significant aspect of social oppression. Thus it is particularly when meeting people 'he considered important' that the father tries to conceal his inferior social status and education (*La Place*, p. 60). If the father tries to avoid criticism by politeness and evasiveness, the mother has a more dynamic approach. She tries to imitate middle-class speech, and in public is always well-dressed and made-up, in order to maintain her position (*Une femme*, p. 56). In *Les Armoires vides*, the mother always gives a little more than the term's fees to the teacher so that her daughter will be well regarded: 'faut te faire bien voir' (p. 68). Similarly, when Ernaux invites student friends home, her father makes enormous efforts to welcome them: 'The composition of the meals was a constant worry, "Does Miss Geneviève like tomatoes?"' Her father's discomfiture and anxiety are contrasted with the relaxed way in which she is received by the families of her middle-class friends, who do not need to fear 'a stranger's gaze'. Despite Ernaux's attempts to pre-empt the 'condescending gaze' of her friends by warning them in advance that her parents' home is 'simple', they still use regional expressions when talking to her father, thus demonstrating their awareness of his inferior social status (*La Place*, pp. 92–3). Again, when Ernaux marries, her parents see money as a way of winning social approval, of averting the critical gaze and their sense of inferiority: 'She wanted to help us financially during our final year of study, later always worrying about what we might like to have. The other family had humour, originality, they did not feel they owed us anything' (*Une femme*, p. 71).

Religion becomes an element of the critical middle-class view of working-class mores and manners described above, particularly in the texts in which Ernaux's private Catholic school plays a major role, *Les Armoires vides* and *La Honte*. In the religious domain, the sense of being constantly observed seems particularly strong; thus for Ernaux's mother, religious festivals were opportunities 'to show herself off, in her best clothes and in good company' (*La Honte*, p. 100). Religion for the mother is a way of acquiring a higher social status by 'showing the bourgeois women of the centre of town that a former factory worker, through her piety – and generosity at church – is worth as much as them' (*La Honte*, p. 103). However, the gaze of the church also has more repressive connotations; for Denise at her first confession, the priest's eyes in the confessional, 'those pale eyes which hypnotise me', are powerfully judgemental, and seem linked to the 'eye of Saint Agnes' in a picture on the classroom wall (*Les Armoires vides*, p. 67). The mother, who as we have seen is very closely associated with religion in Ernaux's descriptions of her upbringing, is described as having a similarly powerful gaze in *'Je ne suis pas sortie de ma nuit'*; Ernaux describes her demented mother's comments on one of her visits to the hospital: 'How are you behaving? Aren't you ashamed of yourself?' and her own guilty reaction, since she has just spent the night with a lover: 'How does she KNOW? My childhood belief that her eyes are capable of seeing everything, like God at the tomb of Cain, overwhelms me' (*'Je ne suis pas sortie de ma nuit'*, p. 22). This sense of being constantly under surveillance renders Ernaux's choice of the expressions 'bien vu' and 'mal vu' (well or badly regarded), to introduce lists of behaviour which her Catholic school deemed acceptable or unacceptable, particularly appropriate (*La Honte*, pp. 83–4). The list of unacceptable or 'badly regarded' behaviour concentrates particularly on what should not be seen: books or films that have not been specifically approved by the school and *romans-photo* (picture stories, often romantic fiction).

In the religious context, the gaze thus has a double dimension: the unswerving, critical eye of God, the Church or the private school, or the guilty look which sees what is forbidden. The latter is clearly particularly significant in *La Honte*, where the crisis which sets the narrative in motion seems to be a murderous version of the primal scene: the twelve-year-old Ernaux sees her father, not making love to her mother, but trying to kill her. The comparison with the primal scene seems justified by Ernaux's own comments in the text, firstly linking the scene with the parents' sexual relationship: 'My parents may have referred to the scene of that Sunday, found an explanation, or an excuse, and decided to forget all about it. For example, after making love one night' (*La Honte*, pp. 20–1). Secondly, the scene is presented as a loss of innocence: 'I had seen what I should not have seen. I knew what, according to the social innocence of the private school, I should not know' (*La Honte*, pp. 108–9). However, this particular primal scene has strong social, as well as sexual and psychic, connotations. Earlier in this chapter I discussed the fall from grace associated with the recognition of the limitations and inadequacies of the culture of origin; here the 'fall', as in its original biblical context, is specifically associated with forbidden sights. The knowledge acquired as a result of this look is both sexual, as in Genesis, and social, for Ernaux has seen that which 'placed me in some inexplicable way in the camp of those whose violence, alcoholism or mental derangement fuelled the stories which would end with the phrase "after all, it's terrible to see such things"' (*La Honte*, pp. 108–9).

Despite the mother's collusion with the school, and with religion generally, and her role in policing her daughter's sexual behaviour, the critical eye is turned on her in a significant passage of *La Honte*. Here, the feeling of being 'on the wrong side of the tracks' or in the wrong camp, which has resulted from the guilty gaze at the forbidden scene, is confirmed; this time the mother, and by extension Ernaux herself, is the object, rather than the subject, of the gaze. On returning home from a school trip the twelve-year-old Ernaux is dropped off at her door by the coach; her mother comes to the door dishevelled and wearing only a stained night-dress, with the result that pupils and teacher stare silently at this spectacle of feminine impropriety: 'I disappeared into the shop in order to make the scene come to an end. I had just seen my mother through the eyes of the private school' (*La Honte*, p. 110). Perhaps the most important element here is Ernaux's own internalisation of the critical gaze, the moment when the sense of inferiority and shame, of one's lowly place in the social hierarchy, which is the effect of the gaze, becomes a *modus vivendi*. This internalisation, as I suggested above, forms a link between the oppressive middle-class gaze from 'outside', and the self-policing within working-class culture. Ernaux provides many descriptions of the negative effects of this internalisation on her own sense of self, effects which often become apparent when she is confronted with her image in the mirror. Thus in *Les Armoires vides*, when Denise sees herself unexpectedly in a shop window or mirror, this triggers a stream of self-critical feelings:

> Other girls are graceful, they move easily, they laugh, run and get up to answer without giving it a thought. My body always gets in the way, with the others watching me, I feel like a cripple trying to learn to walk again, frightened of taking a wrong step or falling. I feel as if my parents are strangers, yet I have a way of walking that is like my mother's and I put my hand to my mouth when I laugh just like the other girls in the neighbourhood. (*Les Armoires vides*, p. 126; trans. p. 84)

In a particularly telling passage in *La Honte*, Ernaux describes an evening in a restaurant near Tours during the coach trip to Lourdes which is described near the end of the book. During the evening, both Ernaux and her father are conscious of not belonging in this rather sophisticated environment, and of being badly treated by the waiters. At one point, there is a description of the reflections of the twelve-year-old Ernaux, when she sees a girl of about the same age with her father. The girl is sun-tanned, at ease, laughing and joking with her father, both physically and socially different from Ernaux herself: 'I saw myself in the mirror opposite, pale, looking sad with my glasses, sitting silently next to my father who was staring into space. I could see everything that separated me from that girl but I did not know what I could do in order to be like her' (*La Honte*, p. 125). In both of these examples Ernaux seems to experience her working-class origins as visible, indelibly imprinted on the body and revealed in the harsh light of the critical gaze of middle-class others.[12]

If 'working-classness' is experienced as a form of visible physical inferiority, Ernaux's representations of gender attribute an equally significant role to the gaze and to its objectifying power in relation to the female body. Just as the internalisation of the critical middle-class gaze leads to self-surveillance in the working-class community, Ernaux describes how a network of gazes in her girls' school reinforces the power of stereotypes of female beauty. Thus the younger girls aspire to the physical maturity of the older pupils: 'It seemed to me that we observed them constantly and that they never looked at us. They were the image we aspired to at the top of the school and in life' (*La Honte*, p. 97). In *Ce qu'ils disent ou rien*, Ernaux describes her heroine, Anne, walking through the town, conscious of being watched by 'the many eyes of a vague audience' as if she were presenting a fashion collection (*Ce qu'ils disent ou rien*, p. 14). This sense of being watched leads to the desire for an approving gaze, and in the end to collusion with the hierarchical classification of female bodies which is depicted as a fundamental aspect of patriarchy: 'The equation – beauty, the main factor in being attractive and loved, equals the purpose of existence – goes through me like a knife through butter, and more surreptitiously than ax squared + bx + c = 0' (*La Femme gelée*, p. 63). Thus Anne tries on a new dress, twirling and parading in front of her bedroom mirror, but in the end sits down, 'discouraged by the fact of being alone in seeing myself' (*Ce qu'ils disent ou rien*, p. 39). The desire to please leads Ernaux's adolescent heroines to offer themselves to the male gaze, eventually internalising the resulting objectification to such an extent that their whole identity becomes focused on their physical appearance: 'As I twirled in front of the mirror at the age of fourteen, the only thing missing was the gaze of the other, for myself I was already just appearance' (*La Femme gelée*, p. 66). Later in the same text, Ernaux describes herself as a young woman seeking to break out of this vicious circle, by finding the ideal partner, a soulmate: 'But where is this brother, as I call him, with whom I would make love without the cattle market trading of flesh, without "you've got beautiful hair, breasts like this or that", but with laughter and communication' (*La Femme gelée*, p. 103). Later in the text, the narrator's self-deception in believing that she has found this partner is implied by the threat contained in the reflected image in the mirror. The negative version of the equation lurks in the background, confirming the oppressive nature of the classifying male gaze at women: 'My reflection in the mirror. Satisfying. But at twenty-two, behind the real face, already the threat of another, imaginary, terrible, faded skin, hardened features. Old equals ugly equals solitude' (*La Femme gelée*, p. 120). The fear of ageing and death clearly continues to be a theme of Ernaux's writing, though she has also recently produced texts which seem to celebrate her power and confidence as a mature woman, and where she is an agent, rather than the object of the gaze; 'Fragments autour de Philippe V.', quoted earlier in this chapter, would be an instance of this. It remains to be seen whether in the future the experience of ageing will become, as it did for Beauvoir, a major theme, and whether the need to accept the mother's ageing body which is the struggle and achievement of '*Je ne suis pas sortie de ma nuit*' will influence Ernaux's writing of her own, ageing body.

If the gaze plays a crucial role in Ernaux's representations of gender and class, to what extent do the texts analyse the objectification of otherness in terms of the ethnic diversity of contemporary French society? In *Journal du dehors*, Ernaux extends her discussion of the policing role of the critical middle-class gaze beyond the family, or even the white working-class milieu in which she grew up. At one point she describes a black woman in tradit- ional dress entering a luxury shop: 'Immediately, the manager's gaze becomes a weapon, constant surveillance of this customer who it is assumed has come into the wrong shop, but who does not realise she is not at home (à sa place) here' (*Journal du dehors*, p. 75). *Journal du dehors* is generally the only one of Ernaux's works where race, as well as gender and class, is represented as a source of oppression; since in this case she can only be in the role of observer, it is not surprising that this issue emerges mainly in the text in which she looks outside the self, to contemporary social reality. The only other striking instance where African culture is represented in Ernaux's writing is the image of excision in *Une femme*, also referred to in *Journal du dehors*. Some readings might castigate Ernaux for this negative representation of African culture; alternatively, its inclusion might be considered to broaden, and pro- vide a world-wide context for the discussion of gender oppression.

Another form of social otherness, and its relation to the gaze, which is present in *Journal du dehors* is less distant from Ernaux's culture of origin; the text demonstrates a consistent interest in and concern for those who exist on the margins of contemporary urban society, the homeless. Significantly, the extent of their marginal- isation is measured by Ernaux in terms of their indifference to the surveillance of the public gaze: 'At what point, when one has no work or home, does the gaze of others cease to prevent us from doing things which are natural, but misplaced (déplacées) in public in our culture' (*Journal du dehors*, p. 100). This indifference could, however, also be read as resistance, a possibility which Ernaux herself recognises elsewhere in *Journal du dehors*; she describes two homeless men in a train compartment, having a loud philosophical discussion which encompasses the desire to return to the womb and the war in former Yugoslavia, and which is delivered with ironic verve: 'There are the Serbs! There are the Croats! It's lucky there are newspapers, I would be pretty stupid without them' (p. 103). Ernaux comments on the exhibitionism of the two men, and the embarrassment of her fellow-passengers: 'Unlike the theatre, the spectators of this scene avoid looking at the actors, act as if they heard nothing. Embarrassed by life becoming spectacle, and not by the reverse' (*Journal du dehors*, pp. 104–5). Life becoming theatre is a constant theme in *Journal du dehors*, whether it is intellectuals who exhibit themselves in a television discussion (p. 68) or the employees of a hairdresser's salon: 'Both male and female hairdressers belong to a theatrical, colourful world, they are all dressed in the latest fashion, and would appear eccentric outside the salon' (*Journal du dehors*, p. 33). This colourful and eccentric world seems in some way to be resisting the grey social uniformity outside.

Another anecdote about a homeless man suggests that his ability to play the role of clown creates a distance 'between the social reality of poverty and alcoholism, which his person might remind us of, and the travelling public' (pp. 78–9).[13] If Ernaux represents these acts of resistance positively, she is less impressed by the self-satisfied exhibitionism of a lower middle-class mother and daughter, and the irony which she reserves for the middle classes returns: 'They feel permitted to make all the passengers share their comments, their gestures, visibly convinced of the excellence of their social being and aware that people are watching, and listening to them' (p. 49). In these instances, Ernaux makes herself the subject of the gaze, observing people around her either sympathetically, or ironically, as in the last example. Perhaps in some way she is writing herself out of the objectification and alienation she has experienced as a result of being on the receiving end of the critical middle-class or male gaze. Appropriately, in *'Je ne suis pas sortie de ma nuit'*, Ernaux describes herself resisting the critical gaze in the same way as the marginalised people she has depicted positively in *Journal du dehors*. Here, at last, in the desperate situation of her mother's mental decline, Ernaux is no longer ashamed, able to return the gaze and resist its objectifying force: 'She laughs for no reason. The shop-assistants give us funny looks, appear embarrassed. I look them up and down, arrogantly' (*'Je ne suis pas sortie de ma nuit'*, p. 17).

The Cultural Locations of Social Difference

Culture

The separation between middle-class and working-class culture, as the discussion so far indicates, is a recurrent theme of Ernaux's writing, which she herself highlights in *La Honte*: 'At the time when I was reading *The Young Brigitte* and *Slave or Queen* by Delly, and going to see Bourvil's *Not so Stupid*, Sartre's *Saint Genet* and Calaferte's *Requiem for the Innocent* were appearing in bookshops, in the theatre Ionesco's *Les Chaises*. For me the two series will remain forever separated' (p. 106). The middle-class side of this divide is often characterised in Ernaux's writing by a sense of unreality or unnecessary abstraction. In *La Place*, she describes how her father sees study as having no connection with reality, and is therefore amazed when his daughter speaks English, a language she has learnt entirely at school, to a passing hitch-hiker. Similarly, he does not regard intellectual effort as real work: 'He would always say that I was learning well, never that I was working well. Work was only manual work' (*La Place*, p. 81). At first, as a child, Ernaux shares the father's view; the culture she is acquiring through her education has little or no connection with the rest of her life, it is merely a game, at which she excels: 'Is that what school's about, a load of symbols to repeat, trace on the page, string together? The world of the store was infinitely more real!' (*Les Armoires vides*, p. 54; trans. p. 36).

At adolescence, rejection of the parents and their culture leads to a re-evaluation of the new culture, which seems suddenly to connect with the experience of adolescent disaffection. It is literature which is responsible for this transformation, providing one of the hooks which tempt Ernaux into the change of allegiance and eventually class: 'Different. Infinitely better. The books I'm reading are absolute proof. Sartre, Kafka, Michel de Saint-Pierre, Simone de Beauvoir, I, Denise Lesur, am one of them. I bow under the weight of their ideas inside me' (*Les Armoires vides*, p. 156; trans. p. 105). The new ideas lead to a questioning 'of social convention, religion, money' (*Une femme*, p. 64), and to an awareness of the passive acceptance of the status quo which characterises the respectable working-class culture of the parents: 'With horror, I realised that everything was "like that" for them, they would just criticise individuals, not the system' (*Ce qu'ils disent ou rien*, p. 67). In a further, typically Ernausian reversal, a passage in *Une femme* demonstrates an understanding of the inappropriateness of an adolescent rebellion based on a culture which, although opposit-ional, is in reality profoundly middle-class. Whereas Anne in *Ce qu'ils disent ou rien* speaks as the disaffected adolescent, the auto/biographical 'I' of *Une femme* has acquired an ironic distance from her own past self: 'I was living my adolescent rebellion in the romantic mode, as if my parents had been *bourgeois*. I identified with misunderstood artists' (*Une femme*, pp. 64–5).

If *Une femme* displays an awareness of the middle-class origins of many radical literary movements, *Les Armoires vides* and *La Femme gelée* analyse a further limitation, in relation to gender. The belief that gender is irrelevant to existential questions and their representation in literature is described as a feature of the adolescent enthusiasm for literature: 'The fact that these books were written by men, that their heroes are also men, is something I don't pay attention to, I identify with Roquentin or Meursault' (*La Femme gelée*, p. 94).[14] The narrators of these two texts rapidly realise that literature excludes and marginalises women's experiences: 'Do some work on one of our assigned texts perhaps, Victor Hugo or Péguy. I feel sick at the thought. They have nothing to say to me, there's nothing that corresponds to how I'm feeling now, nothing to help me with what I'm going through' (*Les Armoires vides*, p. 12; trans. p. 8). In the light of this analysis, the angry denunciations of the first three novels can be seen as a response to the inadequacy of existing literary works in terms of their representations of gender. Bringing women's experience into literature is indeed a feature of Ernaux's writing generally, whether in terms of the exploration of the mother–daughter relationship in *Une femme* and *'Je ne suis pas sortie de ma nuit'* or the rehabilitation of 'feminine' popular culture in *Passion simple* and *Journal du dehors*. As the examples cited above show, feminism is a significant part of the critique of middle-class educated culture which underlies Ernaux's work.

Language

The discussion of this cultural divide cannot be pursued without a consideration of Ernaux's treatment of its manifestation in language. Ernaux's representations of class and gender attribute a fundamental role to language in the maintenance of social inequality; this is indicated by the choice of epigram for *La Honte*, a quotation from Paul Auster: 'Language is not truth. It is our way of existing in the world.' This epigram is particularly appropriate since Ernaux's aim in *La Honte* is to explore the 'way of existing in the world' of her twelve-year-old self; in this exploration it is crucial to return to the linguistic limits of that world: 'the words with which I thought about myself and the world around me' (*La Honte*,

p. 37). Returning to the linguistic universe of former selves is a constant feature of Ernaux's writing, though it takes very different forms. The fictional 'I' of the early texts permits the use of an appropriately colloquial and violent adolescent language, whereas the later works separate the old language from the new by a variety of textual markers. The contrast between working-class and middle-class codes is nonetheless analysed in *Les Armoires vides*; for Denise language is a significant aspect of the culture shock she experiences on her arrival at school:

> The teacher speaks slowly, she uses very long words, she's never in a hurry, she enjoys talking, very different from my mother. 'Hang your overcoat carefully on the hooks!' When I come in from playing my mother yells at me, 'Don't throw your sweater on the floor, who d'you think'll pick it up? Pull yer socks up!' Worlds apart. (*Les Armoires vides*, p. 53; trans. p. 35)

The representation of this linguistic difference then follows a similar trajectory to that already traced in the sections on space, the body and culture: working-class language at first seems more vivid, and more closely related to the real or concrete. As the educational process progresses, however, it is found increasingly inadequate, and the potential of the new language becomes associated with the discovery of a less limited world: 'These words fascinate me, I want to catch them, keep them with me, put them in my own writing. I take them for myself and at the same time it's as if I'm taking on all the things the books talk about' (*Les Armoires vides*, p. 76; trans. p. 51). As a result of this process, Denise seems to be torn not only between two cultures, but also between two languages: 'I carry in me two languages, the black printed marks you get in books, graceful little grasshoppers, in contrast with the thick, fat weighty words which hammer you in the stomach or in the head, make you cry at the top of the stairs on the cookie tin or laugh under the counter' (*Les Armoires vides*, p. 77; trans. p. 51).

This sense of a double inheritance is maintained in Ernaux's later works. If Denise in *Les Armoires vides* and, still more consistently, Anne in *Ce qu'ils disent ou rien* rebel against the language of their culture of origin, it undergoes a kind of rehabilitation in *La Place* and *Une femme*, where Ernaux develops the technique of presenting the words and phrases used by her parents, or current in their milieu, in italics, and in quotation marks (see chapter 1, p. 13). In these two texts, although the separation between Ernaux's acquired middle-class language and that of her culture of origin is marked visually, in general the latter is presented without commentary. Despite the apparent 'objectivity' of the presentation, the power of this 'mother tongue', indicated by the contrasting images in the quotation above, is in fact the source of considerable ambivalence. The language of origin has clearly never lost the power attributed to it by Denise in *Les Armoires vides*; in *La Honte*, Ernaux suggests that the phrase she used at the time of witnessing the fatal scene – 'gagner malheur' – conveys more of the scene's meaning than the abstract and analytical terminology she now has access to (*La Honte*, p. 31).[15] This colloquial, regional expression is laden with connotations, like the 'weighty words' referred to by Denise, whilst the language of theory merely skims the surface, like the grasshopper words dancing across the page.

In one sense, the ability of words and expressions such as 'gagner malheur' to convey the mood and atmosphere associated with a particular experience, or indeed a whole culture or phase of life, is clearly a positive attribute. In *La Place* Ernaux suggests that the working-class language of her childhood is precise and to the point. She justifies its inclusion in the text as follows: 'Simply because these words and phrases convey the limits and the colour of the world my father lived in, and which I also inhabited. And in that world, one word was never mistaken for another' (*La Place*, p. 46). Similarly, in the description of the days immediately following her mother's death, Ernaux comments that everyday language has now acquired a new dimension. She recognises its ability to capture her experience: 'The feeling of emptiness when I think: this will be the first spring she will not see. Now I feel the force of ordinary phrases, even clichés' (*Une femme*, p. 21). However, if this language is laden with meaning in a positive sense, the use of adjectives such as 'heavy' and 'dense' to describe it also implies oppression, the idea of being weighed down and constrained. In her representations of working-class culture, Ernaux is concerned not to idealise, by concealing the 'humiliating limits of our condition' (*La Place*, p. 54; see also chapter 2, p. 39). The phrase used here – 'les barrières humiliantes' – is significant: just as the family is confined spatially and culturally by barriers imposed by a society based on inequality, so language confines them, and their class, to a particular and limited view of the world. Thus in *La Place*, phrases such as: *'On ne peut pas être plus heureux qu'on est'* (*we couldn't be any happier*; p.

77) , or: *'Il y avait plus malheureux que nous'* (*there were people worse off than us*; p. 44), which are italicised in the original, indicate the passive acceptance of inequality referred to above (see also chapter 7, p. 165). These phrases, better than any theory, convey the reality of oppression where transgressive or rebellious thought is annihilated by exhaustion, repetitive routine and the desire to 'better oneself'.

In *Une femme*, the dimension of gender is added to this sense of the oppressiveness of the language of origin:

> Thus, I am writing in the most neutral manner possible, but certain expressions ('if you have an accident') cannot be neutral for me in the same way as other more abstract terms ('denial of the body and of sexuality' for example). At the moment when I remember them, I have the same sinking feeling as at the age of sixteen. (*Une femme*, p. 62)

This sentence is completed by the image of the African mother holding her daughter during excision already discussed. The violent image reinforces the notion of the oppressive force of the words, which in this case are doubly powerful, because they evoke not only the moral codes and conventions imposed on women in a particular time and social milieu, but also because of the implication that they were spoken by the mother, the dominant figure in Ernaux's upbringing, and arguably her life. The phrase 'mother tongue' which I used earlier is, in this sense, appropriate; in general the mother is the child's linguistic model, and given the particularly important role played by Ernaux's mother, it is not surprising that her words are recorded verbatim in four of Ernaux's nine texts (*La Place, Une femme, La Honte, 'Je ne suis pas sortie de ma nuit'*). The 'white shadow' of Ernaux's childhood is thus also omnipresent in linguistic terms, providing a mother tongue which both comforts and constrains (see p. 66).

A further dimension of the phrase 'mother tongue' which is relevant in this context is the fact that Ernaux depicts her language of origin as an almost exclusively spoken language. Ernaux has commented on the links between the factual tone and brevity of letters between her and her parents, and her mature literary style (*La Place*, p. 24; see also chapter 2, p. 31); in *La Place*, she describes her mother's difficulty in writing to her as a student away from home: 'She did not know how to joke in a language and with expressions which were already difficult for her. Writing as she spoke would have been even more difficult, she never learnt how to do it' (*La Place*, p. 89). For Ernaux herself, on the contrary, writing appears almost to have compensated for the uneasiness in speech which results from the gap between the two languages; Denise in *Les Armoires vides* has most difficulty in acquiring the spoken forms of her new, middle-class language, despite the fact that her written work consistently receives top marks (*Les Armoires vides*, p. 77). Even her voice changes when she returns home: 'As soon as I get home, I recover my normal way of speaking, I leave behind the genteel, affected voice of school, I chuck my satchel on the floor' (*Les Armoires vides*, p. 69; trans. p. 46). Similarly, the narrator of *La Femme gelée* becomes aware of having two voices, in this case determined by the exigencies of femininity; the voice she uses in her professional life, as a teacher, is energetic, mimicking 'masculine authority', whilst the private voice is 'anodyne, bird-like' (*La Femme gelée*, p. 174). The child-like tones of the language of intimacy adopted by the newly married couple conceal latent conflict and block real communication (*La Femme gelée*, p. 133). It is perhaps because of the feeling of inauthenticity associated with the acquired middle-class and feminine way of speaking that for Ernaux her mother's voice has a particular significance: 'For me, there is always her voice. Everything is in the voice. Death is, above all, the absence of a voice' (*'Je ne suis pas sortie de ma nuit'*, p. 80). In her talk at King's College, London, Ernaux frequently used the phrase 'trouver sa voix' (to find one's voice).[16] There may be an unconscious play on words here, since *voix* (voice) and *voie* (way) sound the same in French: finding one's voice is as difficult and important as finding one's way or place in the world – 'sa place dans le monde' (*Une femme*, p. 89).[17] Both processes are complicated and even blocked in a society based on exclusion and domination of some groups by others.

Linguistically and culturally, Ernaux seems to be attempting to achieve a balance between a working-class speech and culture characterised by its roots in concrete reality and evocative power, and the grace and expansiveness of middle-class language. On the one hand, words seem heavy, pregnant with meaning, conveying a culture which contains, but at times stifles; on the other hand they are light and airy, the vehicles of a freedom which, as we saw in the analysis of space in Ernaux's works, is almost frightening. Finding one's way or place in the world perhaps mean having both roots and the freedom to move: the tension between these two poles underlies the representations of the two cultures and languages in Ernaux's writing.

Notes

1. In a review of *Passion simple* published in *Libération*, Michèle Bernstein commented negatively on this passage (Bernstein, 1992; see chapter 6, p. 154).
2. For discussions of the importance of the gift in Ernaux's writing, see chapter 2, pp. 52–3 and chapter 5, pp. 134–6.
3. Rue Clopart is a fictional version of rue du Clos-des-Parts, where Ernaux grew up. The real name of the street is used in *La Honte* (p. 46).
4. This is probably a reference to Proust. In this case Proust is not mentioned by name, but the original French makes it clear that the cakes in question were madeleines. In *À la recherche du temps perdu*, it is the taste of madeleines and tea which allows Marcel, the narrator, not just to remember, but to recapture or re-enter the past, thus defeating, albeit temporarily, the march of time. Elsewhere, Ernaux comments on the middle-class nature of Proust's perspective, which of course seems natural and universal, both to him, and to many readers and critics (*La Place*, p. 29 and p. 62; see chapter 6, p. 157).
5. For a discussion of the role of religion in Ernaux's writing, see Vilain's interview with her (Vilain, 1997a, p. 67).
6. Marrone also provides a discussion of the tensions between 'progressive and traditionalist elements' in *Passion simple*, in terms of the representation of the narrator: 'Yet despite the fact that the narrator/protagonist seems to live out personal and sexual freedom, the reader has the nagging notion that beneath a facade of independence is a woman somewhat uncomfortable with her choices' (Marrone, 1994, p. 78).
7. Michèle Bacholle provides a discussion of the sacred and profane elements of *Passion simple* (Bacholle, 1996). She also comments on the significance of the title, and on the parallels with Christ's passion, seeing both a cult of A. as a Christ figure, and Ernaux herself as the suffering Christ, as I suggest here.

Bacholle reads the text as an expression of the increasing secularisation of French society; Ernaux's text is in her view deeply profane in that it depicts an adulterous liaison in religious terms.

8. Ernaux discusses this in *La Honte* (pp. 57–8):

> Because of the colour of the dust caused by the demolitions and reconstructions of the post-war period, and of the films and schoolbooks in black and white, the dark capes and overcoats, I see the world of 1952 in a uniform grey, like the countries of the Eastern block. But there were roses, clematis and wisteria pouring over the gates and walls of the neighbourhood, blue dresses with red patterns printed on them, like my mother's.

Colour is one of the utopian aspects of the representation of childhood in *Les Armoires vides*, and its relegation from the later texts seems to be linked to the 'fall from grace' experienced at the age of eleven in *La Honte*, and in adolescence generally in the other works. The 'fall from grace' involves feeling ashamed of the working-class background, parents and eventually the self; shame is followed by guilt about this betrayal, and attempts at reparation. The discipline of writing within a strict code, 'l'écriture plate', involves the abolition of sensuous memory including colour, which thus becomes part of the reparation, or penance. However, colour occasionally reappears, as here, almost in parenthesis, and at precisely the moment when its importance is denied (see also the discussion of the rejection of memory, and the quotation from *La Place*, chapter 2, p. 37). The repressed in this sense returns. See chapter 4, p. 95).

9. See chapter 2, p. 51 for a discussion of the representation of 'feminine' culture in *Journal du dehors*, and chapter 6, p. 152 for comments on its representation by critics.

10. Object relations theory has developed from the work of Melanie Klein, and as its name would suggest, emphasises the significance of early relations with the mother, as opposed to the Freudian notion of inherent drives in psychic life. Nancy Chodorow has argued that the dominant role of the mother in caring for small children creates an imbalance between the genders, in that the daughter inevitably identifies more strongly with the mother than the son, who on the contrary is encouraged to separate from her. Despite her recognition of the problems which the resulting lack of strong ego boundaries

may raise for women, Chodorow argues that the female child's highly developed ability to empathise with and relate to others is positive (Chodorow, 1989). This summary is based on the relevant entry in Elizabeth Wright's *Feminism and Psycho-analysis: A Critical Dictionary*, which has a much fuller discussion (Wright, 1992, pp. 284–90). Susie Orbach and Luise Eichenbaum have popularised some of these ideas, focusing particularly on the problems for heterosexuality which result from the attrib-ution of the caring role almost entirely to the female parent. Christiane Olivier has published an accessible text which follows similar lines in France, though her approach combines feminism with a strong Freudian basis (Olivier, 1980). In her discussion of the 'recuperation' of romantic fiction in Ernaux's writing, Siobhán McIlvanney also refers to Chodorow's theories. According to McIlvanney, the latter might be used to construct a positive view of the romance's emphasis on the importance of relationships (McIlvanney, 1996, p. 250, note 21).

11. This text is translated in appendix 1 and discussed in more detail in chapter 4, pp. 101–2.
12. This could be described as a form of reversed mirror-phase; in general the many references to mirror images of the self in Ernaux's writing could suggest a Lacanian analysis. However, the texts make the social rather than psychic causes of these crises of recognition and misrecognition abundantly clear. It is perhaps more appropriate to read them as a metaphor for the auto/biographical act itself. They are both textual markers of the socially constructed nature of identity and moments of slightly uncomfortable self-reflexivity: the persona constructed, in this case by the text, seems to look back at the narrating subject, as if to underline the tension between coherence and fragmentation which is a feature of Ernaux's representations of the self (see chapter 2, p. 45, and chapter 4, pp. 99–100).
13. *Le public* in French means both the public and the audience; the use of the word in the phrase *'public-voyageur'* here seems to suggest that the people in the train are both the travelling public and an audience, implying a lack of clear boundaries between theatre and real life.
14. Meursault is the hero of Camus's *The Outsider*, and Roquentin of Sartre's *Nausea*.
15. The Normandy expression 'gagner malheur' means 'to be driven mad with grief or shock'. In the January 1997 discussion

of *La Honte* in *Bouillon de Culture* the phrase, in Ernaux's handwriting, was projected onto the wall (see chapter 6, p. 148).

16. Talk given by Annie Ernaux at King's College, London, 8 March 1994.

17. I am indebted to one of my former students at the University of North London, Christine Hochleitner, for this observation.

4

Identity, Femininity and Loss

*I*n this chapter I will explore Ernaux's representations of femininity in greater depth, focusing particularly on the problematic nature of identity in her writing. In my discussion of the representation of the body in *Passion simple* in chapter 3, I indicated that in the depiction of gender relations Ernaux's texts might have some elements in common with object relations theory (p. 71). Some support for this idea might be found in Ernaux's own references to the 'good mother' and 'bad mother', which suggest an awareness of the work of Melanie Klein (*Une femme*, p. 62; *'Je ne suis pas sortie de ma nuit'*, p. 84). Here, I would like to reintroduce these theories, in order to explore the themes of separation, feminine identity and loss in Ernaux's work in more depth.

Ernaux herself has argued that the 'I' of her texts is 'an impersonal form, almost without gender, sometimes more a word belonging to the "other" than to "me"' (Ernaux, 1994b, p. 221). Sheringham takes up this point in his discussion of the usefulness of the auto/biographical 'I' for women writers. He finds in the work of Woolf and Ernaux a common desire to use the auto/biographical voice in order to acquire distance from personal experience, and particularly to explore the role of others – Woolf's 'invisible presences' – and of historical circumstances in that experience. Sheringham comments that whilst it is possible to identify some male writers who have followed a similar trajectory from fiction to autobiography, the genre has 'much to offer particular self-defining communities held together by such links as gender, ethnicity, or historical experience' (Sheringham, 1998, pp. 6–7). Over and above this political dimension, Sheringham also points to the significance of the mother figure in women's writing as a factor in the choice of many women writers to adopt the auto/biographical mode. Although he does not explore this notion, Sheringham concludes more generally: 'Ernaux's attempt to piece together the reality of her life – to make sense of it – is not designed to produce an identity, another self-image, but rather to identify the process through which selfhood is constituted by the incorporation of otherness' (Sheringham, 1998, p. 24). In this chapter I will attempt to look in more detail at this construction of a relational self in Ernaux's life-writing. In doing this I will provide not only a discussion of a significant aspect of Ernaux's work, but also a case-study of a woman writer who is drawn to auto/biography in part because of the opportunity it offers to question and transform the boundaries of the self. This analysis may thus provide a further elucidation of Sheringham's notion that the 'greater communality found among women writers on this score' may have some con-nection with a different mode of relating to others, particularly the mother (Sheringham, 1998, p. 6). Sheringham includes Leduc and Duras in his discussion of the 'invisible presences' in women's life-writing; here Marie Cardinal's *Les Mots pour le dire* and, even more strikingly, Beauvoir's *Une mort très douce* spring to mind as intertexts (Beauvoir, 1964; Cardinal, 1975). Catherine Montfort has provided a feminist account of the similarities and differences between Beauvoir's text and *Une femme*, and the literature on the mother–daughter relationship in contemporary French women's writing is a growing area (see Montfort, 1996, p. 362, note 7). Although my purpose here is not comparative, this chapter does constitute a contribution to that literature, and it may pave the way for further exploration of the relationships between auto/ biography as a genre and the social and psychic construction of femininity. The parallels between these women writers, like the bonds between them and their mothers, may have a complex psychological dimension, as well as a political *raison d'être*.

One of the basic tenets of object relations theory is the importance of the mother to psychic life and development (see chapter three, note 10). It will by now be clear that the mother is represented as a deeply significant figure in Ernaux's narratives of her life, and that she appears to be particularly influential in terms of Ernaux's analysis of the development of her feminine identity. Nancy Chodorow, a leading feminist exponent of object relations theory, has argued that because of the difference of gender, the boy finds it easier than the girl to separate from the mother, whilst same gender identification results in a high degree of merging between mother and daughter: 'Specifically I shall propose that, in any given society, feminine personality comes to define itself in relation and connection to other people more than masculine personality does' (Chodorow, 1989, p. 45). The phrase 'in any given society' in this sentence might be read as an indication of the tendency to universalism which has often been the subject of critiques of object relations theory.[1] Ernaux herself often vigorously rejects psycho-analytical explanations of behaviour, favouring a social and political approach: 'I expect nothing from psychoanalysis or a psychology of the family whose rudimentary conclusions – dominant mother, father who annihilates his submission in one fatal gesture, etc. – have been obvious to me for a long time' (*La Honte*, p. 31). Nonetheless, object relations theory does at least see gender as socially constructed, and attributes importance to aspects of the social context, such as the dominant role of women in the care of young children in most societies. In Ernaux's case (and perhaps in that of other women auto/biographers) there does seem to be some degree of fit between this particular psychoanalytical theory and literary representations.[2]

If femininity is constructed in relation to others as Chodorow suggests, the consequences for women are, in her view, mixed. On the one hand, Chodorow argues that this highly developed feminine ability to relate to others is both valuable and under-valued in patriarchal society. On the other she describes the problems experienced by women in separating from the mother and establishing the boundaries of the self: 'Various kinds of evidence suggest that separation from the mother, the breaking of dependence, and the establishment and maintenance of a consist-ently individuated sense of self remain difficult psychological issues for Western middle-class women' (Chodorow, 1989, p. 58). In this essay Chodorow differentiates between Western middle-class women and others, though, as she observes, generally only the former become the subject of psychoanalytical studies. She discusses ethnographic research in more matrifocal societies, including Young and Willmott's study of working-class families in East London, in order to argue that in these contexts, where the mother has more status, the problem of low self esteem and confused ego boundaries in women may be less acute (Young and Willmott, 1966). This seems to correspond to Ernaux's represent-ation of her mother and other working-class women as stronger and more independent than their middle-class counterparts.

However, Ernaux's ambivalent representations suggest that even in subcultural contexts where women may in some ways play a more powerful role, the dominant patriarchal view of women reasserts itself, impinging on the psychological development of most women.

The 'relational' female ego described by Chodorow corresponds to Ernaux's literary project as a whole, in a number of ways. As we have seen, her texts, like Ernaux herself in *Journal du dehors* (p. 69), are traversed by the voices of others (see chapter 1, p. 13 and chapter 2, p. 36). In *La Place* and *Une femme* Ernaux has contributed to the relatively new genre – allography – discussed by Nancy K. Miller, where the description of another's life inevitably leads to an exploration of one's own history (Miller, 1996, p. 2; chapter 1, p. 4). The relevance of Chodorow's theory to Ernaux's writing is thematic, as well as formal, insofar as it may illuminate Ernaux's many descriptions of a state where her identity is fused with that of a significant other. The most obvious and recurrent case of this is her depiction of the mother–daughter relationship. Initially, intimacy to the point of fusion with the mother is represented extremely positively, a crucial element of the descriptions of early childhood as a kind of Eden before the fall in *Les Armoires vides*. In *Une Femme* also, early childhood is represented as a golden age, marked by an untroubled intimacy with both parents, and particularly the mother:

> Her flesh bulged through the criss-cross of laces, which were joined together at the waist by a knot and a rosette. No detail of her body escaped my notice. I thought that when I grew up I would become her.
> One Sunday they are having a picnic on the edge of an embankment, near a wood. The memory is of being between them, in a warm nest of voices, flesh and continual laughter. On our way back, we are caught in an air raid, I am on the cross of my father's bike and she is going down the hill in front of us, sitting up straight in the saddle, which is buried between her buttocks. I am afraid of the bombs, and of her dying. I believe we were both in love with my mother. (*Une femme*, p. 46)

A Freudian analysis of this passage would perhaps emphasise the notion of being between the parents, and the possibility of jealousy of the father. It could certainly be read as a confirmation of the importance of the mother, and the difficulty of transfer of desire

from her to the father which Freud sees as significant aspects of
the female psyche in some of his later writing (Freud, [1931] 1977).
In object relations terms it might also confirm the 'emotional
triangle' in which girls grow up, and in which 'their father and
men are emotionally secondary, or at least equal, in importance
to their mother and women' (Chodorow, 1989, p. 77). A similar
memory of physical closeness to both parents is recounted in *Les
Armoires vides*: 'When I wake up early, I slip into their bed, with
their smell, snuggled up against them. The store shrinks, becomes
a house with a roof of blankets and walls of warm flesh that hold
me tight and protect me' (*Les Armoires vides*, p. 28; trans. p. 19).
Both in *Une femme* (pp. 49–50) and in *Ce qu'ils disent ou rien*,
however, an image of physical intimacy with the mother alone is
also evoked, when mother and daughter are described taking a
Sunday afternoon nap together 'like two dogs curled up in the same
box' (*Ce qu'ils disent ou rien*, p. 60). The most striking aspect of
all of these images is their intense physicality, confirming the
association, in Ernaux's writing, of the culture of origin with the
body, and the importance of the mother in the former (see chapter
3, p. 66).

The sense of being contained and safe which is conveyed by the
above quotation from *Les Armoires vides* points to the mother's role
as nurturer and comforter, analysed more explicitly later in *'Je ne
suis pas sortie de ma nuit'*; Ernaux describes an occasion in her
childhood when she visited an uncle in hospital: 'I was so sad and
so happy that my mother was there, strong and protective against
illness and death' (p. 35). In this instance, and in the examples
above, the mother's solid flesh, and the experience of an identity
which is merged with rather than separate from the mother, seem
to be a protection against threats of any kind. At the same time the
mother is constantly associated with loss and death: 'Frightening
to realise the extent to which my mother has always been a figure
of death for me' (*'Je ne suis pas sortie de ma nuit'*, p. 76). As the
quotation from *Une femme* suggests, these idyllic moments of fusion
carry within them the threat of total and traumatic loss; if the
merger is so complete, and so comforting, then the threat of its
disruption must become devastating. At the end of *Une femme*,
Ernaux describes how her memories of her mother have become
in some way distilled: 'Her image tends to revert to the one I
imagine I had of her as a small child, a big white shadow above
me' (*Une femme*, p. 105). Similarly, in *La Femme gelée*, the mother is

described as 'the white woman whose voice echoes inside me, who envelops me, my mother' (p. 15). This image is taken up again in *'Je ne suis pas sortie de ma nuit'*: 'My fantasy representation of her: a patch of white, her shopkeeper's overall, constantly behind me' (p. 82). In all of these images the mother is described as a constant nurturing presence, capable of holding and containing her small daughter's fears and anxieties. However, the colour white links this subliminal image of the mother to the song about the little boy who brings white roses to his mother's grave every Sunday (*Les Armoires vides*, p. 99). Significantly, the song is referred to again at the end of *'Je ne suis pas sortie de ma nuit'*: 'Thinking about the song "The White Roses" which used to make me cry as a child. I cry again when I think about that, about that song' (p. 109). In *Une femme*, the mother as a separate person is described in colour: 'Always vivacious and strong, generous, with red or blond hair (. . .) she climbs through the grass on the cliff, in her dress of blue crêpe patterned with huge flowers' (p. 59). The colour white seems to refer to the mother of the original, merged identification of early childhood, and at the same time to the blankness and emptiness of total loss. As we saw in chapter 2, the threat or even the reality of loss can only be combated by writing: 'It was only the day before yesterday that I overcame the terror of writing, at the top of a *blank white* page, as if beginning a book, rather than a letter to someone, "my mother is dead"' (*Une femme*, p. 21).[3] However, like the mother, who slipped out of her black mourning clothes to don the flowery dress described above, Ernaux's writing accepts the constraints of bereavement: colour is only rarely permitted to enter a predominantly black, white and grey world (see chapter 3, note 8).

Death, as the ultimate threat to the intimacy with the mother, is prefigured in Ernaux's narratives by an earlier rift. The processes of early identification and painful separation at adolescence described by Chodorow and others are coloured not only by social constructions of gender, but also by the class issue. As we have seen, Ernaux describes how she was accepted, through the school system, into the culture of the mind, and in this process lost the emotional intimacy and physical pleasures associated with the culture of origin. In *Les Armoires vides* the heroine's most profound losses are her own body, innocent of the guilt and shame which school and church are later to inculcate, and the freedom to enjoy the physical world and her own sexuality. In *Une femme*, on the other hand, the mother's death seems to bring to the surface the repressed and painful emotions resulting from the loss of the mother's culture, where the most significant intimacy has been experienced. Changing class has necessitated a rejection, not only of this culture, but also of the mother's body, which in childhood, as the quotations above indicate, was associated with plenitude and nurture: 'I began to notice the ideal image of femininity I found in *L'Echo de la mode,* and in the mothers of my middle-class school friends: slim, discreet, good at cooking, calling their daughters "darling". I found my own mother loud' (*Une femme,* p. 63). The last sentence here, 'Je trouvais ma mère voyante' in the original, suggests that the mother's body is now associated by the daughter with socially unacceptable excess: it is too visible, too much, neither slim nor discreet. Although Ernaux's descriptions of early child-hood contain an image of a nurturing mother, acceptance into middle-class culture means that the mother has to be devalued and denied; as we saw in chapter 3, Ernaux begins to see her mother through the eyes of the private school, and is obliged to distance herself from her love and nurturing body. It is therefore not surprising that in *Une femme* and *'Je ne suis pas sortie de ma nuit'* Ernaux has written out her grief for her mother, and that the loss of the mother's body is a recurring theme of her accounts of bereavement: 'One evening in April, she was already asleep at half-past six, lying on top of the sheets in her slip; her legs were raised, showing her sex. It was very warm in the room. I started to cry because she was my mother, the same woman I had known in my childhood' (*Une femme,* pp. 95–6).

If class compounds the difficulty of the separation process, forcing Ernaux to cut herself off from her emotional roots, the effect on the writing is, as we have seen, the choice of narrative structures based on grief or the search for the lost intimacy. Loss of various kinds is the common theme of all the texts; even *Journal du dehors,* which apparently focuses on external social reality, can be read as an expression of the search for intimacy and for the lost past, as the final sentences of the text suggest (see chapter 1, p. 20). If loss, whether of the culture of origin, the mother's body or the uninhibited childhood self, is a constant theme, the first-person narrator of Ernaux's texts is also perpetually seeking to compensate, turning in the classic manner to men for succour. In *Les Armoires vides* Denise seeks to replicate lost physical and emotional intimacy with the mother through her relationships with more socially acceptable objects of desire – middle-class boys. The same could be said of Anne in *Ce qu'ils disent ou rien*, and of the narrator of *La Femme gelée*, who searches for and believes she has found 'an incestuous brother' (p. 118). In *Une femme* men are largely absent; the narrator is divorced, and her only sexual relationship, 'with a man who repelled me', is the result of her increasing distress over her mother's illness (p. 93). In *Passion simple*, there are clear parallels between the description of the passion for A. and of the early childhood fusion with the mother. The total merging with the beloved and lack of boundaries between self and other are common features: 'I would fall into a half-sleep, where I had the impression of sleeping in his body' (p. 21); 'Once, lying on my stomach, I made myself come, I experienced this as if it was his orgasm' (p. 54).

Again, object relations theory can provide further elucidation of this linking of intimacy or fusion with the other, and a lasting sense of loss and grief. Like Chodorow, Luise Eichenbaum and Susie Orbach, who have popularised the theory in Britain and America, argue that the fear of loss which is inherent in any experience of love or intimacy is more intense for daughters. In their view this difficulty is compounded by the fact that as a result of gender conditioning in patriarchal society, the daughter receives mixed messages from her mother, and takes from the mother–daughter relationship not only her mother's positive nurturance of her, but also her mother's ambivalence about her own neediness (Eichenbaum and Orbach, 1983). At the points of separation from the mother, as for example at adolescence, the daughter does not depart from the secure emotional base which would result from internalisation of her mother's positive response to her as an infant, and as a result she replays this insecurity and the trauma of separation in her adult relationships. In this sense Ernaux's texts exemplify the theories of Eichenbaum and Orbach: 'Even though a daughter comes to look toward men, she still yearns for mother's support and care. From girlhood to womanhood women live with the experience of having lost these aspects of maternal nurturance. This nurturance is never replaced. Women look to men to mother them but remain bereft' (Eichenbaum and Orbach, 1983, p. 52). In *'Je ne suis pas sortie de ma nuit'*, Ernaux's self-analysis seems to echo Eichenbaum and Orbach's arguments. There is a strong sense of the relationship between mother and daughter as an encounter of unmet needs on both sides: 'I want to cry when I see this need for love which she feels in relation to me, and which will never again be satisfied (I loved her so much when I was a child). I think of my own need for love from A., now, when he is leaving me' (p. 32). Ernaux is also lucid about the constancy of these unmet needs in herself, their origins in the relationship with her mother, and their effect on her life: 'Everywhere I have searched for my mother's love in the world' (*'Je ne suis pas sortie de ma nuit'*, p. 103).

Despite this sense of unmet needs, and the undermining of the images of the nurturing mother by the 'bad mother' in Ernaux's work, the notion of the merger with the mother persists in the texts depicting the adult, as opposed to the childhood or adolescent, self. In *Une femme*, grief after the mother's death is described using a particularly striking image of merged identity:

> During the ten months when I was writing, I dreamt of her almost every night. Once, I was lying in a river, where two streams met. From my belly, from my sex, which was smooth again like a little girl's, the thread-like strands of plants seemed to grow floating loosely. It was not only my sex, it was also my mother's. (*Une femme*, p. 104)

The uncertain boundaries of the female self are here conveyed by an image of liquidity; the female body is associated with flow, with the natural world, and with a confused sense of the boundary between self and other. This version of femininity may also be reflected in the water images in *Les Armoires vides*, which Carol Sanders has commented on (Sanders, 1993, p. 21). The sensations experienced in the early stages of the abortion are described as 'a warm tide' and Denise wishes that: 'the sun would move across my body, melting flesh and muscle into a pulp that would trickle out gently through the tube' (*Les Armoires vides*, p. 12; trans. p. 8). The significance of these images of liquidity and decomposition is emphasised by their recurrence at the end of the novel: 'The bottles of cider used to ferment during a heat wave, the corks would pop and there'd be yellow froth all over the cellar floor. Empty' (*Les Armoires vides*, p. 181; trans. p. 122). Sanders comments that the dichotomies present throughout the text 'between her past and her present, growth and decomposition, pleasure and pain' come together in this image (Sanders, 1993, p. 21). The explosion of the cider bottles is clearly symbolic of the abortion, and the fact that cider drinking is traditional in working-class culture in Normandy emphasises the association of this physical trauma with the pain involved in changing class. The image thus confirms the indissoluble linking of gender, class and sexuality in Ernaux's writing.

Sanders's idea of the dichotomies present in the image can be developed: Ernaux's representations of the female body, and more specifically the working-class female body, seem ambivalent. The original French version of the cider bottles image describes them exploding 'like flowers', and the bright colour of the yellow froth can be linked to the colourful depictions of childhood sensuality earlier in the text. Similarly the animal imagery and the evocation of the elements, particularly fire and water, in *Les Armoires vides* can seem beautiful and poetic, suggestive of a harmony between the female body and nature. At times in *Les Armoires vides* menstruation seems to be associated with an almost anarchic potential: 'I celebrate all night in a nightclub. The champagne's on me. I feel suffused with grace and light (. . .). The bench sticks to my skirt, I wallow in champagne, flesh, and the warm waves flooding out intermittently onto the pad between my legs. A real flood' (*Les Armoires vides*, p. 175; trans. p. 118).[4] Here, just as the flow of blood blurs the boundaries of the body, Denise has successfully crossed a social boundary through her educational success. Yet, the victory is pyrrhic: there is also something threatening, resulting from the context of the imminent pregnancy and abortion, and from the association elsewhere in the text of liquidity, or pouring out, with decomposition, loss and death.

Chodorow comments that experiences such as menstruation and childbirth, and, one might add, abortion, can represent 'some challenge to the boundaries of her body ego' for a woman (Chodorow, 1989, p. 59). Like Beauvoir, and, in Chodorow's view, many Western women, Ernaux's sense of self appears at times to be threatened by experiences which challenge the boundaries of the body.[5] Chodorow argues that this is hardly surprising given 'a Western woman's tenuous sense of individuation and of the firmness of her ego boundaries' (Chodorow, 1989, p. 59). The fear of loss of self which is expressed in an indirect and metaphorical way in the earlier texts becomes more explicit in some of the recent writing. In *'Je ne suis pas sortie de ma nuit'*, the sense of being merged with the mother becomes increasingly threatening: 'I sat in her armchair, and she sat on a chair. A terrible feeling of a double existence, I am myself and her' (p. 23). Beauvoir makes a similar observation in her description of her mother's last weeks in *Une mort très douce*. She describes how 'someone other than myself was weeping inside me' and tells Sartre how her mother's mouth seemed to express her whole being: 'He told me that my own mouth was no longer under my control: I had superimposed my mother's mouth on to my own face and despite myself I imitated all its grimaces' (Beauvoir, 1964, pp. 43–4).[6] The fusion with the mother, which Ernaux represented as idyllic in the texts depicting early childhood, has become deeply disturbing: 'The experience of self in the original mother-relation remains both seductive and frightening: unity was bliss, yet means the loss of self and absolute dependence' (Chodorow, 1989, p. 71). In *'Je ne suis pas sortie de ma nuit'*, this fear of loss of the self in the relation to the other is compounded by fear of death, and of the passing of time. The adolescent struggle to establish boundaries is here taken up with an almost desperate edge, since identification renders the mother's death symbolic of her own inevitable demise: 'Blindingly obvious: she is my old age, and I feel in myself the threat of the demise of her body, the wrinkled skin of her legs, the folds of her neck, revealed by the haircut she has just had' (p. 36).

The struggle for identity thus seems to be waged both in relation to the universal threats of time and death, and in relation to specifically feminine fears of loss of a clear sense of self. The latter seem to result both from the negative definitions of femininity inherent in patriarchal social structures and, according to object relations theorists, from the dominance of the mother in the raising of children, and particularly daughters. Whether the aforementioned theories are generally applicable is not my concern here, but the match between their insights and Ernaux's depiction of the family and social dynamics within which she struggled for her own identity suggests some relevance in this case. As we saw in chapter 2, writing is Ernaux's defence against threats to the self; this chapter makes it clear that for Ernaux such threats are both universal and gender-specific, and that becoming a writer has been particularly important in the development of a positive female identity. Only writing can defend Ernaux against the dangers of losing her mother or becoming her mother. Writing fills the blank page, and gives form, meaning and solidity to an otherwise overwhelming flow of grief:

> Now the meaning of that day is apparent to me. It was one evening in May, there was sunshine. She was lying down, asleep. My childhood, the Sunday afternoons when we took a nap together, came back to me. Then Sées in 1958, when I was shivering on my bed, obsessed by Claude G., or because of A. in 84. The same, the only love. (*'Je ne suis pas sortie de ma nuit'*, p. 107)

The link between love and writing is still more apparent in 'Fragments autour de Philippe V.', in this case in a sexual context: 'Writing and making love. I feel there is an essential link between the two. I can't explain it, I can only record those moments when this appears most clearly to me' (Ernaux, 1996, p. 26). This short text provides an intense account of Ernaux's preoccupation with the boundaries between self and other, returning, interestingly, to the images of liquidity and merger discussed in relation to the earlier texts:

> He wanted to know what kind of picture the mixture of his sperm and my menstrual blood would make.
> Afterwards we looked at the paper, the damp picture. We saw a woman whose face was being devoured by her thick mouth, whose body seemed to fade and flow, formless. Or perhaps it was the northern lights, or a sunset. (Ernaux, 1996, p. 26)

In this piece the sense of merging with another which is often described as a threat elsewhere in Ernaux's writing seems doubly contained, by the 'damp picture' and by the written text. The picture, 'something similar to a work of art', seems symbolic of the writing process; the flowing formless body of the woman is contained by the piece of paper, just as for Ernaux, the fragile and threatened boundaries of the self are strengthened or even created by writing. Here the subject matter of the text emphasises this positive element. Menstruation is no longer the threat to the boundaries of the female self described by Chodorow, but an opportunity for a playful re-enactment of the almost uterine fusion with the mother, without the associated sense of menace.[7] If the body of the woman in the picture seems formless, Ernaux's writing certainly is not: each word is carefully chosen, as the text reconstructs an encounter where intimacy is combined with clear boundaries. The emphasis here is on difference between self and other, in this case difference of age and gender; separation becomes a pleasurable space, rather than a threat: 'After he left, the next day, I re-ran the scenes of the night (. . .). I kept going back to my gesture, my hand in his hair, without which nothing would have happened. The memory of this gesture, more than anything else, filled me with intense, almost orgasmic pleasure (jouissance)' (Ernaux, 1996, p. 26).[8] In 'Fragments', writing seems to represent a way of combating the traditional and oppressive limitations imposed on women, the sense in which, like Ernaux, most women find themselves 'surprised by the fact of not doing something, not going to a certain place because I am a woman' (Vilain, 1997a, p. 70). In many ways this short text represents both for reader and writer a rare moment of satisfying closure, or even *jouissance*, in Ernaux's writing.[9] In the two texts which follow it, Ernaux returns to the evocation of painful aspects of the past, so that it remains to be seen whether the celebration of the links between writing and life, and the affirmation of a powerful version of feminine identity will be explored in future texts. Perhaps, in the era of postmodernity, such affirmations of identity can only be ephemeral; these are fragments among many.

Notes

1. Critiques of object relations theory have argued that it tends to focus on the mother–child dyad in isolation from the social contexts in which this relationship takes place: this can lead to a lack of sensitivity to cultural and social differences. Object relations theory has also been accused of essentialism on similar grounds (see Wright, 1992, pp. 284–9).
2. Furthermore, I am not alone in drawing on Chodorow in the analysis of Ernaux's texts. See for example, Lucille Cairns's article on *Ce qu'ils disent ou rien* (Cairns, 1994, p. 79).
3. The italics here are mine – they emphasise the significance of the colour white.
4. A more detailed analysis of the representation of menstruation in Ernaux's writing than I am able to provide here would cast more light on this question. Like Marie Cardinal in *Les Mots pour le dire* (*The Words to Say It*), published only one year after *Les Armoires vides*, Ernaux is flouting the taboo surrounding this subject generally in the culture, and specifically in literature. Interestingly, the heroine of *Ce qu'ils disent ou rien* expresses her disillusionment and rebellion against patriarchal codes of behaviour (enforced by the mother) by ceasing to menstruate (*Ce qu'ils disent ou rien*, p. 148). For Cardinal's narrator, excessive bleeding becomes symptomatic of a similar rebellion.

5. Beauvoir's descriptions of the processes of pregnancy, childbirth and breast-feeding in *Le Deuxième Sexe* seem to reveal these fears and her horror of the loss of autonomy involved (Beauvoir, 1949, pp. 67–8). For Beauvoir, menstruation seems to contain none of the positive potential discovered by later feminists: '[the woman's body] is prey to an alien and determined life which makes and unmakes its cradle every month inside her; a child prepares for its birth every month, and is aborted in the collapse of the lacy structure made of blood' (Beauvoir, 1949, p. 67).

6. For Beauvoir, the need to establish a separate identity in order to combat the terrifying prospect of old age and death seems less dominant than a sense of unity with her mother against a common foe. Beauvoir's autobiographical writing seems to depict an early and profound separation from the mother: 'I wanted to build unassailable walls around myself' ('je voulus que mes remparts fussent sans faille'; Beauvoir, 1964, p. 95). However, as her mother's death approaches, these defences seem to crumble, replaced by identification and merger, based on the shared will to live: 'My mother loved life as I do and in the face of death she felt the same rebellion as me' (Beauvoir, 1964, p. 132; see Montfort, 1996, pp. 354–6).

7. Some readers may nonetheless see a threat in this image, given the dangerous potential of such mixing in the era of HIV. Generally in Ernaux's work both sexuality and writing are associated with a sense of danger and risk. This may be present here, alongside the positive and celebratory aspects of the text.

8. See also chapter 3, pp. 71–2, and appendix 1, note 1.

9. This comment does not imply a negative judgement: the general absence of closure, or more accurately, of the 'happy end', is associated with Ernaux's commitment to disturb and question established certainties. 'Fragments' simply represents a difference in tone and subject.

Part 2

5

Reading for Passion and Pleasure

Introduction

*I*n the final section of chapter 2 I provided an analysis of the reader–writer relationship and the implied reader constructed in Ernaux's texts. I hypothesised that Ernaux's auto/biographical pact, exemplified by the many instances of direct address to the reader in her texts, can be seen as a challenge, or an attempt to unsettle or disturb the reader. This is also a view which Ernaux herself has expressed.[1] At the same time, I suggested that this particular version of the auto/biographical pact might lead to a strong sense of the writer as a real person, whose avowed struggle for authenticity in her writing can be read as a guarantor of her trustworthiness and sincerity. These two aspects of the relationship between reader and writer are not necessarily in contradiction, and both may be in play to varying degrees in readings of Ernaux's work. The study of readers' letters which I embark on in this chapter is in part an opportunity to put those hypotheses to the test, and to see how these dynamics are played out in responses to Ernaux's writing.

My purpose here is also broader. Reader-response criticism was a topic of some interest in literary theory in the 1970s and 1980s, as the publication of two anthologies of seminal essays in the area seems to attest (Suleiman and Crosman, 1980; Tompkins, 1980). By 1987, however Elizabeth Freund concluded that 'reader response criticism, on the evidence of its own premises, suggests that it has a past rather than a future' (Freund, 1987, p. 10). In his introduction to literary theory published in 1983, Terry Eagleton provides a review of the various versions of reader-response criticism, and the conflicts between them. These conflicts seem to result mainly from polarised views of the location of meaning, with theorists such as Stanley Fish arguing in favour of the reader's power and freedom, and others, such as Iser, placing more emphasis on the constraining power of the text. Eagleton concludes that reader-response criticism provides us with the now uncontentious information that 'a literary text does not have a single "correct" meaning', and that 'the reader does not come to the text as a kind of cultural virgin' (Eagleton, 1983, p. 89). Nonetheless, Eagleton points out that there is a difference between theoretical acceptance and practical application of these ideas:

> Most of us recognise that no reading is innocent or without suppos-itions. But fewer people pursue the full implications of this readerly guilt. One of the themes of this book has been that there is no such thing as a purely 'literary response': all such responses, not least those to literary *form*, to the aspects of a work which are sometimes jealously reserved to the 'aesthetic', are deeply imbricated with the kind of social and historical individuals we are. (Eagleton, 1983, p. 89)

If Eagleton comments that literary critics have perpetuated the fiction of their own objectivity, I would add that in general they have shown little interest in the readings of 'social and historical individuals' outside the academic world. It is notable that whereas in the realm of media/cultural studies the interest in the audience which developed in the 1980s has led to a number of detailed studies, examples of readership study in the literary field are relatively few and far between, and tend to be concentrated in the area of popular fiction.[2] It is also significant that feminist criticism has been the source of most of the work engaging with actual readers, as opposed to implied or ideal readers of texts. This probably results in part from the interdisciplinary nature of much feminist work, which has facilitated a greater openness to the influence of cultural and media studies than is found in more mainstream literary criticism. The political commitment of feminist critics to the questioning or even removal of the boundaries between popular and 'high' culture has certainly also led to the interest in readers of popular, particularly romantic, fiction already referred to.

The work of feminist critics such as Sara Mills and Lynne Pearce is particularly significant in that it is concerned with readers of literary as well as popular texts. Mills discusses the responses to a feminist poem of a sample of seventy-four male and female staff and students in educational intitutions (Mills, 1994). In her recent book, Pearce analyses the responses of feminist academic readers in Britain and Canada to Margaret Atwood's *Death by Landscape*. Her aim is to explore aspects of the reading process, such as the role of the social context or interpretive community which forms the audience for the reading (Pearce, 1997). Whilst the work of Mills and Pearce does extend the range of texts studied in relation to their reception to the literary or high culture field, unlike my project here it is concerned with academic readers attached to educational institutions. This has the advantage of diminishing the tendency for the 'researched' to become the objectified 'other' of the researching subject, and of enabling self-reflexivity. However, it may have the disadvantage of confining interpretations of literary texts to academic readers, which in turn may perpetuate the notion of literary criticism and literature as a separate and superior category, thus guaranteeing, as Bourdieu has argued, the social status of the practitioners (see chapter 6). Despite this reservation, this feminist work is both academically and politically significant in its attempt to render transparent the processes of critical reading, and the relationship between an affective and a trained response to literature. The impact of gendered identities on readings is also a significant area of analysis, particularly in the collection edited by Mills (Mills, 1994). Although significant, this work is still a notable exception; in the wider field, or at least in the field of French literature, despite contemporary theories which would suggest the contrary, the actual practice of criticism seems to lend a certain finality or solitary air to the literary text, often analysed without reference to the contexts of its production and reception.

It seems appropriate, given Ernaux's own expressed desire to remain 'below literature', to adopt an approach to her work which, in encompassing the study of the readership, is outside the parameters of most literary criticism. Just as Ernaux brings her parents and with them 'a whole social class' into literature,[3] I aim to bring readers into criticism, and to analyse the texts not as closed systems, but as part of a site of social signification. As I argued in the preface, contemporary literary texts are inevitably read inter-textually through the network of critical and journalistic writing and media representations which they generate. Readers' letters in turn become part of that network, which both reflects and participates in the ideological discourses of a particular social time and place – in this case contemporary France. In discussing the letters a delicate balance has to be maintained between awareness that they are constructed texts, and need to be analysed as such, and the notion that they reflect or contain contemporary social realities. In relation to this question, which all empirical work poses, my position is similar to that presented by Jackie Stacey, in her study of female fans of Hollywood stars (Stacey, 1994). On the one hand: 'audiences' reponses are not self-evident truths about what the media means; this would completely ignore the ways in which subjectivities are constituted through ideological discourses' (Stacey, 1994, p. 76). Like Stacey, I have treated these letters as texts, seeking the discourses which run through them, rather than attempting to portray the 'real readers' (the limitations of the information available in this form would, in any case, have made such an enterprise impossible). However, as Stacey points out, there is clearly a difference between such material and fictional texts; readers' letters, albeit constructed within a specific set of codes and conventions, are part of a social reality beyond the literary text itself, and can indicate some of the ways in which the latter functions within its contexts of reception. Again, like Stacey, I hope to have adopted 'a method of analysis that takes what audiences say seriously' (Stacey, 1994, p. 77). In this chapter, then, Ernaux's work is presented in relation to the context of its reception, and as part of a network of signification which is historically, culturally and socially situated.

Methodology

The methodology which I have adopted is typical of a large number of existing audience/readership studies in that it relies on the written word. I have argued elsewhere that in the study of the audiences of media texts, discussion groups and interviews have the advantage of providing a context which bears some similarity to 'real' social situations where such texts might be discussed or referred to (Thomas, 1995a). It is doubtless the case that as well as removing some of the artificiality characteristic of methods such as questionnaire surveys, research based on talk in a social context facilitates analysis of the impact of that context on the readings of texts. In this way a richer, often contradictory picture can emerge, where it is possible to comment not only on what is said, but on what, in a specific social context, appears to be unsayable. Any simple sense that people say what they mean can be avoided, replaced by a more sophisticated understanding of how readings of texts can contribute to the construction of identities in everyday social communication.

This perspective must, in the analysis of readers' letters, be more difficult to achieve. The letter is no longer part of everyday communication, even if, in the shape of the 'e' mail, it may have acquired a modern form. The social context of a letter to an author is not observable in the same way as the cultural space, including both possibilities and interdictions, created by a discussion. It exists only as a basic paradigm. Whilst some generalisations can be made about this paradigm, its particular inflection in each case can only be inferred from the reader's own words. There is no social interaction to observe, and the researcher is only present after the event. In this sense the responses to literature found in letters to the author can seem rather disembodied: one-way communications outside ordinary social relations. They are almost certainly very different from the discussion of literary texts which may occur in conversation.

With these caveats in mind, the study of readers' letters still seems to present significant points of interest. Precisely because they are outside everyday social life, representing a perhaps abnormal recourse to communication with a stranger, they are likely to be more revealing of profound emotional responses than talk. These letters, often written with the hope, but no certainty, of a reply, might be compared to the confessional or the therapy session. The author is present as an addressee, but only minimal response is expected, or even perhaps, in some cases, desired. Whilst the presentation of the self is as constructed in a letter to an author as in a social interaction, the letter form seems more likely to invite self-revelation than most social encounters, certainly with a researcher present. This greater degree of self-revelation is not automatically more interesting or significant than the social personality constructed in a discussion group, but readers' letters do have the advantage of being innocent of the influence of the researcher's presence, the impact of the knowledge that one is being 'researched'. The letters are spontaneous, and in this sense real acts of communication.

Whilst I am far from denying that Ernaux's texts do have a social presence and at times play a role within relationships (see pp. 135–6 below), I would like to suggest a perhaps obvious difference between the contemporary reception of literary and media texts. Whereas media texts are without doubt a major topic of conversation in a range of social settings, providing a significant source of identifications and identities, this may be less the case for literature. In most social contexts, people are probably more likely to claim a particular identity through their expressed allegiance to a TV soap opera than to a contemporary novel. As a result, the discussion group is an appropriate method for the study of the reception of media texts, but it may be more artificial in relation to literature. Reading always was, to a great extent, a private affair, but now, in the age of the world-wide web, it can be seen as a slow, solitary and slightly old-fashioned activity. The equally antiquated letter may thus be a singularly appropriate response, both activities acquiring a special and significant status as remnants of past traditions. Literary texts and readers' letters can perhaps become the repositories of secrets which the speed and technological nature of the telephone, 'e' mail or fax would discourage. The letters I have studied certainly seem to represent particularly intense moments of communication, or self-analysis, the recourse to the communication medium of a previous age heightening their significance and setting them apart, just as a highly valued photograph might be placed in an old-fashioned silver frame. Reading and analysing them is, in research terms, an unusual privilege.

The final caveat concerns the nature of the sample. Firstly, readers' letters do not provide systematic information on socio-economic grouping, age, sexuality and ethnic origin, though gender is almost always obvious (if only thanks to the inflected nature of the French language). Furthermore, the samples I studied were chosen by the author and were not necessarily representative, in terms of age, class and gender, of the whole group.[4] It is therefore not possible to say that, for example, 75 per cent of the letters were from working-class readers in manual occupations, or that 25 per cent were Swiss bankers. The size of my samples varied. In total I read 333 letters, sent to the author between July 1974 and March 1997, though mainly in the years immediately following the publication of *La Place* (1984), *Une femme* (1988), *Passion simple* (1992), *La Honte* and *'Je ne suis pas sortie de ma nuit'* (1997). For the early texts, *Les Armoires vides* and *La Femme gelée*, I read only six and five letters respectively. Although *Ce qu'ils disent ou rien* was mentioned in a number of letters, there were no letters specifically in response to this text. Clearly, as Ernaux has become well-known, the number of letters she receives has increased.[5] It is also possible that some of the early letters have been lost or mislaid. For all the later texts except *Journal du dehors,*where I had only 12, I read a considerable number of letters: 82 for *La Place*, 45 for *Une femme*, over 100 for *Passion simple* and 62 for *La Honte* and *'Je ne suis pas sortie de ma nuit'*.[6] In the case of the last two texts I studied the 'first flush' of letters: the publication date was January 1997, and Ernaux gave me the sample on 21 March of the same year.

Despite the limitations of the information, it is possible to say that the subject matter of the text which has inspired the letter plays a role in determining what is revealed. In the small sample of letters about *Journal du dehors*, three speak in defence of the homeless or very poor who are described in the text, and one of these letters is written by a self-declaring 'Rmiste' (person receiving benefit, the equivalent of a minimum wage). Occupation and class background are mentioned more often in response to *La Place* and *Une femme* than to *Passion simple*, whilst letters about the latter almost invariably give details of sexual and family relations. In an article on the reception of *Passion simple*, Ernaux confirms my impression:

> The range of occupations seems wide, teachers, shopkeepers, employees, shop assistants, but more narrow than that of the readers of *La Place* (no agricultural or manual workers in the letters about *Passion simple*). The male readers seem more educated than the women. The readers always give their marital status, single, married, divorced, and that of the person who is the object of their passion. This is clearly a major factor in an affair of the heart. (Ernaux, 1994a, p. 27)

Although it was possible to determine the gender of the readers in all but two or three cases, the unrepresentative nature of my samples necessitates caution. Because of the existence of the article by Ernaux mentioned above, precise comparisons between my sample and the totality of letters received can be made in the case of *Passion simple*. I read 121 letters, of which 52 were from men, and 69 from women. It would, however, be erroneous to conclude that more women wrote about this text. In her article, Ernaux states that she received a total of 700 letters, slightly more from men than from women (Ernaux, 1994a). Nonetheless, it does seem significant that out of a sample of 45 letters about *Une femme*, 36 (i.e. 80 per cent) were from women, suggesting that the title and subject matter have played some role in attracting women readers to the text. This is supported both by the author's own impression and by the content of the letters, a number of which were most interested in the representation of the mother–daughter relationship. In this sample there was a much less marked majority of women writing about *La Place* (33 out of 50; or 65 per cent), and *La Honte* and *'Je ne suis pas sortie de ma nuit'* (39 out of 62; or 63 per cent). Ernaux commented that she received a more or less equal number of letters from men and women for *La Place* and *La Honte*, but that *'Je ne suis pas sortie de ma nuit'*, like *Une femme*, attracted more women readers. A further 32 letters in the *La Place* sample were from a class of *première* pupils (age sixteen), mainly girls, with an accompanying letter from their teacher.

In terms of age, the sample ranged from adolescents to octogenarians, though Ernaux's comment on the letters about *Passion simple*, that most readers were between thirty and fifty, can also be applied to the other texts. Similarly, the range of occupations was broad, and the sample included letters from people who were only just literate, as well as barristers, doctors and university professors. Whilst the sample contained representatives of all social classes, the dominant group was probably the lower middle class. Frequently, people in this group had, like Ernaux, working-class origins, and were thus particularly likely to respond to her work. It is not surprising that the author's own social trajectory, an omnipresent theme in the texts, was a defining factor in terms of who chose to write to her. The number of teachers in the sample was particularly striking. On the basis of the letters I read, the 'typical' Ernaux reader is a teacher in her late thirties or forties, married with children, and of working-class origins. It would, however, be equally true to say that there is no 'typical' Ernaux reader. In what follows I aim to go beyond these generalities, and to provide a sketch of the roles played by the work of a successful contemporary writer in the lives of her many and diverse readers. It is perhaps at this point that the nine slim Gallimard volumes will really come to life.

Desperately Seeking the Author

My analysis of readers' letters has enabled me to identify three discursive categories as dominant, if not all-exclusive, focusing, respectively, on the author, the reader and the text. There would of course be other ways of analysing or organising this material, and the structure I have adopted here is one of several possible interpretations. I should also emphasise that the categories overlap in many of the letters, as is evidenced by some of the quotations, which could illustrate two or even all three discourses. The same three discourses may be in evidence in letters to other authors, particularly of autobiography, though the lack of comparable research makes this difficult to explore. Their specific inflection in these letters is nonetheless linked to the particularities of Ernaux's writing and her media image; it is to the analysis of that specificity that I will now turn.

The first category concerns the large number of letters or parts of letters where the focus of interest is very much the author as a real person. In these letters the desire to enter, or catch glimpses of, the reality of the life behind and beyond the texts seems to motivate the writing. In the analysis of what I would like to call the 'author discourse' I shall be concerned with modes of address and linguistic register, as well as content. As a prelude to this analysis, I would suggest that two factors may be largely respons-ible for the strong focus on the author in terms of her personal qualities found in these letters. Firstly, as I have already argued, the name 'Ernaux' has an existence beyond the texts themselves, encompassing the network of reviews, articles, interviews and television appearances which literary success has generated, particularly since *La Place* won the prestigious Renaudot prize in 1984. Readers thus have access to many representations of 'Ernaux', and are not solely dependent on the brief and discreet biographical note provided by Gallimard. The fact that many sources of inform-ation are available, and that they include audio-visual images, may contribute to a cult of personality in the reception of the work of any contemporary writer. This may be intensified in Ernaux's case because of the auto/biographical nature of her work. The combination of self-revelation in the texts and mediatisation seems particularly powerful, resulting in an 'author discourse' which bears some similarity to the discourses of stardom analysed by Richard Dyer (see below; Dyer, 1979). Finally, as the examples given below illustrate, the gender of the author seems to be of great significance in determining these responses.

Perhaps one of the most immediately noticeable aspects of the 'author discourse' is the mode of address adopted. The choice of the correct phrase to open or close a letter is particularly difficult in French, since the possibilities are numerous, complex and subtly nuanced. Many readers described their uncertainty about the appropriate mode of address to adopt, commenting that the feelings of empathy and identification inspired by the books make the technically correct mode of address to a stranger – Madame – seem too formal. Taking the *Passion simple* letters as a case-study, I observed that whilst the majority did opt for the neutral Madame, a significant number of readers adopted more intimate modes of address. This was particularly striking in the case of women readers, where about twenty of the circa seventy letters began with the kind of opening normally reserved for friends, most commonly 'chère Annie', but also 'Annie', 'Bonjour (Annie)', and in one case 'chère amie' (dear friend). In the whole sample, *tutoiement* (the use of the familiar form of the second-person pronoun) occurred, but was rare, with the vast majority of male and female readers preferring the polite 'vous' form. The latter might be seen as a recognition of the reality of writing a letter to a stranger, but it was often combined with references to Ernaux as a sister, twin sister, or even, for one young woman, mother, and for another 'blood sister'. One woman reader of *La Honte*, aged seventy-four, finds so many similarities between her own and Ernaux's life-history that she concludes: 'Clearly, we are almost sisters', whilst over twenty years earlier, a male reader of *Les Armoires vides* described the book's heroine, Denise Lesur, as 'a bit like a younger sister for me'.

These formulations can be read as expressions of a fantasy where the author can become a member of the family or a close friend. A more overt version of this is the significant minority of readers, mainly women, who invite Ernaux to dinner or lunch, or for a holiday in the south of France or the Pacific! Perhaps male readers, conscious that an invitation might imply a desire for more than friendship, feel more constrained. Interestingly, one of the women who hopes to meet Ernaux finds it necessary to affirm that she is 'neither women's lib nor "ambivalent"', the latter presumably in relation to her sexuality. More often, the invitation is offered unselfconsciously, and the culture of friendship between women, sometimes with feminist overtones, is invoked: 'Another, less rational reason: the desire to talk with you about life, death, writing, oblivion, whilst striding along paths through mountains, the thyme-scented scrubland of the south, or by the sea' (F., aged 57; 5/3/97).[7] This and other letters in similar vein are reminiscent of

Felski's work on feminist confessional writing, characterised, she argues, by the implied woman reader, or confidante, in the text. Whilst Ernaux's work and its reception cannot be encompassed by Felski's definition, interpreting the text as the outpourings of an imagined intimate woman friend is nonetheless one significant mode of reading. For women readers, who find a representation of their own gendered experience, the texts function as a kind of literary consciousness-raising group, and Ernaux becomes a dear, if fantasised, friend.[8]

A corollary to this, again, mainly among women readers, is what some readers consciously term the 'groupie' syndrome, where like a film star or pop-singer, Ernaux becomes a cult figure. One woman asks: 'Do you realise when you begin a new book, that someone, some would say a "groupie", is already waiting for the next Annie Ernaux?' (F., 10/2/92). The contradiction between this discourse, which emphasises Ernaux's 'star qualities', and the desire to see her as a sister or friend, the 'writer next door', is similar to the tension in star images which Dyer analyses, where discourses of ordinariness and the special or magical coexist, despite the evident contradiction (Dyer, 1979, p. 49). Ernaux's readers, like the fans of a film star, are simultaneously fascinated by her everyday life, the confirmation of her ordinariness, and convinced that she possesses exceptional, even magical qualities. Thus, just as film star fans scan the gossip columns for details of a particular star's favourite breakfast cereal, the minutiae of Ernaux's domestic life are fascinating for some readers: 'Last year, after *Passion simple*, I would often say to myself in the morning "Perhaps Annie Ernaux is having her coffee". And then, irritated, "And supposing she drinks tea?" Not knowing was very disturbing for me' (F.). The contradiction between ordinary and extraordinary found in many star images has a particular nuance here, in that the auto/biographical nature of Ernaux's writing brings with it a further contradiction, between sameness and difference, Ernaux as intimate friend, or revered idol. The auto/biographical genre creates possibilities for identification, and a sense of knowing the author intimately, whilst her increasing celebrity emphasises the distance between her and her readers, making the 'fan' or 'groupie' response identified above seem appropriate. Some readers are aware of this play of contradictions: 'It's really very odd to feel so emotionally close to someone, and yet so far away in every other sense – I mean way of life etc.' (F., retired teacher, 12/2/88). Although overtly most letters focus on the similarities between their own and Ernaux's experiences, these poles of sameness and difference, distance and closeness are often in play in the writing. Thus one young woman comments that she addresses Ernaux as 'Madame' in order to express her own 'indisputable insignificance compared to you'. She goes on to describe the complex feelings which the thought of meeting her 'idol' inspires: 'The possibility of meeting you? I don't know. What else would I have to say to you? I would prefer to listen to you. Not entranced, but in search of your wholeness. To steal from you that indestructible strength which you transmit' (F., journalist, 17/1/88). For another, the conviction that her own experiences are identical to those described by Ernaux is combined with intense admiration and idealisation of the author: 'This book [*Passion simple*] was my bible for many months, I dragged it about with me, everywhere. It was in my bag and my memory. Your book was my guiding light in my destructive relationship with a man. You were my model, I admired you for being able to face the final break-up' (F., aged 26). This emphasis on the book as a physical object is not uncommon; it becomes a symbol in the cult of the author:[9] 'It's my bedside book, I've even stuck a photo of you cut out of a TV listings magazine onto the last page' (F., aged 50, 14/3/92).

As I will discuss in more detail below, the letters often describe this kind of activity – collecting pictures of the author, or following all of her media appearances. This avowal of 'fan behaviour' of a type which is often associated with low social status and stupidity seems unusual in the context of letters addressed to an established writer published by one of France's most prestigious publishing houses. They would be less surprising if addressed to the star of a TV soap opera or sitcom and perhaps indicate both the effects of the mediatisation of Ernaux and her work, and the very great enthusiasm and loyalty which the latter inspires. On reading the letters, it is noticeable that the same names reoccur: Ernaux clearly has a following, a group of readers scattered throughout France, or even living abroad, who read her books the minute they come out, devour the reviews and magazine articles, and would not miss a radio or TV appearance for the world. It is clear from the letters that a number of male readers are in fact 'fans' of Ernaux's work, adopting some or all of these modes of behaviour. On the whole though, women seem more able to describe themselves openly as fans or groupies, and to recount 'irrational behaviour' which is vaguely reminiscent of the 'aberrations' described by the author in *Passion simple*. Perhaps the knowledge that the author herself has a close, if complex, relationship with popular culture makes the avowal of all of this possible. A woman reader might have thought twice about describing to Beauvoir her delight in discovering she wore a turban and almost always ate out! More seriously, it is significant that Ernaux has managed to combine the acquisition of the revered status of 'intellectual' in French society with wide personal popularity. This is a particularly difficult balancing act for a woman in French culture, and it has its own dangers, as chapter 6 will reveal.

Comments on Ernaux's physical appearance seem to be part of this focus on the author as a person. They reflect the contradictions discussed above, with Ernaux's appearance at times interpreted in terms of her emotional complicity with her readers, and at other times as a sign of her superior 'star' qualities – exceptional beauty and femininity. It is not surprising that these comments are often inspired by Ernaux's television appearances and by photographs of her in the press, and that as a result, they are a phenomenon of the increasing mediatisation of her more recent books (from *La Place* and the award of the Prix Renaudot onwards). Again, the subject matter of the text may have played a role; comments on the author's appearance were most common in response to *Passion simple*, where the auto/biographical 'I' is combined with the depiction of a physical passion. The increased size and social diversity of this readership was, however, probably a more significant factor, since many readers were clearly not habitual consumers of literary texts, and were therefore less aware of the impersonal conventions of literary criticism, or of letters to an author. The comments on Ernaux's appearance are only rarely overtly sexual, even in response to *Passion simple*; the author herself remarked that contrary to her expectations she received no obscene letters after the publication of *Passion simple* (Ernaux, 1994a). A very small number of male readers of this text do write to tell Ernaux that they find her desirable, or even, in the case of one reader, that she is the woman he has been waiting for all his life. More generally, it is common for both male and female readers of Ernaux's works from *La Place* onwards to describe their discovery of Ernaux through a media appearance. This is often, though not inevitably, associated with a reaction to the image itself, whether a photograph of Ernaux, or her appearance in a television programme. One reader described how 'everything began with a photo: your face in a TV listings magazine' (M., retired; 5/2/92). A woman reader described how she saw Ernaux interviewed by Bernard Pivot on *Apostrophes*[10] and then read *La Place*: 'Immediately you were wonderful and so were your femininity, gentleness, knowledge and your serene face. I bought your book and read it over and over again' (F., aged 50; 19/3/92). The same reader later saw Ernaux again on television after the publication of *Passion simple*, finding her still 'wonderful' but 'with a less serene face than before, like mine (marked by something (. . .))'. This is quite typical of the comments on Ernaux's appearance, in that her expression or even colouring are often read as signifiers of a particular sensitivity and vulnerability. Ident-ification with the author is also present, and the reader seems to be constructing her own identity as a woman who has loved passionately and painfully through these comments on *Passion simple*. Identification is taken one step further by a female reader writing after the publication of *La Honte* and *'Je ne suis pas sortie de ma nuit'*: 'Blond with blue eyes myself, I feel as if I have your sensitive and fragile face' (F., aged 53; 19/1/97). I will discuss the question of identification at greater length later in this chapter, but here it seems relevant to highlight the lack of boundaries between self and other/author which the fixation on Ernaux's physical appearance reveals in this case.

A more common form of merging is the confusion of the author's physical appearance and her writing. For one man, even her clothes become a signifier for her literary style: 'Give us more of that purity, that stillness, that steady sobriety which you carry within you, and which emanates from your face, and your black garments of that evening' (M., 22/1/92). Ernaux's facial expression is often, as here, read as an embodiment of the themes of her work: 'On Friday night you were beautiful, the whole time you had that gaze which is directed at the people present and which seems to carry another world, the world you come from, from which you originate, . . . and the world still to come, which frightens you' (F., 3/2/92). A woman reader, writing after the publication of *Une femme*, and Ernaux's subsequent appearance on *Apostrophes*, makes a similar link between the author's physical presence and her writing: 'The words of the book, printed, bought in a bookshop, have found a face, have taken a voice, have adopted attitudes. The initial magic resided in this' (F., 2/2/88). The desire to know a person, character-istic of the author discourse, is clearly manifest here: for this reader the texts themselves become more powerful, or indeed magical, when they can be attached to an image (and resulting fantasy) of the author as a real person. However, this fantasy work is sometimes rendered more difficult by the author's real, physical presence, particularly when there seems to be a contradiction between Ernaux's appearance and the subjects of her writing; one woman commented after seeing Ernaux at a book fair that she was 'belle et glacée' (a glacial beauty), in her smart suit, and felt she could only really get close to Ernaux through writing to her: 'As I write to you, your suit doesn't exist any more. What remains is the woman who wrote *La Place* and *Une femme* in order to feel less alone and artificial' (F., aged 31; 25/1/88). Ernaux's clothes are here being read in the same way as her published texts. The choice of a suit carries with it the same dangers as a metaphor, in that it expresses the social distance between its wearer and her working-class origins. At the same time, wearing a dress bought at Monoprix on *Apostrophes* would be as obvious and artificial a choice as writing in the dialect of the pays de Caux (the part of Normandy where Ernaux was born and brought up). The woman writer may well wish for the greater neutrality of male garb.

All of these references to Ernaux's appearance, whether as sources of identification or evidence of a merging of the persona of the writer and her texts, are profoundly influenced by the gender of the author in question. Although she writes, and therefore 'acts', Ernaux is obliged to 'appear', and thus to participate in the social construction of femininity (Berger, 1972). The extent to which Ernaux's readers relate to her not only as a woman, but as the embodiment of the socially constructed fundamentals of femininity (sensitivity, grace, beauty, vulnerability and so on) can be illustrated by a final quotation from a man who has seen Ernaux on television, hounded by at least one male critic. It is indicative of the gendered nature of Ernaux's celebrity in French culture that the writer of the letter declares that he has not read any of Ernaux's books, and is therefore only responding to a media appearance. The fact that there is no widely accepted feminine form for the word 'écrivain' (writer) may seem indicative of a gender-neutral space in the culture. In reality, it seems that Ernaux is often seen first of all as a woman, and secondly as a writer. For this man, Ernaux represents an essential femininity, inspiring a corresponding gallantry on his part: 'A woman as intelligent as gorgeous. Refined as well as feminine. Who then is this peasant who dares to be critical? Isn't he moved by this universe of feminine refinement?' (M., 12/2/ 92).

Those who have actually read the books are equally keen to spring to Ernaux's defence, when the critics weigh in. The most common reaction is to argue that the critics are disqualified by their lack of relevant experience. This emphasis on the value of the works as *témoignage* (testimony) again indicates the importance to many readers of the knowledge that the author is recounting her own, real experience, and their interest in her as a person. At the same time, readers often defend Ernaux against the criticism that her style is too simple, and that her work is not literature,[11] on the grounds that her language is suitable for her subject matter, and that her ability to move her readers, often to tears, is an indication of literary value. This letter, sent after the publication of *Une femme*, is typical: 'Those who have not been through this hell cannot understand. Especially those who spoke of your style being too sparse, too flat. My mother, like yours, is already in a world beyond language, where I cannot follow her. Only this extreme economy can translate such a reality' (F., 19/3/88). This type of defence is common after the publication of *Passion simple*, where the journalistic criticism was particularly vehement, and readers' identification with the recounted experience intense. Some of the defences of Ernaux against her critics are, however, political as well as personal, showing an awareness of the class- and gender-based prejudices which often seem to motivate professional critics. A male reader, commenting on a radio interview after the publication of *La Honte* and *'Je ne suis pas sortie de ma nuit'*, argued that the criticism seemed to be aimed more at Ernaux as a person than at her work.[12] He concludes by asking whether this could be an instance of class-based criticism (M., writer; 19/2/97). Some women readers are aware of the misogynistic tendencies revealed by some critics, particularly in response to *Passion simple*: '[These reviews] were absolutely disgraceful, the fact that they were written by men says it all . . . They don't like truth, and for them sexuality does not exist in women' (F., retired primary schoolteacher; 5/3/92).

Often, the readers' defence of the author aims to comfort and support her, with phrases such as 'don't let yourself be beaten down' (M., 9/2/94) or 'don't listen to them' (F., 1/5/92). Just as readers are comforted by the knowledge acquired in reading Ernaux's books that they are not alone, in turn they attempt to provide the author with similar consolation: 'Thank you for making me realise that one is rarely an isolated case. And thank you for being yourself. I thought you were sublime on Pivot's programme, *Bouillon de Culture*, and be reassured, people like you' (M., aged 27; 21/3/92). This desire to comfort the author manifests itself not only in defending her against critics but also in more general terms. This is perhaps not surprising, given the predominance of the themes of loss and grief in texts such as *La Place*, *Une femme* and *Passion simple*. Nonetheless, it is part of the 'author discourse' in that it implies a response to, and interest in, a person, rather than a text. After the publication of *Passion simple*, for example, a male reader expressed his concern, on seeing Ernaux on television, 'for everything suggested that your suffering was great' (M., 9/2/92). Advice on how to conduct the relationship with A. was offered by at least one (male) reader, and many expressed concern about the outcome of the relationship and Ernaux's state of mind.

If for many readers Ernaux becomes an object to be cherished and revered, for a small number of others, she is the epitome of abjection. These letters, focusing on the author as a person, do so in order to criticise, or even insult. Although these letters are only a tiny minority, their violence is surprising. In this sample, though there were a few letters which made critical comments in response to all of the works, only *Passion simple* and *Journal du dehors* inspired the most extreme responses. Like the much greater number of positive letters, they reveal the extent to which the author's gender has affected the reading. Here, it is often the representation of an active and desiring female sexuality in the two texts which has inspired the negative reaction. The association of female desire with the unclean can be observed in phrases used by one woman reader who refers to *Journal du dehors* as a 'tissue of filth' and a 'success of the sewers'. What really seems to have upset this reader is the expression of sexual desire by a woman of fifty:

> This absence of lucidity, of psychology which causes you to regret that a young layabout of twenty-five is more interested in your handbag than your fifty-year-old person. Have you lost your senses, Madam, to such an extent that this sexual obsession which is transparent in many of your works should make you lose the most elementary modesty? (F., teacher; 9/1/94).

Excessive sexuality is castigated here, whilst in other cases, absence of emotion, that necessary condition of femininity, is the crime.

Ernaux is accused of being an intellectual woman, who in *Passion simple* has produced a book which is as 'cold and hard as a stone' (F., writer; 18/3/92). This 'coldness' is sometimes associated with Ernaux's profession: with other teachers, she shares 'that emotional poverty' which threatens future generations (F., 22/1/92). If the negative letters at times bear witness to the unpopularity of the teaching profession, it is the author's gender and her willingness to make the repressed culture of femininity the subject of her writing which are at the root of the most violent rejections. The male reader of *Journal du dehors* who sees in the work 'girlie philosophy, an atmosphere of tampons, frequent showers, clean fingernails' expresses overtly the horror of femininity, and the misogyny which underlies some of the journalistic writing (see chapter 6). Among the readers' letters such intensely negative responses are the exception to the rule. The author discourse may reveal a strong interest in the gendered person 'behind' the texts, and may in part be the result of their mediatisation, but generally it is also indicative of the enthusiasm and loyalty which the texts themselves inspire. In the section which follows I will look at one of the factors which engenders this enthusiasm – the possibility of making links between the texts and the readers' own lives.

Reading as Construction of the Self

The 'reader discourse', an equally common feature of the letters, moves the focus away from the author, and onto the reading self. In the letters or parts of letters where this discourse dominates, reading is far from being a passive experience; on the contrary, these readers are keen to tell their own stories, and to construct their own identities, often using Ernaux's texts as a springboard. In her article on *Passion simple*, Ernaux argued that the readers' appropriation of the text was very clear (Ernaux, 1994a, p. 28). My argument here is similar, in that the fascination with the other discussed above is complemented in these examples by the desire to express aspects of the self. In writing to the author about themselves, these readers are constructing themselves as the subjects, rather than passive recipients, of a creative process. In part, I would interpret this as an example of the 'active audience' which has been identified and analysed in the fields of media and cultural studies.[13] I would also agree with Ernaux that the desire to recount the self is particularly strong in response to auto/ biographical writing: 'More than any other kind of writing, an autobiographical text implicates its readers, and obliges them to situate themselves in relation to what is expressed – in short, to reply "yes, me too" or "no never"' (Ernaux, 1994a, p. 27). Ernaux's remark, in her article on the reception of *Passion simple*, is clearly based on her experience of reading hundreds of readers' letters over many years. The sample which I am analysing here entirely bears out her observation. The readers do seem to be implicated in the way she describes, with the majority writing to affirm that they recognise the experiences and emotions which Ernaux's texts depict.

This discourse, or mode of reading has been described as 'authentic realism' by Sara Mills, in a historical account of feminist reading strategies (Mills and Pearce, 1996). According to Mills's definition, 'authentic realist' readers seek some correspondence between their own lives and that recounted in the literary text, which is then judged in terms of the level of authenticity attained. In feminist contexts particularly, authentic realism has attributed a political function and value to the act of reading: the (woman writer's) text raises the reader's awareness of oppression, and becomes the catalyst for social and personal change. Some of the readers' letters analysed below do, in fact, claim this kind of relation to Ernaux's writing (see p. 129). More generally, recognition of a particular experience leads to an account of their own life histories. Whilst I would agree with Sara Mills that 'authentic realism' has its limitations as a critical practice, as this study demonstrates, it is a widespread and pleasurable mode of reading, and as such deserves serious attention. In response to *Une femme*, twenty-five of the thirty-six letters from women readers, and five of the nine letters from men (i.e. 66 per cent of the total sample) included accounts of the readers' own lives. It seems that Ernaux's auto/ biographical act has stimulated their own, validating their experiences and providing a sense of justification and confidence. This tendency seems to be related to, rather than in conflict with, the focus on the author described above, in that it may be part of the fantasy of a relationship with a person, a desire to be recognised by Ernaux, just as one has recognised oneself in her work. The political role of these recognitions should not be ignored: as the example of *Une femme* cited above suggests, for many women, and some men, Ernaux's texts do raise awareness of the social causes of individual suffering, and thus empower. In the analysis of extracts from readers' letters in this section, I will attempt to explore in more detail these affirmations of the self, and the desire for recognition which some of them express.

In one particular facet of the discourse, the reading process itself becomes the subject of a narrative. It is as if these readers are keen to impress upon the author the reality of their lives, and to provide an equivalent of, or response to, Ernaux's descriptions of the act of writing. They paint vignettes of themselves reading, as if attempting to preserve a particularly significant moment of their lives, just as the author aims to 'save' her life from oblivion by writing. Perhaps taking their cue from Ernaux's texts, where the emotional connotations of objects and everyday scenes are constantly implied, and at times explored, these readers often describe the circumstances in which they read in minute detail: 'It is 10.43. In the "American" bar – alone. On the table there is a coffee, a glass of water, a pencil, an ashtray and a book. In spite of the laughter and exclamations of my anonymous companions, I only see and hear *Passion simple*' (F., aged 18; 6/3/92). A more unusual, humorous narrative by a male reader of *La Place* describes reading Ernaux in snatched moments while simultaneously reading an adventure story aloud to his small daughter: he declares himself very lucky 'not to have faced the fight against the terrible "Gogotes" all alone' (M., 7/4/84). The manner, as well as place or context of reading is often commented on, with many readers of all nine texts, but particularly the more recent, short volumes, describing how they read the books at one sitting, in a highly emotional state. A woman reader of *Passion simple* combines this sense of the urgency of her need to read the book with description of the rather unusual context in which she read it: 'Read, is perhaps an understatement, Devoured, would be more accurate – at each red light as I was on my way home, impatient for the next stop' (F., 12/1/?). For a reader of *La Place* a train journey provided the opportunity to read the whole text, between Bordeaux and Bayonne. Here, however, the discourse of literary theory is invoked by the use of words reminiscent of Barthes such as 'jouissance' (ecstatic or orgasmic pleasure): 'I got off the train feeling drunk with that specific inebriation born of what I can find no other word to describe, the ecstasy (jouissance) of language. I was in love with your italics' (F.).

The large number of teachers, writers and artists within the sample may have resulted in an exceptionally high number of responses of this kind, where the reading process is described as both an intellectual and emotional engagement with the text. Some readers send to the author many pages of detailed commentary. One reader of *Passion simple* describes his relationship with the book as replicating the passion described in the text, veering, in the process, between the languages of literary criticism and of romantic love:

> Furthermore, the book never leaves my side. I open it frequently, at random, I re-read a passage, and then with a kind of disordered passion, I note, on well-filled pages, the impressions, the emotions, the fleeting ideas, the associated memories which throng within me; I put together phrases which are in different parts of the text, think of themes to develop, observations about the style, the vocabulary: this is how I pursue my reading, entering into a dialogue in favour of which my life is temporarily suspended. (M., teacher; 5/2/92)

Another reader of *Journal du dehors* provides thirty examples of references to eroticism in the text, 'intrigued' by what he sees as their masculine tone, and comparing Ernaux to the 'feminine writing' produced by authors such Cixous or Irigaray (M., 14/5/93). Comparisons, particularly with other women writers, as diverse as Yourcenar and Duras, occasionally occur, illustrating the parallels between professional literary criticism and at least one mode of writing to an author.[14] The construction of the reading subject is here marked by the desire to affirm one's status as an intellectual, capable of addressing the author as an equal. A woman reader of *Passion simple*, who teaches literature, describes herself as split between the analytical mode of reading and a more personal response. She emphasises her professional status as much as her emotional empathy with Ernaux:

> On my second reading I wanted to return to your remarks on the nature of writing, its finality, its relationship to the real, the time of passion and the time of writing. Having said that, and from this you will recognise our common profession, it was obviously with the desire of finding myself in your book that I read you first of all. This desire was fulfilled, at last. (F., literature teacher)

This tension between the need to affirm one's status as critical reader and personal engagement with the text was also observed by Pearce in her study of feminist academics' readings of Margaret Atwood (Pearce, 1997, p. 233).

For the majority of readers, however, the status of critical reader is less important than the expression of emotion. Many readers describe the process of reading Ernaux as a highly intense experience, though in most cases, the emotion is more raw, and expressed more simply than the above: 'I read *Une femme* last night: I began reading late, thinking I would stop when I felt sleepy. Sleep did not come, but tears did, very quickly: I wiped them with the sheet, gently, so that I would not wake up my husband' (F., aged 40; 21/1/88). This description of nocturnal, avid reading and of a strong emotional response on the basis of identification with the content of Ernaux's works is typical of the letters received about all of the texts. In the article cited earlier, Ernaux herself commented on the very large number of letters she received from men and women in response to *Passion simple*, expressing a strong ident- ification with the experience of passion the text describes. Women use phrases such as 'I saw my reflection in your mirror' (F., 22/4/ 92), revealing the complete merging of identity noted above. Men, on the other hand, are sometimes surprised to find themselves identifying with a woman narrator: 'I found myself, not in A., but in you' (M., lecturer; 24/4/92). As Ernaux herself comments, *Passion simple* seems to have freed some readers from self- censorship. If such an experience can be the subject of a serious literary work, published by Gallimard, then it is possible for individuals to free themselves from guilt, and to avow their own feelings. The accessibility of Ernaux's texts, rather than the originality of her subject, is crucial here. It could be argued that many works of the French literary canon are concerned with the theme of obsessive passion; Proust's *À la recherche du temps perdu* immediately springs to mind. However, the possibilities of recognition, identification and liberation which the work might offer are available only to those who can cope with the complexity of Proust's vocabulary and syntax (see chapter 6, p. 157). It is not surprising, in this context, that readers often express their surprise at finding that Ernaux's texts, published with all the literary and social prestige of the house of Gallimard, speak to them and seem relevant to their own lives. Many comment that they have never identified in this way with a book before – 'no other book has ever given me this strange sensation of being my story – told by myself' (F., late fifties; 20/3/92).

This sense of surprise is particularly strong in the response to the works dealing with Ernaux's change of social class. It may result from the fact that, unlike obsessive love, working-class experience and the feelings resulting from the move from working-class to middle-class culture are under-represented themes in French literature.[15] Indeed, in general, as Ernaux herself points out, the experience of working-class life is either caricatured or repressed by the dominant culture. In this context, it is not surprising that many readers write not only to express their identification with the feelings of loss and shame which Ernaux describes, but also to thank her for bearing witness to this experience. Thus, a woman of working-class origins, and of Ernaux's generation, who has become a doctor describes Ernaux's work as crucial in her understanding of herself, and of her feelings of alienation and isolation: 'However, it was *Les Armoires vides* which affected me the most, since for the first time, actually, despite the fact that I read a lot, I saw situations and feelings described which I thought I was alone in experiencing, and which weighed heavily in my life, and still do' (F., aged 50; 12/9/88). A young man of twenty-two describes his disaffection from his literary studies, and from contemporary French literature generally, until he discovered *La Place*. Despite the sorrow inspired by the book's themes of loss and grief, he is happy to discover his own cultural heritage in a work of literature:

> The delight, first of all, of seeing the world of my grandparents re-emerging from the depths of my childhood, spent in lower Normandy. The pleasure of finding them on the white pages of a 'folio' edition. My grandfather shaving as only men of that period knew how. My grandmother oppressed by all the weight of the social conventions of the time. (M., student; 22/7/94)

For many readers, like the woman doctor cited above, this validation of their experience through its literary expression has a therapeutic effect, providing a new sense of direction and of being able to cope with conflicting emotions. Thus a young woman who has left a peasant background in France to build a new life in New Zealand writes using the familiar 'tu' form of address: 'I am writing to you, Annie, to thank you for giving me back my memory. I had forgotten so many things. I nearly went mad. Now I have a base from which I can act – that's it' (F., aged 25; undated letter). A woman in her late sixties states quite clearly that Ernaux has helped her in her psychotherapy, commenting that 'You cannot know how much good you have done me' (F., aged 67; 4/3/97).

Although many of the people who write to Ernaux have had similar experiences, whether of changing class, watching a parent die of Alzheimer's disease, or of passion, the identification is not necessarily based on precise parallels. Thus a gay man describes how he identifies with the feelings of shame described in *La Honte*, and draws strength from Ernaux's writing: 'And so to be able to read, as an adult, the words of someone who seems to have felt similar feelings (for other reasons, of course, my shame, my shames naturally have different causes from yours), this makes it possible to anchor one's consciousness of existing, to face other people' (M., primary schoolteacher/singer, 1997). Similarly, some readers write at times of extreme crisis or tragedy, not because Ernaux describes precisely the same situation, but because of the powerful emotions she depicts and evokes. A woman whose daughter committed suicide at the age of seventeen writes after the publication of *La Honte* to tell Ernaux 'how much books like yours help people to survive'. As I suggested in the introduction to this chapter, the author plays the role of therapist or priest in these letters, providing a neutral and separate space in which repressed feelings can be expressed: 'It's your books, Annie Ernaux, which are unbearable. They have trapped me in such an intimate identification that my modesty prevents me from sharing them with anyone other than you, the author herself. And fortunately I do not have to look her in the eye' (F., aged about 57, English teacher; 7/2/97). The use of the third person here is indicative of the necessary, and liberating, distance between the writer and Ernaux, her addressee. This extract is also interesting because of the ambivalence expressed by words such as 'unbearable' and 'trapped'. Earlier in the letter the reader describes herself sobbing as she reads, 'completely drained' by the force of the childhood memories which the text has evoked. This letter, and many others, indicate that Ernaux's writing can be disturbing, as well as beneficial (see chapter 6, p. 151). Another reader describes how he will keep Ernaux's books on a special shelf, along with a few other works which 'terrorise' him (M., 18/2/92).

Recognition is not, however, confined to personal experience, but can include the pleasure of recalling a historical period, such as the description of the early 1950s in *La Honte* – 'I found myself completely taken back to the year 1952, when I was thirteen years old' (F., aged 58, librarian; 1/3/97). A sixty-year-old woman reader thanks Ernaux for recording the language of the period: 'for making those typical, dated expressions come to life again' (F., aged 60, doctor), whilst a third is particularly sensitive to Ernaux's technique of developing narrative from the description of old photographs: 'I particularly liked your descriptions of photos which appear like signposts in some of your books. In every house there are some of those old photograph albums, so resonant of a period, and so strangely similar, so that I really felt I could see those old photos of yours' (F., late 60s, 11/3/97). Identification with experiences, place or period is sometimes accompanied by political analysis: 'Although ten years separate us, in the sixties I had feelings which were just as violent and painful, because of the social injustice which reigns in our town, and of course, in our country' (F., aged 44; 3/2/97). This reader of *La Honte* shares with Ernaux not only an experience, but its interpretation – she is responding to the many indications in the text that the shame recounted is social, rather than psychological in its origins.

It would, however, be incorrect to conclude that all of those who write to the author see such a close correspondence between their experience and her texts, or share her views. Ernaux, as a teacher of literature, and highly trained literary theorist herself, is part-icularly well-equipped to present and discuss her work. It has been argued that she is unusually concerned to predetermine its reception, both through the constant authorial interventions in the texts and through her comments in press interviews (Charpentier, 1994).[16] My analysis of the 'author in the text' in chapter 2 and of the journalistic reception of Ernaux's works in chapter 6 have, in general, led me to agree with Charpentier's view. However, the success of these efforts on the part of the author must of necessity only ever be partial, and it is likely that the author herself would not have it otherwise, being fully aware that 'reception is always unpredictable' (IN). The text is powerful, but not all-powerful, and oppositional readings, as defined by Stuart Hall, remain possible (Hall, [1973] 1996).[17] Such readings, are, indeed, illustrative of the now widely held view that readers are not merely the passive victims of ideology, but active in the process of meaning con-struction.

Thus, a small but significant minority of Ernaux's readers enjoy and appreciate the writing, whilst questioning the universality of the experiences recounted. A number of readers have changed class, like Ernaux, but question the negative feelings she describes, in this case in *Les Armoires vides*:

I found in your book the world of my childhood and adolescence. (. . .)
And of all of this I have excellent memories, I've never despised my
parents, never been ashamed of being 'the grocer's daughter'. On the
contrary, I was proud. So why is there so much anger in your book?
Why were you ashamed of your parents' condition, and why did you
only see vulgarity and pettiness in the people who came to their shop
and café? (F., aged 38, primary school teacher; 22/3/79)

It is not surprising that *Les Armoires vides* should inspire this
response, given the violently angry tone, and rejection of both
working-class and educated middle-class culture which it
describes. This rather one-sided view is replaced, from *La Place*
onwards, by a sense of being torn between the two cultures; the
more positive and affectionate representation of working-class
culture in the later texts facilitates the positive identifications
described above. However, there are still a small number of readers
who do not recognise the painful feelings described by Ernaux.
For a retired English teacher, for example, 'social class does not
exist'. Although she enjoys Ernaux's use of language – 'the clichés
you pick out bring back memories, and make me laugh a lot' – she
does not identify with the feelings of loss, guilt and alienation. She
concludes her letter by hoping that Ernaux can learn to be more
relaxed about this! This is, in many ways, an unusually oppositional
reading, with the reader refusing to follow the guidelines provided
in the text for the correct mode of reception. There is, in this case,
some irony in the fact that this reader is refusing Ernaux's 'high
culture', serious version of the change of class: she refuses to enter
the angst-ridden world of the intellectual, and remains firmly and
happily rooted in popular culture: 'On reading your text, I seemed
to hear the voice of Arletty,[18] and her saucy reflections, and I often
laughed, even though the subject dealt with was serious' (F., 10/
6/88). The class of *première* pupils who read *La Place* present a
different kind of 'oppositional reading'. To some extent, their
questioning of the author's world view can be seen as the result of
the intellectual debate which the classroom reading of literature is
designed to initiate. It may also be seen both as evidence of the
pupils' lack of experience and as an indication of the cultural gulf
between them and the generation who were young in 1968:

However, according to your novel, and the study we have made of it
in class, you see a difference between the worlds of the bourgeoisie

and the working class. I agree that this difference existed in the time of your father and grandfather, but it seems to me that now this difference has disappeared. With ten years of hindsight in relation to your writing, do you still believe in this social difference? If you do, what do you mean by the term 'bourgeoisie'? (F., schoolgirl; 1995)

The markers of academic writing present here – the use of the impersonal verb 'it seems to me', the terminology of argument ('however', 'I agree') and the demand for precision embodied in the final question – are indicative of the distance on the road to intellectual culture which this particular pupil has already travelled. This comment could be made about all of these letters, which are very different from the rest of the sample – written, with varying degrees of success, in clear paragraphs, constructing an argument, requiring Ernaux to define her terms, to justify her position. Ironically, in writing letters which are part of the process of learning correct, middle-class linguistic and social conventions, these pupils are completely unaware of what is happening to them. Like Denise Lesur, they see themselves as free, facing the universal human problems of existence as defined by the heroes of Sartre or Camus (*Les Armoires vides*, p. 157). Social class, gender and race do not, yet, enter the equation.

The 'Words to Say It'

The interest in the author, or in the reading self and his or her history, does not exclude an equally strong focus on the texts themselves. If letters consisting of pages of detailed textual analysis are a rare, though interesting occurrence in the sample, many readers demonstrate an intimate knowledge of the text. It is quite common for readers to quote from the text, or to reuse words or phrases found in the text, as if Ernaux's writing has provided a language and structure for the comprehension and expression of disavowed or repressed experiences. Lynne Pearce has observed something similar in her discussion of academic responses to Atwood's *Death by Landscape*: 'What has happened here, indeed, is that the text has become overlaid with the reader's own parallel story: traces of the original show through in places, but as the reader lets go of the need "to make a reading", another reading, which is also a writing, begins' (Pearce, 1997, p. 240). Here, the need to 'make a reading' may generally be less in evidence, but the reading which becomes a writing is certainly, as we have seen, a feature of these letters. In this section, I am concerned specifically with those moments when the original 'shows through', the appropriation of Ernaux's actual words.

Many readers of *Passion simple* thank Ernaux for finding the words to express their experience, and some adapt passages from the text:

> 'From November '94 to March '95 I spent my time waiting for a phone call, a man's visit, I know I won't see him again, he is not free.' I thought of writing that, and then I heard you on France-Culture and I understood that you had written what I had experienced and wanted to write. Thank you for these pages. (F., late fifties)

If the opening lines of *Passion simple* inspire this kind of adaptation, the closing sentences of *Une femme* also seem particularly powerful in this sense. A number of readers repeat Ernaux's words in order to express their own grief, or anticipated loss: 'My parents are very old, but still alive . . . but I know that when they die, I will also have lost – if I may use your moving phrase – "the last link" or at least the strongest "with the world I came from"' (F., aged 45, teacher; 8/2/88); 'On 24 April, with my father, I too lost the last link with the world I came from' (F., 11/5/88). These examples illustrate how Ernaux's readers enter her linguistic universe, identifying and reusing keywords and phrases. The word *lien* (link) is one of these key words, often taken up by readers, who perhaps share with Ernaux the desire to construct a coherent identity, precisely by making links between past and present, cultures of origin and acquisition. One woman reader of *Une femme* reworks the title of *La Femme gelée* to describe her own life-history: 'A woman transfixed (figée) at twenty, not quite thawed out (dégelée) by forty' (F., aged 50, 12/4/88). The words 'don' and 'donner' (gift, to give) which recur in Ernaux's writing are also frequently taken up by readers (see chapter 2, pp. 52–3). Ernaux's notion of writing as a gift seems to be as evocative as the idea of making links, through reading and writing. Some readers reply to the rhetorical question – 'isn't writing a way of giving?' at the end of *Une femme*: 'Isn't writing a way of giving? Yes, that's what I felt – a real voice which gets close to our most difficult feelings' (F., 2/4/88). The phrase used at the end of *Passion simple* – 'un don reversé' – to describe

Ernaux's sense that in writing the book she is in some way reciprocating the gift of passion, is also reworked: 'The French teacher I am feels, even more than he understands, the "kind of reciprocal giving" (don reversé) which the book constitutes. You have presented me with a gift, a very great gift' (M., 11/6/95). Or again: 'I welcome your "reciprocal giving" as the most beautiful present and perhaps it will be comforting for you to know that the words born of your suffering will help me live through mine' (F., teacher; 23/3/92).

A number of readers see Ernaux's books as a gift in this way, and feel the desire to give something back to the author, perhaps by replying to her rhetorical questions. On p. 65 of *Passion simple* Ernaux wonders whether she writes 'in order to find out whether others have done or felt similar things, or whether they find such feelings normal'. Several letters respond to this, often giving the page reference, and always 'reassuring' the author that they do have similar experiences. Ernaux's comments on the writing process often receive 'replies'. A reader of *Une femme* comments on the opening line of the penultimate paragraph ('This is not a biography, or a novel of course, perhaps something between literature, sociology and history'): 'And supposing it was a letter? This is how I "received" it' (F., aged 67; 6/2/88). She is not alone in reading Ernaux's text as if it were addressed to her personally; many readers comment that they felt a particular text had been written for them. A reader of *La Honte* describes how she reads Ernaux's books 'as one reads a letter, at other moments than those reserved for reading' (F., 20/1/97), whilst for another reader, *Passion simple* is 'like, but better than, a telephone conversation' (F., 13/2/92). On one level, these comments are related to the author discourse discussed in part of this chapter, where the fantasy of the author as personal friend is expressed. They are also illustrative of the strong tendency among Ernaux's readers to appropriate the texts and enter into a dialogue with them. The fact that these responses tend to be in relation to the frequent authorial inter-ventions suggests that the latter play a particular role: the doubts and difficulties of the writer which are expressed seem to open up the text, and to invite comment and response.

A further illustration of both the openness of the text and the evocative power of Ernaux's notion of writing as a gift can be found in the numerous letters which describe the act of giving the books to a friend, relative or lover. In many ways this activity ties together all the strands of the reader discourse discussed here. The books are sometimes offered as a way of expressing an identity. A woman of Norman origins, now working as an actress in the United States, describes precisely this appropriation of the texts: 'It was habitual for me to refer to you when someone asked me who I was, or where I came from. "Read Annie Ernaux, she's remarkable, and you'll learn a lot more about me than I could recount"' (F., actress; 27/4/92). For others, this kind of self-revelation would be too threatening, and Ernaux's books cannot be exchanged as lightly as other works: 'I could not lend *La Place* or *Une femme* to my colleagues without telling them about all the feelings which overwhelmed me as I read, and without thus laying bare my own heart' (F., 38, librarian). However, the desire to communicate with a loved one often overcomes the qualms of modesty. For a young student *La Place* will be evidence of the love he feels for his father, whilst for a mother of nine, *Une femme* will be a link between her and her four daughters. Appropriating the author's words is particularly common in the responses to *Passion simple*, which is often offered to the object of the reader's passion. One male reader asks Ernaux to dedicate a copy of the book to his lover, exhorting her to respond to his desires, but 'in your own style, of course' (M., late fifties). A school librarian describes how she will be sharing this book, not with her pupils, but with 'the only person who was, like me, touched to the core' (F.). A woman whose shame because of her working-class background has prevented her from forming a close relationship also hopes that Ernaux's words in *La Honte* will be able to speak for her: 'Then your book came out, it gave me new hope, new energy. If I love a man again, if I have to commit myself, these writings will perhaps serve as an intermediary for me, your words will speak on my behalf, there won't be much to add except to give the book, will I have the courage?' (F., aged 49). Despite the highly personal nature of some of these appropriations, they confirm the social nature of the reception of a literary text, which becomes an object of exchange, creating and reinforcing networks and communication. For the majority of readers it is the 'gift' of Ernaux's life-writing rather than her literary prestige which is of value, as the texts become 'turning points' in their own life-histories.

Notes

1. In a talk on writing in the first person given at King's College, London, on 8 March, 1994, Ernaux made the following comment: 'The use of the first person implicates the reader enormously and can lead either to a feeling of uneasiness or to enthusiasm, in both cases of an extreme kind.'
2. A well-known example of this would be Janice Radway's study of women readers of romantic fiction: Radway, 1984–7.
3. From an interview with Ernaux by Jean Royer, quoted in Day, 1990, p. 75.
4. Ernaux commented that in choosing the samples which she gave to me, she had removed letters and cards which merely offered formal congratulations, for example at the time of the Prix Renaudot. The letters she chose all expressed 'a real relationship with the text, a personal reaction' (Unpublished interview with the author, 23 May 1997).
5. Ernaux did not have precise figures for the total number of letters received for each text as she files them by year, not by text. Nonetheless, the increase in Ernaux's popularity can be seen in the fact that whereas for *Les Armoires vides* and *Ce qu'ils disent ou rien* she received about twenty and ten letters respectively at the time of publication, for *Une femme* the number was about 300, and for *Passion simple* about 700. Ernaux also commented that the number and timing of the letters depends very much on the text; thus, for *La Femme gelée* she continues to receive letters, since the gender inequality described is still a determining factor for many women's lives. *Journal du dehors* inspired fewer letters, because its content is less personal than the other texts, in Ernaux's view (Unpublished interview with the author, 23 May 1997).
6. Since *La Honte* and *'Je ne suis pas sortie de ma nuit'* were published simultaneously, the letters often responded to both texts
7. Where I have not already provided the information in my text, I note the occupation, age and gender of the reader (M. or F.) and the date of the letter after each quotation. Where one or more of these pieces of information is absent, this is because the letter did not provide the relevant information.

8. Readings based on the relationship between Ernaux's texts and lived experience are discussed in more detail on pp. 124–133 of this chapter.
9. For a discussion of the almost fetishistic importance attached to books in French culture see chapter 6, p. 148.
10. *Apostrophes* was a successful literary discussion programme on French television, which survived for fifteen and a half years, and was presented by Bernard Pivot. It has now been replaced by *Bouillon de Culture*, also presented by Pivot.
11. See chapter 6.
12. See chapter 6, pp. 152–5 for an analysis of the same tendency to focus on the person rather than the work among professional critics.
13. David Morley was the pioneer of empirical work in the media/cultural studies area. He questioned the concept of the passive spectator which film criticism of the 1970s, based on Althusser's theories of ideology and known as '*Screen* theory', had promulgated (Morley, 1980). Amongst others, David Buckingham has espoused and developed the idea of the active audience in his work on soap opera (1987), and on children and television (e.g. Buckingham, 1993).
14. In her article on the reception of Ernaux's work by journalists and librarians, the French sociologist Isabelle Charpentier uses Bourdieu's term 'lectores' to describe professional critics, whose role is to 'divulge legitimate versions of the practice of reading, and to find their own status enhanced as a result' (Charpentier, 1994, p. 48). Comparisons with other writers might be seen as part of this legitimate, and legitimising, practice. See also chapter 6.
15. For a useful list of other writers of working-class origins, and summary of their treatment of these themes see Marie-France Savéan (1994) pp. 200–21.
16. Charpentier argues, convincingly, that the author's ability and determination to provide interpretations of her own works render the traditional role and activity of professional critics superfluous. She sees this act of 'provocation' as the cause of the hostility unleashed on the publication of *Passion simple*. See chapter 6.
17. In this influential paper, Hall developed the notion of three codes of reading: dominant, negotiated and oppositional. A dominant or preferred reading 'decodes the message in terms

of the reference code in which it has been encoded', producing an almost perfect correspondence between the meanings encoded in the text and the reading (Hall, [1973] 1996, p. 47). The match is less perfect in a negotiated reading, where there is a mixture of acceptance of and resistance to the dominant meanings in the text. An oppositional reading completely replaces the dominant code with its own oppositional code, and therefore produces a reading which questions or contradicts the meanings encoded in the text.

18. Ginette Vincendeau describes Arletty as 'one of the great populist stars of French cinema' and her performances as 'full of heart and wisecracks' (Vincendeau, 1996, p. 20). Perhaps her most famous role was as Garance, in Marcel Carné's *Les Enfants du Paradis* (1943–5).

6

Reading Critically

Introduction

*I*n this chapter I will turn to readings of Ernaux's works by
professional critics. In analysing these readings it is important
to bear in mind that professional status is constantly being
reclaimed by the critical act. Isabelle Charpentier, whose work
provides a keystone for this chapter, uses Bourdieu's term 'lectores'
to distinguish these professional readers from the reading public,
and to emphasise how they derive their authority and status,
'auctoritas', from their readings (Bourdieu cited in Charpentier,
1994, p. 47, note 5). Clearly, the *lectores* play a significant role as
gatekeepers of legitimate culture, and it is precisely because of her
class and gender-based challenges to these practices that Ernaux
is chosen as a suitable subject for study by the sociologist,
Charpentier. In a sense this chapter is a case-study of the operation
of systems of exclusion from high culture, which may be based on
class, gender, ethnicity or sexuality, but which are generally
expressed in other terms; it is thus an analysis of pretexts, or
rhetorical devices justifying exclusion or disqualification. Toril Moi
and Elizabeth Fallaize have focused particularly on the role of
gender in these systems of affirmation and exclusion in French
literary culture; their analyses of the hostile critical reception of
Beauvoir's work in France, drawing, in the case of Fallaize, on
Joanna Russ, will also provide a crucial reference point for my work
here (Moi, 1994; Fallaize, 1995).

The Academic Reception of Ernaux's work

My main focus in this chapter is on the reception of Ernaux's work
by the French media, since, as chapter 5 has demonstrated, they

play a significant role in the wide dissemination of Ernaux's texts, and in readers' responses to the writer and her work. Nonetheless, it would be hard to justify the exclusion of academic writers (such as myself) from the analysis of readings of *lectores*, as defined by Bourdieu; whilst space will not permit a detailed account of every academic piece on Ernaux, some salient points should be noted here.

Firstly, a striking feature of the academic writing on Ernaux is its location in the anglophone world, rather than in France. Even if many articles, interviews and chapters are written in French, they are mainly published in American and British French Studies journals, particularly the former (see bibliography, pp. 184–6). Ernaux was also recently included in three anglophone texts: a collection of articles on contemporary French fiction by women, an edited collection of translated extracts of works by contemporary French women writers, and a history of French women's writing from 1848 to 1994 (Atack and Powrie, 1990; Fallaize, 1993; Holmes, 1996). As this list of subjects may indicate, one of the main reasons why the anglophone academic world is more interested in Ernaux's writing is the greater importance and institutionalisation of feminism in British and American universities. Although some of this work clearly emphasises the importance of class in Ernaux's texts (Day, 1990 being exemplary in this respect), many academics working in American and British universities read Ernaux primarily in relation to feminism generally, and to French feminism or 'feminine writing' more particularly. Thus, for example, Sanders compares Ernaux's style to the 'feminine writing' produced by writers such as Wittig, Cixous or Irigaray (Sanders, 1993). Though this is not the case in the Sanders article, the anglophone emphasis on gender can lead to a slight tension, or perhaps mutual misrecognition, between Ernaux and some feminist academics. In her account of feminist writing in France, Sellers chooses to write about the Ernaux text which can most easily be read as a feminist manifesto, *La Femme gelée*; in her discussion of the work she refers only to Ernaux's deconstruction of gender roles, without mentioning class, despite the emphasis in the text on the relationships between the two forms of oppression (Sellers, 1991, pp. 85–7). Holmes describes how 'English feminists' at a talk given by Ernaux in Birmingham 'made the case for the significance of gender in both the theme and form of Ernaux's writing, but were met by the author's strong reluctance to acknowledge this' (Holmes, 1996,

p. 298). Tondeur comments that for Ernaux, 'belonging to a sex which did not have a voice is less important than coming from a class which has never had the right to speak' (Tondeur, 1996, p. 8). However, it is possible that Ernaux's position on this has shifted over time. Recently she has emphasised the importance of feminism in her work: 'Feminism, as the struggle for equality between men and women in terms of way of life, responsibilities and roles – identical or shared – is always at the heart of my preoccupations' (Vilain, 1997a). In the light of this, and the consistent linking of class and gender oppression in Ernaux's published works, the 'either/or' position described by Tondeur seems currently to be a less accurate account than Day's earlier interpretations (Day, 1990). Ernaux is happy to be described as a feminist writer (IN), and her emphasis on social class seems salutary in these 'post-Marxist', postmodern times. Despite these tensions, it is important to recognise the role played by feminist academics in carving out a space for work on Ernaux's writing in anglophone countries.

Ernaux's works are taught in universities in several anglophone countries, and the resulting scholarly editions and commentaries on her work are also an indication that this inclusion in the curriculum extends to schools (Wetherill, 1987; Day and Jones, 1990). On this latter point, Ernaux is received in a similar way by the French educational system: her works are studied as set texts, and an edition of *La Place* containing questions and essay topics, as well as a dossier on *La Place* and *Une femme*, have been published by Gallimard (Savéan, 1994 and 1997). The fact that Ernaux's texts have been taken up by teachers in France and elsewhere can be seen partly as a result of their brevity, plain style and accessibility. Ernaux herself has commented that the interest in her work in schools is linked to the dominant theme of her writing: the painful process of changing class through education – a process experienced by many secondary level teachers, and equally relevant to pupils (IN). It is reinforced in France by her willingness to reply to letters from whole classes of *lycéens*, and even to participate in videotaped discussions with them.[1] As yet, there are no completed French doctoral theses focusing on Ernaux's work, though she has received copies of around fifteen or sixteen *maîtrise* (M.A.) dissertations.[2]

Francophone journals in countries such as Canada and Switzerland have published a few articles on Ernaux (such as Bacholle, 1995; Vilain, 1997a and b; Meizoz, 1996), and in France, Ernaux has been included in some anthologies (Garcin, 1989; Prévost and Lebrun, 1990). However, an equivalent of the small but growing corpus of work on Ernaux published in Britain and America cannot be found in France. Although there are two books in French on her work as a whole, one was written by a Swiss academic working in the United States, and published in Holland (Tondeur, 1996), and the other was published by a fairly small and little-known publishing house based in Monaco (Fernandez-Récatala, 1994). It is intriguing, given the high status of her publisher Gallimard, and the award of the Prix Renaudot in 1984 for *La Place*, that French academics have paid relatively little attention to Ernaux's writing. Indeed, one of the main manifestations of interest in her work in France is among sociologists rather than literary critics (Charpentier, 1994; Mauger, 1994). Mauger concludes that if Ernaux's literary project is, as she claims in *Une femme*, 'below literature', it is 'not very far from sociology' (Mauger, 1994, p. 44). This conclusion is entirely in tune with Ernaux's comments, in *Une femme* and elsewhere, and her interest in and sympathy with the discipline of sociology has clearly fostered positive communication between the writer and this group of academics. On the other hand, Ernaux's refusal of literary artifice and her constant questioning of the cultural hierarchies in which literature and literary criticism are embedded seem to lead to a less enthusiastic response from French academics working in the latter domain. The examination of journalistic criticism of Ernaux's work which follows may shed further light on this relationship, particularly since I will pay special attention to those bastions of the French literary establishment – the 'quality' papers, and television cultural debates.

The Reception of Ernaux's Work by the French Media

In this discussion I will draw on Charpentier's article, and my own analysis of the press reception of Ernaux's work, which focuses particularly on reviews of the two most recent publications at the time of writing – *La Honte* and *'Je ne suis pas sortie de ma nuit'*. My discussion will encompass Ernaux's television appearances, as well as the press reception, since they arguably play an equally significant role in mediating Ernaux's writing. The analysis is presented in three sections: firstly, a chronological overview of the reception; secondly, an analysis of recurring discourses in the media texts on Ernaux; and finally, following Charpentier, a discussion of the writer's own interventions in this mediatisation of her work. In the last section I will focus particularly on Ernaux's television appearances, on the grounds that the sheer size of the television audience renders them perhaps the most effective site for authorial intervention in the construction and contestation of readings of her work.

The first and most striking feature of the media response to Ernaux's work is the sheer volume of the coverage: the publishers, Gallimard, currently hold seventeen dossiers of press cuttings, and after each publication, Ernaux is systematically invited to discuss her work on a range of radio programmes and on television. Isabelle Charpentier found that the press reception of Ernaux's work was predominantly positive until the publication of *Passion simple* (Charpentier, 1994, p. 48). Bernard Pivot, the presenter of the cultural discussion programme, *Apostrophes*, and its more recent replacement *Bouillon de Culture*, confirms this view, if, clearly, on a more impressionistic basis, in a remark addressed to Ernaux: 'It has to be said that you have always been used to the press singing your praises' (*Bouillon de Culture*, 8 March 1992). My own perusal of the press reviews of *Les Armoires vides, Ce qu'ils disent ou rien, La Femme gelée,* and a selection of the reviews of *Une femme* and *La Place* allowed me to arrive at a similar conclusion; it is important to note at this point that if one considers the journalistic writing on Ernaux as a whole, praise is very much more prevalent than blame. This chapter will inevitably give a more negative impression, firstly, because I am attempting to explore and identify the controversial aspects of Ernaux's writing, and secondly, because it is often in the more negative reviews that ideological subtexts are revealed. Thus, even in the earlier reviews, a small proportion of articles reveal some of the symptoms of the negative responses which were to follow the publication of *Passion simple.* For example, in a generally positive article on Ernaux and Duras, the communist paper *Humanité Dimanche* comments: 'Mesdames, bravo! with two blows of the spoon – one in the Goncourt soup, the other in the Renaudot – you are tasting these prizes today' (Boué, 1984, p. 12). Despite the humorous tone, this introduction of the language of cookery, and hence the association of women writers with the domestic sphere, is indicative of the gender stereotypes which will emerge fully in the response to *Passion simple*. In a review of *Une femme* published in the right-wing *Figaro-Magazine*, it is Ernaux's class origins which seem to inspire a subtly superior tone, expressed in the form of comments on grammatical 'errors' and stylistic improprieties: 'Annie Ernaux, who has won the right to express herself, owes it to herself to be as attentive and rigorous as possible' (Nourissier, 1988, p. 41). Charpentier also notes the adoption of a 'a distant tone' in the specialised literary press, and a significantly more enthusiastic response from the left-wing and regional press than from the Paris-based right-wing or centre-left nationals, which nonetheless generally remained 'moderate' until 1992. She also comments that her survey of Ernaux criticism since 1974 found no overtly negative review written by a woman journalist (Charpentier, 1994, pp. 51–2).

However, as Charpentier remarks, it is with the publication of *Passion simple* that the ambivalent response of some critics to Ernaux's writing is fully expressed: 'The guarantors of the value of Ernaux's work are more fragile than it appears, as the reception of *Passion simple* demonstrates. (. . .) This work will provide an opportunity for certain critics to devalue the body of earlier work published by the author' (Charpentier, 1994, pp. 48–9). If the extreme right-wing press is most virulent in its critique of *Passion simple*, Charpentier finds that many of the male critics writing in the mainstream press, both left- and right-wing, are hostile to the work. Perhaps the most striking examples of this are Jean-François Josselin's piece in the centre-left *Nouvel Observateur*, and Eric Neuhoff in *Madame Figaro*. In the former, Josselin refers to Ernaux throughout as 'la petite Annie', a phrase which in part refers ironically to the brevity of her texts, but also clearly infantilises and ridicules the writer. Both critics attack the popular culture version of femininity which the text represents, and Josselin seems disturbed by the expression of female desire in literature, labelling the book 'a touch obscene' (Josselin, 1992, p. 87). The fact that gender-based lines of battle are drawn up in the journalistic controversy surrounding *Passion simple* is also illustrated by Josyane Savigneau's defence of Ernaux in *Le Monde* in an article entitled 'Le courage d'Annie Ernaux'. As Charpentier remarks, *Passion simple* became so controversial that a radio programme, 'Le Masque et la Plume', was devoted to it, with participants representing both sides of the argument. In his television discussion programme, *Bouillon de Culture*, Bernard Pivot opened the discussion of *Passion simple* by asking Ernaux repeatedly how she had dared, not only to write such a text, but to speak about it on television. In the end, the writer retorts: 'Is what I have written so surprising, so scandalous that I should hide myself away?' (*Bouillon de Culture*, 1992). Josyane Savigneau's article, as its title would suggest, also emphasises Ernaux's courage. She comments on a passage where Ernaux describes her indifference to her grown-up children at the height of her passion:

> The masculine desire to stereotype women is out of luck here: Annie Ernaux is at the opposite end of the spectrum from Emma Bovary. In her work there is no guilt, and that's what is disturbing. No hysteria, no theatre. Just a commitment to write the truth about her passion, even when it shocks the common-sense view. (. . .) Is a woman entitled to write like this? (Savigneau, 1992, p. 23)

The media controversy surrounding *Passion simple*, with opposing sides admiring Ernaux's bravery or castigating her lack of discretion, seems to indicate that even in the final years of the twentieth century, in France, she is not.

The media reception of the post-*Passion* texts combines enthusiastic rehabilitation of Ernaux's image with lingering traces of the negativity unleashed at this key point. Most recently *La Honte* and *'Je ne suis pas sortie de ma nuit'* have received a more balanced response than *Passion simple*, although as the section which follows will demonstrate, the terms in which Ernaux's writing is discussed are strangely repetitive. Unlike Charpentier's earlier analysis, my study found no clear distinction between national and regional press, with 21 per cent and 22 per cent negative or mixed reviews respectively (see appendix 2 for details of the study). However, like Charpentier I found the specialised literary press more critical of Ernaux (50 per cent negative or mixed reviews), which suggests that Ernaux's ambivalent literary status persists, despite, or perhaps in part because of, the commercial success of her books and the amount of media attention she receives. Although women's magazines were almost universally positive about the two texts (only one out of seven reviews was negative), Charpentier's finding that only positive reviews were written by women journalists is no longer accurate, with at least four critical pieces written by women. I also found, in the reception of both *La Honte* and *'Je ne suis pas sortie de ma nuit'*, and in relation to earlier texts, that the same discourses were mobilised in negative reviews by women as are found in the texts by male writers. Thus, Michèle Bernstein, writing about *Journal du dehors* in *Libération*, echoes Josselin's distaste for the expression of female sexuality in the texts, finding 'other typically Annie Ernian obsessions in the book. Sex, to put it crudely' (Bernstein, 1993, p. 23).[3] This participation by women in discourses collusive with their own oppression is depressing, if not at all surprising. It is to the analysis of these and other recurring discourses in the critical writing on Ernaux that I will now turn.

I have identified two dominant discourses in the journalistic reception of Ernaux's work, around which a number of sub-categories or themes can be grouped. The first is the attempt to disqualify Ernaux from the literary sphere, to argue that although her writing may be moving, powerful or popular, it is not literature. The second dominant discourse is the tendency to focus on the writer as a person, rather than on the texts themselves. In the first of these discourses it is possible to see the most obvious expression of the gatekeeping role of literary criticism, its function in excluding certain texts and writers from the literary canon. The discourse often takes the form of questions: thus a report on the 1997 Salon du Livre in the *Journal du Dimanche* is entitled 'They write, but is it literature?' (Sauvage, 1997, p. 18). Ernaux is one of the writers discussed in the article, and although it is accompanied by a positive account of her writing, the very fact that the question is asked clearly sets the agenda. The title of a review of *La Honte* in *L'Humanité* – 'The true and false clues to writing in Annie Ernaux's work: what is literature?' – echoes this concern (Lebrun, 1997, p. 19). Again, even if the conclusion is positive, the fact that the question is posed, and that a defence of the writer has to be mounted, is significant. In some ways this kind of argument prepares the ground for those critics who draw the opposite conclusion; *Le Figaro*, for example, commented on *'Je ne suis pas sortie de ma nuit'*: 'it is not certain that this has much to do with literature' (Matignon, 1997, p. 33).

A number of techniques or rationales for disqualification are located within this discourse. The first of these relates to the symbolic importance of the book as a physical object in French high culture. Indeed, Ernaux comments that her mother's cultural aspirations were expressed by the great respect she showed for books, even washing her hands before touching them (*Une femme*,

p. 57). The *Nouvelle Revue Française* collection published by Gallimard is characterised by distinctive cream covers, with red wrappings bearing a word or phrase summarising the content of the work. This minimalist and yet striking design seems to epitomise the delicate balancing of the commercial and cultural roles of such a publishing house. The cultural value symbolised by this design, and by books generally, is underlined by the technique used in television discussion programmes such as *Apostrophes* or its more recent incarnation, *Bouillon de Culture*, of foregrounding the book as physical object. Thus, the books to be discussed are laid out on a coffee table in front of the presenter, Pivot, who at the appropriate moment brandishes them, or, demonstrating his own cultural competence, reads from one of the pages he has marked. All of this cultural theatre is reinforced by the graphics: when a writer begins to speak, s/he is shown in a frame half-filled by the book itself; then, during the presentation, periodically the book glides across the screen, temporarily disembodying the writer's voice. The set for *Apostrophes* was often a book-lined room, so that books also provided the background for the 'talking heads'. *Bouillon de Culture*, in January 1997, has a rather more sophisticated set, redolent nonetheless of all the connotations of high culture: the bookshelves are still visible, though less dominant, and extracts from the texts to be discussed, in the writer's own hand, are projected onto the walls, alongside diaphanous, vaguely antique statues (*Bouillon de Culture*, 1997). I have not seen anything similar on British television (or indeed a precise equivalent of *Bouillon de Culture*), and would argue that there is a particular fetishisation of the literary text in French culture.

Ernaux's texts seem to contravene this cult of the book by their very brevity, which is a constant theme of the negative reviews. It is as if, in producing thin volumes, Ernaux is threatening the cult itself; her short texts embodying the fear that the fetishised object will disappear completely, thus epitomising rather than protecting against fears of loss and disintegration. I feel justified in drawing these rather psychoanalytical conclusions by the obsessive repetition of this theme. As we have seen, Josselin justifies his phrase 'la petite Annie' in this way: 'small also in recognition of the brevity of Madame Ernaux's texts, which is the critic's delight' (Josselin, 1992, p. 87) and Neuhoff describes *Passion simple* as 'a passion summarised in forty little pages (at most)' (Neuhoff, 1992). Jean Vedrines, writing in *Valeurs Actuelles*, refers to *La Honte* and '*Je ne suis pas sortie de ma nuit'* as 'deux livricules à la mode' (two fashionable bookettes) and is also affronted by Ernaux's technique of leaving blanks on the page: 'pages as white and empty as the life which is recounted there' (Vedrines, 1997, p. 65). Pascale Frey, in *Elle*, produces a term parallel to *livricule*, in her reference to *La Honte* as 'le second opuscule' (Frey, 1997, p. 36). Perhaps the most extreme example of the association of symbolic and physical weight is provided by A.H. in a review of *Passion simple* published in *L'Express*:

> The simplicity of Madame Ernaux is no longer anything more than bankruptcy, or even silliness in this account whose twenty or so pages of typescript the publisher and printer have struggled to make into a volume. If we proceed in this manner, we will certainly need a thirty wagon goods train to transport Roger Martin du Gard's *Les Thibault*. (A.H., 1997, p. 100)

Brevity, in the French context, is clearly not considered the soul of wit. In the critique of Ernaux's style, which is often associated with comments on brevity, her texts are also seen as contravening the conventions of great literature. Hence the title of Jérôme Garcin's article on Ernaux and another contemporary writer, Philippe Djian – 'The Hatred of Style':

> One reads these two thin, dry works [*La Honte* and *'Je ne suis pas sortie de ma nuit'*] (. . .) with the emotion which naturally these admissions provoke, but also with the perplexity which results from her approach to literature. For, in attempting to strip writing of everything which characterises it, and to reduce its function to the act of naming, the writer ends up being nothing more than an accountant of facts, a court clerk of feelings. (Garcin, 1997a, p. 63)

Garcin seems in the end to see both Ernaux's and Djian's challenge to the conventions of literary language as a threat to literature, concluding that 'some days literature must wonder whether it still exists'. In fact critics are divided on this aspect of Ernaux's writing, with some seeing Ernaux's unadorned style as classically precise and clear, and others seeing it as an absence of literary quality. Exactly this argument occurred in the edition of *Apostrophes* which discussed *Une femme*, with one of the participants (Geneviève Gallet) finding the style 'deliberately bare and dry' and wondering whether this impaired the emotional effect. Pivot immediately expressed the contrary opinion, and was supported by another participant, Huguette Bouchardeau, who argued that 'this lapidary style, this apparent dryness transmits an extraordinary level of emotion' (*Apostrophes*, 1988). This argument has thus been running for at least ten years, and as an instance of the powerful gatekeeping function of critics and commentators, it seems likely to continue in the future.

Ernaux's style may be controversial, but her subject matter provides further grounds for questioning the texts' literary value. Disqualification by content is one of the tendencies identified by Joanna Russ in her humorous discussion of the reception of women's writing: 'She did (write it), but look what she wrote about' (Russ, 1984, p. 40). The auto/biographical genre, when it focuses on experience outside the male, middle-class mainstream of French literature, seems to become highly dubious, and Ernaux's determination to base her writing on her own life can lead to a variety of charges, particularly in the more specialised, literary press. Marie-Laure Delorme, writing in *Le Magazine Littéraire*, comments that *La Honte* left her feeling uneasy: 'as if it was time for the author to take up another story' (Delorme, 1997, p. 73). At least one anglophone literary critic expressed a similar view, concluding her review with the 'readerly hope' that having expressed the origins of her sense of shame in *La Honte*, Ernaux would 'venture into fresh literary territory' (McIlvanney, 1997, p. 246). Bernard Plessy perhaps delves deeper into this desire for novelty, when he accuses Ernaux of narcissism. He comments on '*Je ne suis pas sortie de ma nuit*': 'Why remind us she has had an abortion, a divorce, why allude to nights of love, her books, her prizes, her appearance on *Apostrophes*, her presence at the fête de l'Huma?[4] (. . .) One ends up feeling that the mother's illness is a pretext for the daughter to talk about herself' (Plessy, 1997). These comments encapsulate much of the unease felt by some critics when faced with Ernaux's work. Firstly, the difficulty of fitting the texts into generic categories – here biography or autobiography – is a source of irritation. Secondly, Ernaux's success seems to grate on the nerves of those perhaps anxious to establish or maintain their own position ('her prizes, her appearance on *Apostrophes*'). Finally, her introduction of personal experience into literature is seen as a social gaffe, and Ernaux is castigated for her *impudeur* (immodesty, shamelessness).

The term *impudeur* is strikingly recurrent in Ernaux criticism; this is significant, since it suggests both a fear of the personal and a set of codes of propriety which women, particularly, should adhere to. It is also, like Ernaux's style, a theme which can be used in either a negative or positive way, underlining the arbitrary nature of such judgements, or more accurately, the fact that they are motivated by factors other than the texts themselves. This notion of impropriety is applied most frequently to *Passion simple* and *'Je ne suis pas sortie de ma nuit'*. Thus Marie-Laure Delorme comments on the latter text: 'More than once, one is exasperated by so much immodesty, facility, narcissism' (Delorme, 1997, p. 73), whilst for *Le Figaro* 'what was exorcism becomes exhibitionism' (Matignon, 1997, p. 33). However in *L'Express*, we read about *La Honte* that: 'Annie Ernaux's book was written with a complete lack of modesty (une impudeur totale), which, however, does not make a spectacle of itself, never allowing us the time to become voyeurs.' Clavel concludes this positive account by describing both books as 'overwhelming, like a lightning flash' (Clavel, 1997, p. 76).

In a similar way, the expression of sadness, shame and guilt in Ernaux's writing can be seen positively or negatively. The review of the 1997 publications in *Le Figaro Magazine* carried the headline: 'Annie Ernaux: Writing as Therapy' (Nourissier, 1997, p. 76), and a number of reviews emphasised the books' therapeutic qualities: 'One learns with her to overcome the pain of being alone from now on, an adult orphan. Ernaux throws out words like stones, heavy with emotion, creating a path which others – anonymous readers – will continue to tread' (Laval, 1997, p. 33). This is in sharp contrast to reviewers who complain that, for instance, 'Annie Ernaux's life is not very jolly' (Frey, 1997, p. 36). A regional paper, *L'Opinion Indépendante*, uses the titles of Ernaux's books in its slightly laboured ironies: 'She had frozen us with *La Femme gelée*, made us cry over *La Place*, traumatised us with *Journal du dehors* (. . .) What has she got in store for us in her next book? We are already trembling . . .' (Authier, 1997, p. 5). Tremble they may, for Ernaux's critics, on both sides of the divide, make it clear that her books are not comforting: 'That is to say that she disturbs, by presenting herself so naked, so impoverished on the great ship of French literature' (Clavel, 1997, p. 76). The discourse of the disruptive text is frequently deployed, and it is one of the few critical discourses which Ernaux takes up herself, or engages with. Generally the troubling nature of the writing is used as a proof of the texts' literary status, a positive response to the question 'is this literature?'. However, texts which disturb, because of their unconventional and unclassifiable subject matter and style, irritate and annoy some critics: 'Annie Ernaux writes dry books, as hard and devoid of flesh as the bones she continues to throw at the dogs which pursue her. They want to bite, leave her no respite, bark at her heels' (Clavel, 1997, p. 76).

Much of this barking and biting is in fact aimed at the writer as a woman, rather than at the works themselves. This tendency, the second dominant discourse which I have identified, is remarkably similar to a major topos of Beauvoir criticism discussed by Moi, and it can be neatly summarised by Moi's phrase 'reducing the book to the woman' (Moi, 1994, p. 77). The level of hostility expressed towards Ernaux in the French press is not on the same scale as that endured by Beauvoir, but the fact that very similar discourses are deployed indicates that fifty years after the publication of *The Second Sex*, the reception of women writers in French culture is still, at least in part, determined by their gender. It would perhaps be more accurate, following Moi, to point to the combination of gender and political views as the source of the hostility: 'together these two factors – her sex and her politics – are fatal to her reputation as a writer' (Moi, 1994, p. 74). In Ernaux's case, one could perhaps add class origins to this list, since her insistence on this theme seems to make critics particularly uneasy. Class, perhaps more than ever, is a taboo subject, and the person who raises it, in British or French social contexts, is likely to be accused of 'having a chip on their shoulder', and to be required to find fresh inspiration.

The reduction of the work to the person often takes the form of an attack on the references to popular culture in Ernaux's work. Clearly, few critics are bold enough to attack the descriptions of poverty found in both *La Place* and *Une femme*, thus subscribing to the myth of the noble peasant. However, when said peasant's tastes in reading or music are identified as shared by the author it is a different story. Furthermore, it is the inclusion of a particular, gendered popular culture, combining two kinds of low status, which seems to incense critics. For Josselin, this popular culture version of 'femininity' has no place in the French literary canon, as the disdainful tone of his comments on *Passion simple* betrays: 'She buys underwear sets, watches soap opera, and has a little cry when Sylvie Vartan sings the superb "C'est fatal, animal"' (Josselin,

1992, p. 87). Neuhoff opines that 'the reader wonders whether a text from the Harlequin collection [Mills and Boon] has strayed into the sober covers of the NRF' (Neuhoff, 1992). Neuhoff's comment is also an illustration of the threat to the fetishised object, the Gallimard edition, which Ernaux's writing constitutes. In her discussion of the personality topos found in Beauvoir criticism, Moi has identified the sub-category of the *midinette* (frivolous city-girl or shop-girl) to describe this association of women's writing with the trivial or banal (Moi, 1994, p. 78). It is in fact the very same Neuhoff who commented on *Adieux: A Farewell To Sartre* that Beauvoir's travel-writing was 'like a *midinette* sending postcards to her family' (Neuhoff, 1981, quoted in Moi, 1994, p. 78). If the repetition of this topos in relation to Ernaux can be seen as the consistent sexism of French high culture, it is heartening that in the 1990s women are capable of defending themselves (see the section on Ernaux's defensive strategies, below). In his 1993 review of *Journal du dehors*, Josselin refers to Ernaux throughout as Madame Ernaux, concluding with the phrase 'la grande Annie'. Even though he cannot resist the ironic flourish of using the journalist's first name, there is some acknowledgement that he has been corrected by Josyane Savigneau of *Le Monde*: 'We will be careful, from now on, not to call her "la petite Annie", dear Josyane' (Josselin, 1993, p. 99).

As was the case for Beauvoir, Ernaux's membership of the teaching profession permits the deployment of what Moi calls the 'bluestocking' topos. Ernaux is sometimes portrayed as an intellectual of the most tedious kind: 'Annie Ernaux has had the kindness to explain *La Honte* to us step by step and to sell us for the same price, with these grudgingly given words, an unforgettable pedagogic commentary on their meaning and universal significance. Dogmatic, she speaks in a haughty tone, has her view on everything and goes in for aphorisms' (Vedrines, 1997, p. 65). The notion of the 'false intellectual' is reinforced in Ernaux criticism by associating her with the domestic and provincial, a charge which could not be made against Beauvoir. The linking of these two features may seem quite arbitrary to an outsider, but there is clearly a sense in which recognition as a serious artist in France depends on a good Parisian address, and never being seen in a supermarket. Thus for Neuhoff, *Passion simple* is 'as gay as a suburban semi on a rainy Sunday in November. Put on slippers before entering' (Neuhoff, 1992). In similar terms Michèle Bernstein mocks the passage in *Passion simple* where Ernaux describes her indifference, during one of A.'s visits, when she burns a hole in the carpet with a hot coffee-pot: 'from this one concludes that if one goes to see Annie Ernaux outside the time of a passion, one had better wipe one's feet' (Bernstein, 1992, p. 23). In an American academic journal, Marie Naudin adopts the same mildly ironic tone: 'All is rather discrete, contained in a suburban house full of flowers, clean washing, towelling bathrobes and little snacks to nibble at' (Naudin, 1993, p. 386). If in these examples Ernaux is portrayed as excessively feminine, rooted in an unfashionably suburban and domestic lifestyle, at other times she is seen as devoid of 'normal' feminine emotions, capable, again like Beauvoir, of sacrificing even her own mother for her attempt at art: 'Adding her phobic fear of emotion to that of literature (. . .) she transforms this final song of love to the deceased into an obscene description of physical degradation' (Garcin, 1997a, p. 63).

Perhaps, however, as for Beauvoir, the area in which the most powerful gender-based attack can be mounted is in relation to sexuality. Here we see the confusion of the books and the woman at its most complete, and the full force of the discourse epitomised by the word *impudeur*. The quotations from Josselin and Bernstein cited earlier are illustrative of this tendency (see p. 145 and p. 147, above), as is Jean Vedrines's outraged cry: 'she prostrates herself before her religion of the body, present on every page of her innumerable and interchangeable mini-works' (Vedrines, 1997, p. 65). However, the most violent attack followed the publication in 1997 by Philippe Vilain of a work describing his relationship with Ernaux – *L'Etreinte* (*The Embrace*). Unfortunately, this has provided an opportunity for the *Nouvel Observateur* to relaunch its attack, by casting aspersions on Ernaux's sexual behaviour: 'one must assume that in future it will be sufficient to have obtained the favours of the famous author in order to be published by her editor. If other lovers of the novelist *lay* their reminiscences on paper, will it be necessary to create a collection?' (Garcin, 1997b, p. 126). The fact that the article is supposedly a review of the work of another writer, and yet in fact is dominated by a personal attack on Ernaux, is an extreme example of the concentration on the woman, rather than the texts. In this case, there simply was no text by Ernaux, an absence which allows the critic to get on with the real work of depicting Ernaux as a 'loose' or promiscuous woman. On the brink of the twenty-first century, and in a culture which prides itself on its sexual tolerance, it may seem extraordinary that writing is as dangerous for a woman's reputation as acting was in the time of Shakespeare.

If the attack on Ernaux represents her as the embodiment of all that is alien and threatening in patriarchal versions of the feminine, clearly it also colludes with the first dominant discourse identified in undermining her literary status. References to the nineteenth-century novelist, Flaubert, in the journalistic writing on Ernaux are a particularly interesting instance of this. The fact that the references abound is perhaps not surprising: both writers hail from Normandy, and are associated with realism, albeit of a very different kind, and Flaubert is an acknowledged influence on Ernaux's work (Tondeur, 1995a, p. 41). *Le Canard Enchaîné* coins the adverb 'flaubertiennement' to describe Ernaux's writing, while *Le Point* descibes her as having learnt and understood the lesson of the master, Flaubert (Durand, 1997, p. 6; Amette, 1997, p. 76). This need to describe Ernaux's writing in terms of the literary style of an established bastion of the male literary canon does at least have some positive elements. However, the equally recurrent comparison with one of Flaubert's most well-known female characters is more troubling; the desire to make Ernaux into a fictional character can be read as an extension of the general desire, analysed above, to discuss her as a personality, rather than focusing on her works. Thus, the title of Josselin's piece on *Passion simple* is 'Un gros chagrin. Ou comment dans *Passion simple* Annie Ernaux se prend pour la petite nièce de Madame Bovary' ('A big trauma. Or how in *Passion Perfect* Annie Ernaux fancies herself as Emma Bovary's great niece'). Pierre-Marc de Biasi, in *Le Magazine Littéraire*, also produces a long critique entitled 'Les petites Emma 1992' (De Biaisi, 1992, pp. 59–62). The comparison with Emma Bovary is maintained in reviews of *La Honte* five years later; a positive review in *L'Evénement du Jeudi* is entitled 'Annie Ernaux: Le bovaryisme est un humanisme', and includes the remark 'Madame Bovary, c'est un peu elle', paraphrasing Flaubert's own 'Madame Bovary, c'est moi' (Delbourg, 1997, p. 82). In all of these cases a woman *writer* is compared with a male novelist's female *character*, indicating the difficulty in French culture of seeing women as writing subjects, rather than objects of the male gaze or textual mastery.

Contesting Media Representations: The Writer's Role

In the final section of this chapter I will consider Ernaux's response to the at times ambivalent reception of her work by French journalists. Charpentier comments that Ernaux has developed a number of strategies which aim to predetermine her reception, as well as attempting to counteract the attacks on her work (Charpentier, 1994, pp. 63–75). My analysis of the authorial interventions in the texts in chapter 2 also illustrates this tendency. At times these textual interventions seem almost to engage directly with the critics; thus in *Journal du dehors* we find Ernaux apparently responding to the *midinette* discourse produced in the criticism of *Passion simple*: 'it's impossible – or inadmissible – for me to read the horoscope and behave like a *midinette*. The "I" shames the reader' (*Journal du dehors*, p. 19). Here I will focus on Ernaux's strategies of self-presentation in the metatexts surrounding her work, so that this chapter will complement the analysis of the 'author in the text' in chapter 2.

Ernaux presents her work in a variety of different contexts: she is interviewed by journalists and academics, and has appeared on television programmes as diverse as cultural debates and women's magazine programmes, as well as participating in videos made by schools and universities. It would perhaps be possible to trace an evolution in Ernaux's style of self-presentation: the earlier television appearances are characterised by a combative, almost rebellious approach, whereas more recently Ernaux has appeared calmer, and more in control, even in the face of a more hostile press. In 1981, for example Ernaux appeared on 'Aujourd'hui Madame', a programme aimed at women which included a section where a writer meets a group of three female readers, 'des auteurs face à leurs lectrices'. In the animated discussion of *La Femme gelée* which ensues, Ernaux takes up a feminist position which appears controversial in this rather conservative context. Remaining, of course, polite to the women readers, she nonetheless consistently challenges their liberal readings of the text, insisting that the problems she has described are social not individual in nature:

> Woman reader: But there is no love in this marriage.
> Ernaux: Love is the big word which is used to conceal all kinds of alienation . . .

At times, the discussion is so lively that it becomes unintelligible, as several participants speak at once. Ernaux argues her case passionately and forcefully: 'I knew about the joys of motherhood, but I wanted to talk about the shitty side.' A male presenter (Jacques Garat) chairs the discussion, and at times he intervenes to 'moderate' Ernaux's position, which is thus constructed as extreme, and even old-fashioned, as if by 1981, feminism had won all its battles: 'I think your neighbour [a reader] thinks that we have been listening to this discourse for some time . . .' Interestingly, Garat also has a 'second string', a woman presenter (Christiane Cardinal) who sits next to the readers and seems to have the typically feminine role of 'looking after' these members of the public who find themselves in the strange environment of a television studio. She does not intervene directly in support of Ernaux's views, but does mutter the occasional 'évidemment' (of course), which suggests that this account of the joys of motherhood is not totally alien to her.

In 1984 Ernaux adopted a similarly combative role in the very different context of a discussion programme about the writer Marcel Proust broadcast by TF1 in the *Droit de Réponse* series, and entitled 'Proust, ma chère'. Eleven participants (of whom three were women, including Ernaux) joined the presenter, Michel Polac. The participants were mainly well-known journalists and writers, including Philippe Sollers; the duchess of La Rochefoucauld was invited to give her personal impressions of Proust's social milieu. The lighting and clouds of cigarette smoke occasionally wafting across the screen seemed designed to recreate the atmosphere of a café on the Left Bank. Ernaux's first intervention, well into the discussion, which, as the numbers alone might indicate, did not provide much space for women's voices, was in response to the question 'Did Proust write for the people?' On this occasion it was Ernaux's class-based analysis which scandalised her entourage: her insistence that the complex syntax of Proust's works renders them unintelligible for most of the population, and that the world which Proust depicts is not of universal relevance and significance, caused such a level of protest that the discussion again collapsed into incoherence. At one point Ernaux is even accused of Stalinism, but despite the fact that she is opposed and literally shouted down by her 'colleagues', she raises her voice and continues to reiterate her point.

If *Apostrophes* and more recently *Bouillon de Culture* provide more of a platform, and a more peaceful atmosphere for the writer to present herself and her work than a 'free-for-all' debate of this type, nonetheless there are some attempts at provocation, doubtless with the aim of producing 'good television'. The presenter, Bernard Pivot, at times seems rather torn between this aim and his clear admiration for Ernaux's work, which has been consistent over many years. Thus in the 1992 edition of *Bouillon de Culture* which discussed *Passion simple*, Ernaux was introduced as 'my guest of honour, my main guest, whom it is a pleasure to invite'. However, later in the programme Pivot reads out some of the negative comments on the book in the press, including Josselin and Neuhoff, and asks Ernaux whether the behaviour she describes is not in fact a bit ridiculous. At the end, Pivot clearly crosses a boundary when he asks Ernaux whether A. has read the book:

> Ernaux: I don't know.
> Pivot: But wouldn't you like to know?
> Ernaux: I cannot tell you.

This exchange is followed by a rather awkward silence, and a rapid change of subject and interlocutor. It demonstrates Ernaux's increasing confidence and power in this kind of context: her monosyllablic replies constitute a dignified rebuttal of Pivot's attempts, like the press journalists, to focus on the woman rather than the work. As I have indicated in chapter 5, in recent years many readers have commented positively on Ernaux's television appearances, generally expressing support of Ernaux, and countering any hint of criticism. Despite its obvious mediatisation of the writer and her work, television does nonetheless seem to provide a relatively direct channel of communication between Ernaux and her large and faithful readership.

If the style of Ernaux's media appearances has inevitably evolved, the content of her interventions has remained remarkably consistent, whether it is voiced in press interviews or on television. One of her main policies is the absolute refusal to engage with some of the critical discourses which are mobilised; thus the refusal of literature which is presented in the texts is also part of Ernaux's discussion of her work in the media. Ernaux's reluctance to discuss the aesthetic qualities of her texts, and insistence on their socio-logical and political content, disarm, albeit temporarily, those critics who attempt to disqualify her writing from the hallowed realm of literature. Ernaux consistently presents her writing as research, and the topic of that research as the social world. In 1984, invited to appear on *Apostrophes* for *La Place*, Ernaux insisted on her desire to arrive at some kind of truth about her father's life, and her rejection of literary devices, and of the novel as a form: 'There was also a desire to bring my father's culture to life again.' In an interview in an academic journal over ten years later, Ernaux expresses similar aims: 'My writing seeks to capture what is fleeting, to leave a trace of oneself, but also of others, to fight against the transitory nature of existence, and the rapidity of change in contemporary life' (Tondeur, 1995a, p. 41). Here, the rejection of one discourse, the literary or aesthetic, is accompanied by part-icipation in another: the claim for truth-value or authenticity, discussed in detail in chapter 2 (pp. 33–8). Ernaux seems willing to engage with the discourse which represents her work as both a search for truth and a therapeutic process: 'Sometimes I say to myself that I am empty, or that my writing is empty! Since my first novel, I have been trying to extirpate from myself one single thing, shame. Social shame' (Laval, 1997, p. 32). At the same time, as in the texts themselves, Ernaux's theorisations of her work, part-icularly in the more considered form of the press or academic interview, demonstrate a sophisticated awareness of the con-structed nature of autobiographical 'truth': 'One of the biggest illusions is the belief that reality is there, in front of you, or inside oneself, spontaneously given. (. . .) In fact, when one wants to recount a scene which one has witnessed, it becomes clear that there are many possible points of view, many interpretations' (Hafsia, 1996). Thus, in the description of her literary project Ernaux is at pains to emphasise that this complex relationship to truth is no easy business; partly as a result of this, the critical discourse in which she seems to participate most willingly is perhaps the topos of the 'disruptive text': 'At first I thought of writing as a very violent transgression. Literature is something which should disturb, it's linked to something sexual' (Tondeur, 1995a, p. 42).

An acute awareness of the critical commentaries on her work is also manifest in attempts to counter some of the negative discourses which are mobilised. In an interview given in a Tunisian paper, *La Presse*, Ernaux seems to be countering the charge of repetitiveness, and answering the critics' expressed desire to see her broaching new subjects: 'From the moment when one no longer considers one's lived experience, in the superior, superficial and philo-sophically ill-founded words of Malraux, as a "miserable little pile of secrets", but as a field for research, using the "I" as a tool (. . .), there is no limit to the potential of autobiographical writing' (Hafsia, 1996). Similarly, Ernaux responds to the persistent charge of *impudeur* in an interview published in *Télérama*: 'I don't consider myself to be immodest. Modesty is the preservation of an intimacy. There is no real intimacy. (. . .) There is no "I", no person, no individual. We are the product of different family histories, and of society. (. . .) You see, I am a materialist' (Laval, 1997, p. 32). Here, as in response to the literature/not literature debate, Ernaux has succeeded in redefining the terms of the argument; she is able to draw on her own cultural capital – her knowledge of developments in critical theory and sociology – to deconstruct the liberal humanism which underlies many of the attacks on her writing. At other times she turns the tables on the critics, by criticising their analytical techniques, or the lack of them. In *Bouillon de Culture* she commented on Josselin's article on *Passion simple*: 'A literary critic should, after all, overcome the first, almost visceral reaction which he feels and try to say what the book is about, and how it is written. Is that really all that there is in this book? And here I have the impression that this work had not been done.'

As the above suggests, Ernaux is clearly well-qualified to respond to her critics, given her own background in literary criticism. In Charpentier's view this competence is in itself a significant reason for the ambivalent reception of Ernaux's writing. According to Charpentier, the fact that Ernaux is more than able to provide interpretations and analyses of her own texts is highly threatening to professional critics, who find themselves without a role. Their 'disqualification' of Ernaux's work, particularly after the publication of *Passion simple*, is seen by Charpentier as a defence of the literary world against the incursions of sociological thought, in this case manifest in Ernaux's ethnologies of the self (Charpentier, 1994, pp. 74–5). For Charpentier, Ernaux's redefinition of the subject of the discussion renders her writing project 'aesthetically unassailable' (Charpentier, 1994, p. 65). Although the tactic is, I agree, effective, my own analysis of the reception of Ernaux's texts leads me to conclude that the critical hold on the definition of literature is largely maintained, and that the aesthetic discourse rolls on, regardless of Ernaux's interventions. In the *Apostrophes* discussion of *La Place*, for instance, the presenter Pivot insists: 'What you are saying is completely contradictory. You rebel against art, but you have created art'; this is followed by a fairly lengthy discourse on the stylistic qualities of *La Place*, by Pivot and some of the participants. Nonetheless, I would agree with Charpentier, that Ernaux clearly is perceived as a threat by the French literary establishment. The case of Annie Ernaux is an interesting one, for perhaps more than any other contemporary French writer, she has managed to combine a sustained resistance to the latter's attempts to define and devalue her writing with continuing and widespread popularity.

Notes

1. For example 'Parole d'Ecrivain', Lycée J. Mace, Vitry and C.R.D.P. , Créteil, 1985.
2. This comment is based on consultation of the 'Doc-thèses' database in the Bibliothèque Nationale, Paris.
3. The original French demonstrates the full force of Bernstein's distaste: 'D'autres obsessions bien Annie Erniennes courent dans le livre. Le cul, s'il faut l'appeler par son nom' (Bernstein, 1993, p. 23).
4. 'La fête de l'Huma' is the annual celebration organised by the communist paper *L'Humanité*.

7

Reading in the First Person

As we saw in chapter 2, Ernaux is entirely aware of the dangers of speaking in the first person; whilst 'the third person, (. . .) is always the other, who can do what they want (. . .) the "I" shames the reader' (*Journal du dehors*, p. 18/19). In this chapter, following both Ernaux's example in literature, and that of feminist academics such as Nancy K. Miller in literary criticism, I intend to abandon the uniformly impersonal voice and the 'masquerade of self-effacement' which Miller sees as its fundamental characteristic (Miller, 1991, p. 24). Despite the precedents in the small corpus of personal or autobiographical criticism which Miller has charted, the risks of speaking in the first person in an academic work are probably as great, if not the same as, those faced by Ernaux (Miller in Wright, 1992, pp. 306–11). I might be charged with self-indulgence, with egocentrism, or inappropriate and unnecessary self-revelation. At the very least, I am aware of a less than smooth transition from the authoritative, impersonal tones of previous chapters, to the 'I' of this one, which must encompass former, less confident selves. The parallels between this and the experience of changing class are evident: the fear of making some terrible gaffe, which would instantly reveal me in my true class colours is not a million miles away from the feeling that in breaking the continuity of the impersonal academic voice, I am in some way being impolite, speaking in a loud voice in church, or belching at a tea party in an Oxford college.

Ernaux's metaphors of light and heavy words also seem relevant. Academic analysis leaves the reader and the writer somehow free, in an airy space outside time and social context; by bringing in the reality of the person behind the academic voice, I have the impression of exchanging this lightheadedness for something heavy, clinging and slightly shameful. As previous chapters have shown, the association of mind with middle-class and body with

working-class culture, and the still lower status of the combination
of the latter with femininity, the imprint of class on the female body,
have been constant themes of Ernaux's writing. All of this is in the
background here, constituting the heaviness of this particular 'I',
and the difficulty of leaving the safe ground of an impersonality
which, in its origins at least, is masculine and middle-class. As for
Ernaux, however, the necessity of threatening an earlier coherence
and unity seems to impose itself (*'Je ne suis pas sortie de ma nuit'*, p.
12). My approach, which throughout has recognised the diversity
of possible readings and appropriations of these texts, necessitates
some uncovering of the process of my own reading. In this chapter
I will therefore attempt to explain why Ernaux's writing has been
and is important for me, and how my own experience has coloured
my interpretation of her texts. Nonetheless, by its very nature, this
project has to achieve its own equilibrium, between the continuing
analysis of the works themselves and the uncovering of the
subjective basis of this analysis. The balancing act here is between
the dangers of indulgent and irrelevant self-revelation on the one
hand, and the return to the safety of the impersonal voice on the
other. Of necessity, in order to avoid these extremes, my approach
involves a merging of both voices. In this sense there is a parallel
with Ernaux's approach to literature, her attempt to include both
her present and past languages and cultures in the texts, and to
allow many voices to traverse them. This parallel with Ernaux's
own position as a writer straddling two cultures is, I hope, an
indication of a match between my topic and my approach.

A fundamental question raised when the writer's identity is
reinstated in critical writing is how a particular literary text is
chosen for analysis in the first place. The convention of the
impersonal voice would lead us to believe that such decisions are
made on a purely academic basis. Whilst this may sometimes be
the case, it also seems likely that individuals are often drawn to a
particular writer, text or period for reasons connected with their
own lives and experiences. It could be argued that such engage-
ments are a significant aspect of the reading of the text, and of its
history and place in a specific cultural context, yet these processes
are rarely the subject of analysis. My first piece of published work
on Annie Ernaux was presented in September 1994 at a conference
at the University of Sussex entitled 'Life-History and Learning:
Language, the Self and Education'. The choice of this conference
was in itself significant in several ways; the linking of words such

as 'education' and 'language' to life-history and the self was as resonant for me as similar links in the writing and thought of Annie Ernaux. The adult education background of many of the participants at the conference also differentiated it from standard academic conferences on French literature, with all their connotations and ethos of 'high' culture. Originally I submitted a proposal entitled: 'Losses and Gains: The Experience of Learning in Contemporary French Women's Writing'. My intention was to analyse *Une mort très douce* by Simone de Beauvoir, and *Les Mots pour le dire* by Marie Cardinal, as well as Ernaux's *Une femme*. The thematic links between the three novels were the mother–daughter relationship, intellectual and emotional learning, and formal education. It is clear to me that even at this stage my choice of topic was motivated by the presence of these themes in my narratives of my own life, though my conference proposal makes no mention of this. I justified my choice on the grounds that the three novels 'represent three decades of women's writing in France, and are more accessible than the *écriture féminine* often associated with French feminism in an anglophone context'. Two months later, when I sat down to write the paper, Beauvoir and Cardinal just disappeared. I no longer wanted to write about their novels, which depict the chosen themes in a middle-class context. It was Annie Ernaux's description of the transition from working-class to middle-class culture, mirroring my own, which moved me to write. More recently, this same motivation has sustained my interest in the writing of this book.

Recognition is the first word that springs to mind when I begin to reflect on my reading of Annie Ernaux. Recognition, first of all, of a culture. There are almost certainly great differences between a working-class childhood in 1940s Normandy and in Wolverhampton in the 1950s. Even the term 'working class' would require qualification and elucidation. Nonetheless, the sense of recognising a lost or past culture, also present in Ernaux's texts, is profound: 'Words transmitted from generation to generation, absent from newspapers and books, ignored by schools, belonging to popular culture (originally my own, and this is why I recognise them immediately)' (*Journal du dehors*, p. 70). As I described in chapter 3, Ernaux's writing reveals that she has inherited her parents' sense of material insecurity, which despite her success still seems to prevail, and to impinge on her representations of social reality (p. 56). The descriptions of this anxious relationship to financial survival bring an image to my mind: I am standing in our new

1950s kitchen, which like the scene of June 1952 described in *La Honte*, is lit by sunlight. My father is shaving in front of a small mirror, and my parents are discussing the fact that he has just been made redundant from his job as a pattern-maker. I remember only a confused feeling, as if something terrible might happen. Perhaps my parents are discussing the future, how we are going to hang on to the bright little house which they are struggling to buy. I imagined myself doing something heroic or magical to help my parents. A second example: Ernaux's analysis of her father's acceptance of the status quo, and the general passivity she associates with her culture of origin is, for me, also resonant with images from my past: my two aunts, who were tailoresses, working in a shop where they had both to serve the customers and to *make* the product sold (fur coats), all in two tiny rooms without the most basic amenities, and for a pittance. Yet, they believed this was their place in life, the boss was always right. In *La Honte*, Ernaux describes how this passive acceptance of the status quo is marked by a belief that life is a succession of set times or stages (*La Honte*, p. 59). On reading these sentences I see myself playing with my cousin in the front room of a Victorian terraced house, only slightly ruffled by my Aunty Clara's comment that for me the time for playing will soon be over, it will be time for work. I associate that comment with my aunt's highly polished hall floor tiles and the boiling of sheep's heads to make brawn, in a kitchen with one cold tap, which was her domain.

What is the import of these memories and recognitions? On a social level, I suspect that they reflect the commonalities between two different working-class childhoods. Differences of country, culture and decade are certainly significant, but like Ernaux, I am part of a gradual process of social ascension, across the generations. The position of the parents in this chain is of course crucial, and ambivalent: on the one hand they pass on to their socially still more mobile daughters their own ambition and drive. The many descriptions of the energy of Ernaux's mother attest to this. On the other, they are anxious, uncertain that their material progress can be maintained, with one foot still firmly in the 'things don't change' and 'we're alright as we are' camp. These two sides are present both in Ernaux's texts and in the memories which are triggered by my reading of them. Across the differences they are probably a common point, a specificity of an aspirational or respectable working-class culture.

In the more literary sense, what kind of a reading process am I describing? The similarities between two apparently disparate literary projects – that of Marcel Proust and Annie Ernaux – will by now have become apparent (see chapter 3, note 4). Ernaux has described how a popular song, 'Voyage', can give her back her past, in a way that a work of literature such as *À la recherche du temps perdu* cannot (*Journal du dehors*, pp. 62–3). She may find her past self or selves in a popular song, rather than tea and madeleines, but the obsessive search for identity through return to the past are common points. The similarities between my experiences and the past selves which Ernaux evokes through her writing, and the social specificities which both refer to, seem to make her writing as powerful for me as 'Voyage' is for her, or the madeleines for Proust. If recognition, or mirroring, of a past self is a significant aspect of Ernaux's writing, then my reading becomes a kind of doubling of this process, the text a two-way mirror. The mirror reflects social rather than universal truths, and the recognition promotes not a transcendent reverie on the nature of time, but poignant memories of past realities.

This kind of reading clearly implies a strong identification with the texts and the author. As a result of the readership study described in chapter 5, I am aware that there is nothing unique in this, that Ernaux's novels generate enthusiastic correspondence from many readers with similar backgrounds or trajectories. Ernaux herself has noted this aspect of reader response to her books: 'Twenty years ago, when my first book, *Les Armoires vides*, was published, I received a few letters from readers, including one from a university lecturer, who wrote to me "Denise Lesur is me"' (Ernaux, 1994, p. 27). Here, however, I would like to explore the nature of this identification or recognition, and its relationship to my academic analysis of Ernaux's texts. Most academic work would seem to be based on the split between the researching subject and the object of study. Even if in reality the researcher has strong links with the text or social group s/he is studying, in general the written account of the work will tend to efface these bonds, and to emphasise the researcher's objectivity. Valerie Walkerdine is one of the few researchers to have explored the question of what happens when the boundaries between subject and object of research become blurred; in her article, 'Video-Replay: Families, Films and Fantasy' she has made her own subjectivity as much the object of study as the example of external social reality which she set out to work on (Walkerdine,1986). Because of her working-class background, Walkerdine identifies with the researched, rather than the researcher role. Her article expresses anger towards the middle-class culture she is now part of and she firmly rejects the latter's reading of *Rocky 2*, according to which the film is an expression of dangerous male aggression. In its place she develops a redemptive reading, emphasising the significance of identification with a fighter-hero to an oppressed working-class spectator. Confronted with the culture she has left, and identified by its members, her subjects, as an alien presence, Valerie Walkerdine uses her academic article not only to produce a reading of this family's gendered power relations and response to *Rocky 2*, enriched by her own experience, but also to work through the difficult emotions which the research situation has triggered:

> The film brought me up against such memories of pain and struggle and class that it made me cry. I cried with grief for what was lost and for the terrifying desire to be somewhere and someone else: the struggle to 'make it'. No longer did I stand outside the pleasures of engagement with the film. I too wanted Rocky to win. Indeed I was Rocky – struggling, fighting, crying to get out. (Walkerdine, 1986, p. 169)

Walkerdine simultaneously acknowledges her difference and seeks to affirm her similarity; she may seem on the surface like any other teacher/researcher, but the article brings to light a hidden, earlier identity. This in turn colours and enriches her analysis of the text and its possible meanings, belying the notion of the supreme value of academic objectivity.

Similarly, in writing about Ernaux, my engagement with the texts is, but is not merely, a question of identification. As the Walkerdine article seems to suggest, this desire for self-expression is linked to the emotional costs of the transition, in that it counteracts in some way the dissatisfaction and shame often experienced in relation to the original culture and identity, as part of the process of, or indeed as a motivation for, change. Reading and, as Ernaux makes clear, writing are not a psychoanalysis.[1] However, Ernaux's literary exploration of the twists and turns of a process which, if socially logical, is emotionally contradictory, her naming of the succession of shames, guilts and angers involved, is illuminating, apparently to her readers, and certainly to me. There is also a political motivation; the old identity is not only hidden, but marked by its cultural invisibility, as Carolyn Steedman has pointed out: 'The experience of childhood, particularly of working-class childhood, has not yet entered our general accounts of social history' (Steedman, 1983, p. 26). Part of my motivation to write stems from the desire to question this low cultural status, or the cultural absence of this experience. In an interview with Jean Royer, quoted by Loraine Day, Ernaux herself made the following comment: 'My books are certainly a response to a desire to bring my parents into literature. But with them, I am also bringing a whole social class' (Day and Jones, 1990, p. 75). This significant statement of intention by Ernaux is indicative of the similarity of purpose of Ernaux, the writer, and myself, the reader, resulting in part from a shared political and personal project.

My sense *of* recognition is also in some sense a desire *for* recognition of an aspect of my identity which is no longer obvious. There is a personal pleasure associated with the removal of the mask of uniform 'middle-classness'. In an article on Ernaux, written on the occasion of her lecture tour of England in 1994, Sylvie Marion commented on the disparity between her impression of Ernaux as a sophisticated, serene and self-assured woman, and the tortured narrators of her texts (Marion, 1994). It is as if Marion cannot relate the trappings of material success and 'high' culture tastes which she observes in Ernaux's house to the descriptions of her humble origins in the writing. However, it is precisely the affirmation of the link between her present middle-class self and the working-class child she once was that Ernaux emphasises throughout her texts, and particularly at the end of *Une femme*: 'I will never hear her voice again. My mother, with her words, her hands, her gestures, her way of moving and laughing, is the link between the woman I am and the child I was' (*Une femme*, p. 106). My original analysis of this: 'Ernaux writes in order to ensure that this surface identity is never seen as the whole story' is both a valid interpretation of Ernaux's words and a projection of my own desire onto the author. What I am describing here is not just what writing does for Annie Ernaux, but what reading, and writing about Ernaux's works does for me, in allowing me to reveal a now almost invisible facet of my identity. Through my discussion of Ernaux's writing I am indirectly exploring this earlier identity, and the emotional processes involved in the change of class which is a dominant theme of my own life history as well as of Ernaux's texts.

Like Ernaux, I successfully 'acted the part' of the new class identity which I aspired to, but feelings of inauthenticity, and insecurity persisted, along with a sense of not quite belonging in either world: in Ernaux's terms, feeling *déplacée*. As I have already argued, *Les Armoires vides* contains a vision of early childhood as an idyllic time, marked by a sense of wholeness and *joie de vivre*. The experience of going to school is depicted as the moment when the idyll is shattered, and plenitude and self-assurance are replaced by a sense of almost complete annihilation: 'When I go to school I'm a nobody' (*Les Armoires vides*, p. 62; trans. p. 42). Much later, in *La Honte*, these feelings of annihilation are associated with a specific event, the sight of her parents' violent argument. Whilst the precise timing and circumstances of the 'fall from grace' shift in the various texts, its force is continually present. In *'Je ne suis pas sortie de ma nuit'*, Ernaux reveals that her place in the family, as well as in the world has left her with an uncertain sense of self: 'I was born because my sister died, I replaced her. So there is no real "me"' (*'Je ne suis pas sortie de ma nuit'*, p. 42). In *La Place*, this sense of being the wrong daughter to her parents, as disappointing and problematic to them as they are to her, is already present: 'Perhaps he would have preferred to have a different daughter' (p. 82). Later in the text, Ernaux describes a visit to her parents, whom she finds unchanged: 'I found them as they had always been, without that "sobriety" of conduct, the correct language, which now seem natural to me. I felt separated from myself' (*La Place*, p. 98). The ambiguity of this comment is striking: it could mean that the acquisition of middle-class culture has separated Ernaux from her real self, or, equally, that she now feels out of place and separated from herself in her parents' culture. In either case, the change of class and the family dynamics seem to have led to a fragile and easily disrupted sense of self, and to feelings of inauthenticity and displacement (see chapter 4). These feelings are conveyed in *Les Armoires vides*, and the word *factice* (artificial) recurs: 'I have nothing to say about Gide or anything else for that matter, I'm a fake (je suis factice)' (*Les Armoires vides*, p. 13; trans. p. 9). The association of inauthenticity with the new middle-class identity is repeated at the end of the novel, again using the same key word: 'It's all bluff (Tout ça c'est factice), playing to the gallery, grist to my mill' (*Les Armoires vides*, pp. 174–5; trans. p. 118). At the end of *Une Femme*, Ernaux describes how writing has allowed her to feel 'less alone and artificial in the dominant world of words and ideas' (*Une femme*, p. 106). The most significant words here for me are 'less artificial' and I have translated the original French 'moins factice' more literally than the published translation (which has 'out of place'), in order to emphasise the idea of the acquired middle-class identity as artifice or masquerade.

The inadequate self-image seems to be compensated for by fantasies of an idealised self, which are described in several of the texts as a favourite childhood game; in *Ce qu'ils disent ou rien*, advertisements in magazines are used to make a house, and to tell stories (p. 37). In *La Honte*, the description of this game is elaborated; it acquires a name – 'the game of the ideal day' – and involves the invention of an ideal self, based on the products advertised in *L'Echo de la Mode*: 'The process was always the same. I imagined I was a girl living alone in a big, beautiful house (variation: alone in a bedsitting room in Paris). With each product praised in the magazine I invented my body and my appearance, nice teeth (with *Gibs*), full red lips (*'Kiss'* lipstick), slim figure (*'x'* corset) etc.' (*La Honte*, p. 127). This game appears to be an extension of the stories which Denise Lesur tells at school, at first in order to impress her classmates, and eventually for herself, 'so that I could live in a more beautiful world, purer, richer than mine' (*Les Armoires vides*, p. 77; trans. p. 51). In reality it is education which will permit some kind of realisation of these fantasies of a better self, and access to 'the translucent, insubstantial, rustling world of school, a pure world where I too pretend to be pure' (*Les Armoires vides*, p. 75; trans. p. 50). The price of this purity, as we have seen, is the denial of the body, and the 'pretence' inevitably leads to the feelings of artificiality described above.

Nonetheless, the middle-class, educated world has all the lure of the forbidden path, cottage or castle of the fairy-tales, and education is associated with mystery and unreality – the agent of the desired, magical transformation. Thus, Denise experiences her arrival in Rouen as a university student as almost unbelievably idyllic: 'It seemed almost unreal. Streaks of pale golden sunlight on the walls, a mellow autumn' (*Les Armoires vides*, p. 164; trans. p. 111). The university library, as I have already pointed out, is compared to Sleeping Beauty's castle (chapter 3, p. 60). Even at school, good marks allow Denise to escape humiliation: 'That knowledge made me feel free, warm, protected. I was the little queen again (la petite reine)' (*Les Armoires vides*, p. 73; trans, p. 49). Again, this sudden transformation from frog to princess, or in this case queen, is reminiscent of the fairy-tale. The extreme nature of this reversal, after the feelings of deep humiliation and annihilation inflicted by the school initially, perhaps explains the strong sense in Ernaux's first novel that educational success was the result not of ability and effort, but of a kind of spell. My own experience of the education system has left me with a similar sense of its arbitrariness. Described at primary school as 'slow to grasp new ideas', I became one of the few comprehensive school pupils to win a place at Oxford. At first my efforts to please my teachers received only a very limited success, and then suddenly, I could do no wrong, the top marks seemed to fall into my lap. The explanation is probably linked to the fact that like Denise, I was learning to play the game of school, and that without the cultural advantages of a middle-class home, this took a while. Despite this rationalisation, acquired of course much later, this transition seems to foster the split identity I recognise in myself, and in Ernaux's writing: on the one hand weighed down by some indelible inferiority, and on the other magically gifted, able to soar to the heights.

In *Les Armoires vides*, as we have seen, Denise compensates for these uncertainties by excelling at school, at the same time taking her revenge on the middle-class teachers and fellow pupils who humiliated her when she first arrived: 'More dictations, more subtractions, I quiver, mustn't let them beat me! They may be creeping up slowly . . . To stay ahead, to have my revenge, I entered more and more into the school game' (*Les Armoires vides*, p. 72; trans. p. 47). Compelled by anger and insecurity, Ernaux's heroines, and perhaps Ernaux herself, have to become not only middle-class, but intellectual, thus aspiring to a cultural milieu which Bourdieu has described as 'a Parisian haute bourgeoisie (. . .) combining all forms of prestige and all the titles of economic and cultural nobility' (Bourdieu [1979] 1984, p. xi). In 1929, the psychoanalyst Joan Rivière described how one of her patients, an intellectual woman, compensated for her acquisition of the 'masculine' quality of intellectualism by means of a masquerade of excessive femininity. Although the lack of attention to gendered power relations in Rivière's analysis has been critiqued, her article provides a provocative account of how an insecure or contradictory identity may be compensated for by a masquerade of excess (Heath, 1986). In relation to gender, it is possible to see something similar in *La Femme gelée*, where Ernaux describes how she acquired all the excesses of middle-class femininity, as if to compensate for her intellectual achievements. However, a parallel can also be drawn in terms of social class, where a masquerade of excess compensates for the perceived inadequacy of the original culture. Ernaux does not merely acquire middle-class culture and language, she becomes an expert in the field, able to create her own particular linguistic and literary register, appropriate to the complex identity which she aims to express. My identification with Ernaux results also from recognition of this compensatory drive to excel. If, for Ernaux, linguistic excellence had to be taken to the extreme of becoming a successful writer, in my own case, the excess can be seen both as the adoption of the impersonal, academic register, and as the acquisition of a foreign language. Speaking French for me was another masquerade, where the traces of the original identity still present in my native speech were completely effaced. In the early stages of learning French I became simply an English person speaking a foreign language; I did not take with me into the new culture the connotations and nuances of class position which can be deduced in the English system from pronunciation and accent. Excess and escape become synonymous: for Ernaux, into literature, for me, into French.[2] The irony in Annie Ernaux's case is that this very excess – her excellence in the French cultural field – provides her with a space in which, as a writer, she can explore, and come to terms with, her feelings of insecurity.

Narratives involving transformation, through masquerade, from traditional fairy-tales such as *Cinderella* to recent Hollywood films, such as *Working Girl*, are clearly a deeply embedded aspect of Western culture, and the narratives of life-history are no exception. Like the fairy-tales, Ernaux's adolescent rejection of her parents and their culture can be seen as a version of Freud's *Family Romances*, where the child is disillusioned on discovering that his father is not 'the noblest and strongest of men and his mother the loveliest and dearest of women' (Freud [1909] 1977, p. 225). The child compensates for this disillusionment, and for the inevitable sense of the inadequacy of the parents' love, by constructing a fantasy narrative, in which the real parents are exchanged for nobler beings. The child, like the heroes and heroines of many fairy-tales, believes himself to be a foundling, in reality of aristo-cratic lineage. Ernaux's own references to magical transformations would seem to confirm the suitability of these comparisons. In her first novel, Ernaux describes a similar fantasy: 'The store, my parents couldn't be real, one evening I'd go to sleep and wake up beside a road, I'd come to a manor-house, inside a gong would sound and I'd say "Here I am, Papa!" to an elegantly dressed person being served by a well-trained butler' (*Les Armoires vides*, p. 80; trans. p. 53). As in Freud's analysis, the focus in this fantasy is on the father.[3] The fantasy seems to be a reversal of the scene in the restaurant in Tours, described more than twenty years later in *La Honte*, where the father was humiliated by the bad service he received from the waiters: Ernaux's choice of placing the father in the fantasy scene may be the result of a subconscious linking with this experience. It may also be the case that the father seems to need a more profound transformation than the mother, who at least aspires to middle-class culture. Later, as we have seen, education becomes the magical agent which can effect the transformation, not only of her own being, but also of her parents:

> I'd whisper in their ear what they should do and say, I'd teach them all I know, algebra, history, English, and they'd know as much as me, and we could have intelligent discussions, and go to the theater together. . . . My parents, same faces, same bodies, but totally transformed . . . then I really could love them, stop hating their way of life, their manners, their likes and dislikes . . . (*Les Armoires vides*, p. 117; trans. p. 78)

If, in this first stage, the desire to transform the parents follows almost exactly the course charted by Freud, the publication of *La Place* marks a complete reversal. The desire is no longer to transform the parents by making them middle-class, but to represent them positively as they are. Instead of denying the real parents and replacing them, in fantasy, with grander individuals, here the real parents are being reclaimed, perhaps partly out of guilt about the initial rejection. The anger is turned outward, rather than inward, and the middle classes, rather than the culture of origin, become its butt. The 'I am more than I seem' narrative identified by Freud is here about claiming lowly, rather than grander, origins, and a new affirmation of the former. At the same time, like the conventional narratives of transformation prevalent in our culture, Ernaux's texts evoke the pleasure of the revelation of the 'true self'; in this case a little working-class girl who is queen of her own body ('la petite reine de mon corps'), rather than the beautiful princess whose noble status has been denied (*Les Armoires vides*, p. 49). The traditional 'from rags to riches' narrative is questioned, since the trajectory described by Ernaux involves loss as well as gains. These losses, as we have seen, are at the heart of the structure and content of almost all of Ernaux's nine texts. Thus in Ernaux's writing we see both the conventional, Freudian trajectory, the rejection of the parents and the desire for nobler origins, and its subversion – the reattribution of value to the real parents, however modest their cultural capital. In the first case, my response is one of recognition, in the second, the realisation of a desire. When my aunts and uncles visited me at Oxford, their accents, clothes and conversation sent me into agonies of embarrassment; my own masquerade was revealed as exactly that by this dreaded meeting of my two worlds. Like Ernaux, I also felt guilty that I saw my family through the (imagined) disdainful eyes of my fellow students, the children of civil servants and diplomats. Perhaps, in writing this book, I am at last able to look back, to return the critical gaze, just as Ernaux can return the stares of the onlookers in *'Je ne suis pas sortie de ma nuit'*.

These narratives, in Ernaux's literary texts and in my critical writing, seem to involve the rediscovery of a true self which has been obscured by the masquerade. Postmodernist theories would probably reject such a notion, preferring the infinite play of shifting identities which the masquerade encapsulates. A belief in the historical and constructed nature of identity also clearly underlies Ernaux's writing, particularly in *La Place* and *Une femme*, and in *La Honte* she has made her theoretical position extremely clear. Ernaux rejects unitary notions of identity: 'For me – and perhaps for all those of my generation – whose memories are attached to a summer pop-song, a fashionable belt, to things which are destined to be ephemeral, memory brings no proof of permanence to my identity. It makes me feel, and is the confirmation of, my fragmentation and my historicity' (*La Honte*, pp. 95–6). This sense of the constructed and fragmentary nature of identity is theoretically sound, and fundamental to both my and Ernaux's political positions, but it may, in some ways, be difficult to live. The fact that the old identity is associated with childhood experiences, and significant early emotional attachments, surrounds it with an aura of authenticity. The complex emotions arising from the change of class may result in a nostalgic longing for the childhood self, at ease and competent in a single culture. My analysis of Ernaux's novels is imbued with this nostalgia, and my motivation to write about them is profoundly connected with Ernaux's poignant description of her childhood self. As for Walkerdine, emotion combines with politics, and loyalty to the class and culture of origin predominates. Just as Walkerdine is aware of the impact of her middle-class presence on the family she is observing, Ernaux identifies with the discomfiture her mother experiences in her own daughter's house: 'It took me a long time to realise that my mother felt ill at ease in my own house in exactly the same way as I had done as a teenager when I met people from "a higher class"' (*Une femme*, p. 77). It is this identification which I share, along with the experience of loss which Ernaux has captured in her writing. For me, as perhaps for Ernaux, the process of writing, which affirms my place in middle-class culture, has been in some sense 'justified' by its role in providing an opportunity to express an identity which is no longer obvious. Self-expression and the discovery, in Ernaux's 'écriture plate', of a nostalgic romance of childhood, more than any theoretical conviction, have provided my motivation to write, and the pleasure of writing 'literary criticism'.

Notes

1. In her interview with Gibert, Ernaux commented: 'Writing is not a psychoanalysis. After four books I have not rid myself of what is fundamental' (Gibert, 1985, quoted in Garaud, 1994, p. 214, note 23).
2. The trajectory I describe here is in contrast with that traced by Nancy K. Miller, in her humorous account of the humiliations associated with French-language errors, when one is 'in French': 'The French Mistake' (Miller, 1991b, pp. 48–55). Whilst I recognise and remember vividly those humiliations, speaking French, for me, is still accompanied by a feeling of liberation.
3. Freud attributes this to the uncertainties surrounding paternity:

> When presently the child comes to know the difference in the parts played by fathers and mothers in their sexual relations, and realizes that *'pater semper incertus est'*, while the mother is *'certissima'*, the family romance undergoes a curious curtailment: it contents itself with exalting the child's father, but no longer casts any doubts on his maternal origin, which is regarded as something unalterable.

(Freud [1909] 1977, p. 223) There is some connection between this comment and the very strong sense in Ernaux's writing of the matrilineal nature of her origins. The power of the mother–daughter bond, rather than the difference in reproductive role, seems, however, to be at the heart of this tendency (see chapter 4).

Appendix 1
Fragments around
Philippe V. (Fragments
autour de Philippe V.)

*H*e had written about his desire for me several times in letters, but on the evening we had decided to spend together he seemed intimidated, hardly speaking. Doubtless because he's a student, much younger than me, and I write books. After the theatre – his arm and mine had often touched on the armrest – I invited him for a drink. We went to a pub in rue Monsieur-Le-Prince. I was no longer sure I wanted to make love with him, though for several weeks I had been longing for the relationship to develop. He was sitting opposite me, watching me speak. At the low tables nearby, there were groups of young men and women, sitting on stools. The waitress in a black mini-skirt kept passing by our table. He was drinking a cocktail with alcohol, mine was just fruit juice. It was a moment when all the details of your surroundings seem to have a meaning, because nothing has happened yet, perhaps nothing will happen.

When we left the pub, I invited him back to my house for another drink. He accepted immediately. I still didn't know whether I wanted to make love with him. I was giving myself more time to decide, whilst at the same time realising that in taking him to my house I was making this scenario more and more likely. In the car I put on a cassette of pop songs. Every time I changed gear, my hand brushed past his leg.

In the living-room we sat in armchairs quite a long way apart from each other, without any real conversation ('Do you like sake?' etc.), waiting. It was up to me to make a move, to begin. It was obvious that nothing would happen unless I took the initiative.

I didn't think about exactly what I should do, I just thought that I had to do something. I got up from my chair, walked towards him and stroked his hair. He pressed his head against my body, then he got up and held me in a violent embrace. I could feel the as yet unknown penis pushing against me through our clothes, with a force and rigidity that explained his silence that evening.

After he left, the next day, I re-ran the scenes of the night, the sight of his body, his penis at the moment I first saw it – always an indescribable moment – later half imprisoned in a condom which was too small. I kept going back to my gesture, my hand in his hair, without which nothing would have happened. The memory of this gesture, more than anything else, filled me with intense, almost orgasmic pleasure.[1] It occurred to me that it was of the same nature as the act of writing the opening sentence of a book. That it was based on the same desire to intervene in the world, to *open* a story. For a woman, the freedom to write without shame is connected to that of being the first to touch a man's body with desire.

We made love on a Sunday in October. I was lying on a piece of drawing paper spread out on the bed. He wanted to know what kind of picture the mixture of his sperm and my menstrual blood would make.

Afterwards we looked at the paper, the damp picture. We saw a woman whose face was being devoured by her thick mouth, whose body seemed to fade and flow, formless. Or perhaps it was the northern lights, or a sunset.

We were amazed not to have had this idea before. We wondered if other people had had the same idea. The next day he framed the picture and hung it on the wall of his room.

We did the same thing in the following two or three months. It had become an added pleasure. The impression that the orgasm was not the end of everything, that a trace of it would remain – we wrote the date and the time on the paper – something similar to a work of art.

Writing and making love. I feel there is an essential link between the two. I can't explain it, I can only record those moments when this appears most clearly to me.

Annie Ernaux (in *L'Infini*, no. 56, Winter 1996, Paris: Gallimard); translated by the author.

Fragments around Philippe V.

Note

1. 'Jouissance' in the original. This is perhaps a reference to Barthes, who in *Le Plaisir du texte* associates the word 'jouissance' (enjoyment, orgasm) with the text which disrupts rather than confirms the reader's cultural and literary expectations, and 'provokes a crisis in his relationship with language' (Barthes, 1973, p. 26). An earlier version of 'Fragments', provided by Ernaux, has the word 'satisfaction', suggesting that the change to 'jouissance' is both a significant and a self-aware choice. For Ernaux's own versions of the disruptive text, see chapters 2 (p. 48) and 6 (p. 151).

Appendix 2
The Press Reception of La Honte and 'Je ne suis pas sortie de ma nuit'

(All dates refer to 1997)

Positive Reviews	Negative/Mixed Reviews
Mainstream National Press:	
1. Dailies	
La Croix 12/13 March	Les Echos, le quotidien de
Le Monde (des Livres)	l'économie 21 January
24 January	Le Figaro (Littéraire)
L'Humanité 31 January	16 January
Libération 16 January	
Le Parisien 1 February	
2. Weeklies	
Le Canard Enchaîné 22 January	Le Point 28 February
Le Point 11 January	Le Nouvel Observateur
L'Express 30 January	16 January
Le Figaro Magazine 11 January	
L'Événement du Jeudi	
23 January	
Journal du Dimanche	
2 February	
Humanité Dimanche 16 January	
Télé 7 jours 8–17 February	

Positive Reviews	Negative/Mixed Reviews
Télérama 15 January *Téléjournal* 25–31 January	

3. The Specialised Literary Press
Le Monde (des Livres)
   24 January
La Quinzaine Littéraire
   16–28 February
Lire   February
	Le Figaro (Littéraire)
	   16 January
	Le Magazine Littéraire
	   February
	Le Bulletin des Lettres
	   no.561 March

4. Presse Féminine (Women's Magazines) *Madame Figaro* 25 January *Femme Actuelle* 24 February *Atmosphères* February *Marie-Claire* March *Biba* February *Cosmopolitan* February	*Elle* 3 February

Regional Papers:

1. Dailies
Les Informations Diéppoises
   14 February
L'Echo Le Régional Île de France
   20 February
La Presse de la Manche   15 June
Normandie   1 February
Var Matin   31 January
Nice Matin   26 January
Le Provençal   23 February
Dernières Nouvelles d'Alsace
   27 February
La Voix du Nord   25 February
Ouest-France   21 February
Le Républicain Lorrain
   16 February
	L'Opinion Indépendante
	   25 July
	L'Echo Le Régional Île de France 20 March
	Paris Normandie
	   8–9 March
	Le Méridional 26 January
	Midi Libre 2 February

Positive Reviews	**Negative/Mixed Reviews**
La Nouvelle République du Centre-Ouest 23 January *Le Dauphiné Libéré* 20 January *L'Alsace* 20 January *Le Progrès* 19 January *La Marseillaise* 12 January *La Marseillaise* 28 January *La Croix Nord / Pas de Calais* 11 April	
2. Weeklies *Temps Libre* 9–15 April *La Semaine du Roussillon* no. 44 7–3 February *Centre France Dimanche* 12 January	*Sud-Ouest Dimanche* 26 January

Bibliography

Ernaux's Works

Books

(1974), *Les Armoires vides*, Paris: Gallimard.
(1977), *Ce qu'ils disent ou rien*, Paris: Gallimard. (Not translated; *What They Say Goes*)
(1981), *La Femme gelée*, Paris: Gallimard.
(1984), *La Place*, Paris: Gallimard. (Prix Renaudot, 1984)
(1988), *Une femme*, Paris: Gallimard.
(1992), *Passion simple*, Paris: Gallimard.
(1993), *Journal du dehors*, Paris: Gallimard.
(1997), *La Honte*, Paris: Gallimard. (Not translated; *Shame*)
(1997), *'Je ne suis pas sortie de ma nuit'*, Paris: Gallimard. (Not translated; *'My Night is not Over'*)

Articles/Short Texts

(1985), 'Retours' ('Going Back'), *L'Autre Journal*, April, pp. 70–1.
(1989), 'Ernaux, Annie', in J. Garcin, (ed.), *Le Dictionnaire, Littérature française contemporaine*, Paris: Editions François Bourin, pp. 179–83.
(1994a), 'Lectures de *Passion Simple*' ('Readings of *Passion simple*'), *La Faute àRousseau: Journal de l'Association pour l'Autobiographie et le Patrimoine Autobiographique*, no. 6, June, pp. 27–9.
(1994b), 'Vers un Je transpersonnel' ('Towards a Transpersonal I'), Autofictions et Cie, *Cahiers RITM* no. 6, Université Paris X-Nanterre, pp. 218–221.
(1996), 'Fragments autour de Philippe V.', *L'Infini*, no. 56, Winter, pp. 25–6; translated in appendix 1, pp. 177–178.

Translations into English

(1990), *Une femme,* trans. Tanya Leslie as *A Woman's Story,* London: Quartet Books, and (1990), New York: Seven Stories Press.

(1990), *Les Armoires vides,* trans. Carol Sanders as *Cleaned Out,* Illinois: Dalkey Archive Press.

(1991), *La Place,* trans. Tanya Leslie as *Positions,* London: Quartet Books, and (1992), *A Man's Place,* New York: Seven Stories Press.

(1993), *Passion simple.* trans. Tanya Leslie as *Passion Perfect,* London: Quartet Books, and (1993), *Simple Passion,* New York: Seven Stories Press.

(1995), *La Femme gelée,* trans. Linda Coverdale as *A Frozen Woman,* New York: Four Walls Eight Windows (now Seven Stories Press).

(1996), *Journal du dehors,* trans. Tanya Leslie as *Exteriors,* New York: Seven Stories Press.

Academic Writing on Annie Ernaux

Bacholle, M. (1995), 'Annie Ernaux: Lieux communs et lieu(x) de vérité', *LittéRéalité,* vol. 7, nos. 1–2, pp. 28–40.

——, (1996), '*Passion Simple* d'Annie Ernaux: Vers une désacralisation de la société française?', *Dalhousie French Studies,* no. 36, Fall, pp. 123–34.

——, (1998), 'An interview with Annie Ernaux: Ecrire le vécu', *Sites,* vol. 2, no. 1, pp. 141–51.

Cairns, L. (1994), 'Annie Ernaux, Filial Ambivalence and *Ce qu'ils disent ou rien*', *Romance Studies,* no. 24, Fall, pp. 71–84.

Charpentier, I. (1994), 'De corps à corps: réceptions croisées d'Annie Ernaux', *Politix,* no. 27, pp. 45–75.

Day, L. (1990), 'Class, Sexuality and Subjectivity in Annie Ernaux's *Les Armoires vides*', in M. Atack, and P. Powrie (eds), *Contemporary French Fiction by Women: Feminist Perspectives,* Manchester and New York: Manchester University Press, pp. 41–55.

Day, L. and Jones, T. (1990), *Ernaux: La Place, Une femme,* Glasgow: University of Glasgow French and German Publications.

Fallaize, E. (1993), 'Annie Ernaux', in E. Fallaize, *French Women's Writing: Recent Fiction,* London: Macmillan, pp. 67–87.

Fau, C. (1995), 'Le Problème du langage chez Annie Ernaux', *The French Review,* vol. 68, no. 3, pp. 501–12.

Fernandez-Récatala, D. (1994), *Annie Ernaux*, Monaco: Editions du Rocher.

Garaud, C. (1994), 'Ecrire la différence sociale: Registres de vie et registres de langue dans *La Place* d'Annie Ernaux', *French Forum*, vol. 29, no. 2, pp. 195–214.

Holmes, D. (1996), 'Feminism and Realism: Christiane Rochefort and Annie Ernaux', in D. Holmes, *French Women's Writing, 1848–1994*, London: Athlone Press, pp. 246–65.

Kimminich, E. (1994), 'Macht und Magie der Worte: Zur Funktion des Schreibens im Werk Annie Ernaux', in W. Asholt (ed.), *Intertextualität und Subversivität: Studien zur Romanliteratur der achtziger Jahre in Frankreich*, Heidelberg: Universitätsverlag Carl Winter, pp. 149–59.

Laubier, C. (ed.), (1990), *The Condition of Women in France, 1945 to the Present: A Documentary Anthology*, London and New York: Routledge, ch. 9.

Mall, L. (1995), '"Moins Seule et Factice": la Part Autobiographique dans *Une Femme* d'Annie Ernaux', *The French Review*, vol. 69, no. 1, pp. 45–54.

Marrone, C. (1994), 'Past, Present and Passion Tense in Annie Ernaux's *Passion simple*', *Women in French Studies*, no. 2, Fall, pp. 78–87.

McIlvanney, S. (1992), 'Ernaux and Realism: Redressing the Balance', in M. Allison, (ed.), *Women's Space and Identity*, Women Teaching French Papers 2, Bradford: Department of Modern Languages, University of Bradford, pp. 49–63.

——, (1996), 'Recuperating Romance: Literary Paradigms in the Works of Annie Ernaux', *Forum for Modern Language Studies*, vol. 32, no. 3, pp. 240–50.

——, (1997), 'Ernaux, Annie: *La Honte* and *"Je ne suis pas sortie de ma nuit"*', *Dalhousie French Studies*, nos 39–40, pp. 244–6.

Meizoz, J. (1996), *Annie Ernaux, une politique de la forme*, Geneva: Editions Slatkine.

Miller, Nancy K. (1998), 'Autobiographical Others: Annie Ernaux's *Journal du dehors*', *Sites*, Spring 1998, pp. 127–39

Montfort, C. R. (1996), '"La Vieille Née": Simone de Beauvoir, *Une mort très douce*, and Annie Ernaux, *Une femme*', *French Forum*, vol. 21, no. 3, pp. 349–64.

Motte, W. (1995), 'Annie Ernaux's Understatement', *The French Review*, vol. 69, no. 1, pp. 55–67.

Naudin, M. (1993), '*Passion Simple* Annie Ernaux', *The French Review*, vol. 67, no. 2, pp. 386–7.

Prévost, C. and Lebrun, J.-C. (1990), *Nouveaux territoires romanesques*, Paris: Messidor, Editions Sociales, pp. 51–66.

Sanders, C. (1993), 'Stylistic Aspects of Women's Writing: The Case of Annie Ernaux', *French Cultural Studies*, no. 4, pp. 15–29.

Savéan, M.-F. (1994), *La Place et Une femme d'Annie Ernaux*, Paris: Gallimard.

——, (1997), 'Dossier: *La Place* ', Paris: Gallimard.

Sheringham, M. (1998), 'Invisible Presences: Fiction, Autobiography and Women's Lives – Virginia Woolf to Annie Ernaux', *Sites*, vol. 2, no. 1, pp. 5–24.

Thomas, L. (1994), 'Women, Education and Class: Narratives of Loss in the Fiction of Annie Ernaux', in M. Hoar, M. Lea, M. Stuart, V. Swash, A. Thomson and L. West (eds), *Life Histories and Learning: Language, the Self and Education: Papers from an Interdisciplinary Conference*, Brighton: University of Sussex, pp. 161–6.

—— and Webb, E. (1999), 'Writing from Experience: The Place of the Personal in French Feminist Writing', *Feminist Review*, no. 61.

Tondeur, C.-L. (1995a), 'Entretien avec Annie Ernaux', *The French Review*, vol. 69, no. 1, pp. 37–44.

——, (1995b), 'Le passé: point focal du présent dans l'oeuvre d'Annie Ernaux', *Women in French Studies*, no. 3, Fall, pp. 123–37.

——, (1995c), 'Relation mère / fille chez Annie Ernaux', *Romance Languages Annual*, no. 7, pp. 173–9.

——, (1996), *Annie Ernaux ou l'exil intérieur*, Amsterdam and Atlanta, GA: Rodopi. Vilain, P. (1997a), 'Entretien avec Annie Ernaux: une "conscience malheureuse" de femme', *LittéRéalité*, vol. 9, no. 1, pp. 66–71.

——, (1997b), 'Annie Ernaux ou l'écriture comme recherche' (reviews of *La Honte* and '*Je ne suis pas sortie de ma nuit*'), *LittéRéalité*, vol. 9, no. 1, pp. 111–13.

Wetherill, P. M. (1987), 'Introduction to *La Place*', London: Routledge.

Journalistic Writing on Annie Ernaux

Amette, J.-P. (1997), 'Enfance et adolescence', *Le Point*, no. 1269, 11 January.

Authier, C. (1997), 'Annie Ernaux, la mère souffrance des lettres', *L'Opinion Indépendante*, no. 2260, 25 July.

Bernstein, M. (1992), 'Annie Ernaux: mémoire d'une jeune femme coincée', *Libération*, 16 January.

——, (1993), 'Annie Ernaux: les humiliés et les offensés', *Libération*, 1 April.

Boué, M. (1984), 'Prix littéraires, féminin pluriel', *Humanité Dimanche*, 16 November.

C., A. (1997), 'Tout dire pour s'accepter?', *Les Echos*, 21 January.

Clavel, A. (1997), 'L'enfance à nu d'Annie', *L'Express*, 30 January.

Cusset, C. (1997), 'La romancière qui franchit l'océan', *La Lettre*, January.

de Biasi, P.-M. (1992), 'Les petites Emma 1992', *Le Magazine Littéraire*, July/August.

Delbourg, P. (1997), 'Annie Ernaux: le bovarysme est un humanisme', *L'Evénement du Jeudi*, 23–9 January.

Delorme, M.-L. (1997), 'Annie Ernaux: sans surprise', *Magazine Littéraire*, no. 351, February.

Devarrieux, C. (1997), 'Honte et solitude', *Libération*, 16 January.

Durand, D. (1997), '52, année erratique', *Le Canard Enchaîné*, 22 January.

Frey, P. (1997), 'La vie d'Annie Ernaux n'est pas gaie', *Elle*, 3 February.

Garcin, J. (1997a), 'La haine du style', *Le Nouvel Observateur*, 16–22 January.

——, (1997b), 'Pour l'amour d'Annie Ernaux: Passion simple, suite', *Le Nouvel Observateur*, 6–12 November.

Gibert, J.-J. (1985), 'Le Silence ou la Trahison?' *Révolution* , no. 260, 22 February, pp. 52–3.

H., A. (1992), '*Passion simple* par Annie Ernaux', *L'Express*, 30 January–5 February.

Hafsia, J. (1996), '"On ne peut se contenter de rester à la surface des choses"', *La Presse*, Tunis, 21 October.

Josselin, J.-F. (1992), 'Un gros chagrin', *Le Nouvel Observateur*, 9–15 January.

——, (1993), 'Annie dans la métro', *Le Nouvel Observateur*, 15–21 April.

Laval, M. (1997), 'Ce jour-là, le 15 Juin 1952', *Télérama*, 15 January.

Lebrun, J.-C. (1997), 'La fausse et la vraie piste de l'écriture chez Annie Ernaux. Qu'est-ce que la littérature?', *L'Humanité*, 31 January.

Leclère, M.-F. (1997), 'Majuscules', *Le Point*, 7 February.

Marion, S. (1994), 'Class Action', *The Times Higher Education Supplement*, 25 March.

Matignon, R. (1997), 'Annie Ernaux: l'arrière-cuisine de l'enfance', *Le Figaro*, 16 January.

Mazingarbe, D. (1997), 'Récits: *La Honte, 'Je ne suis pas sortie de ma nuit'* d'Annie Ernaux', *Madame Figaro*, 25 January.

Mertenat, T. (1997), 'La vraie littérature est dangereuse', *Journal de Genève et Gazette de Lausanne*, 22 February.

Neuhoff, E. (1992), 'Un peu mince', *Madame Figaro*, 1 February.

Nourissier, F. (1988), 'Mort et résurrection d'une femme', *Figaro Magazine*, 16 January.

——, (1997), 'Annie Ernaux: le roman comme thérapeutique', *Figaro Magazine*, 11 January.

Plessy, B. (1997), 'Annie Ernaux est-elle un cas?', *Le Bulletin des Lettres*, no. 561, March.

Salvaing, F. (1997), 'L'ethnologue de soi-même', *Humanité Dimanche*, 16 January.

Sauvage, C. (1997), 'Ils écrivent mais est-ce de la littérature?', *Journal du Dimanche*, 16 March.

Savigneau, J. (1992), 'Le courage d'Annie Ernaux', *Le Monde*, 17 January.

——, (1997), 'Ethnologue de soi', *Le Monde des Livres*, 24 January.

Simson, M. (1996), 'Annie Ernaux; Diaries of Provincial Life', *Publishers' Weekly*, 9 December.

Vedrines, J. (1997), 'Une Bovary du pauvre', *Valeurs Actuelles*, 8 February.

Walter, A. (1997), '"La honte n'a jamais cessé de m'habiter"', *Marie-Claire*, March.

General

M. Atack, and P. Powrie (eds), *Contemporary French Fiction by Women: Feminist Perspectives*, Manchester and New York: Manchester University Press.

Bakhtin, M. (1981), *The Dialogic Imagination, Four Essays by M.M. Bakhtin*, trans. C. Emerson, and M. Holquist, Austin: University of Texas Press.

Barthes, R. (1970), *Mythologies*, Paris: Editions du Seuil.

——, (1973), *Le Plaisir du Texte*, Paris: Editions du Seuil.

Beauvoir, S. de (1949), *Le Deuxième Sexe*, Paris: Gallimard.

——, (1958), *Mémoires d'une jeune fille rangée*, Paris: Gallimard.

——, (1960), *La Force de l'Age*, Paris: Gallimard.

——, (1963), *La Force des Choses*, Paris: Gallimard.

——, (1964), *Une mort très douce*, Paris: Gallimard.

——, (1972), *Tout compte fait*, Paris: Gallimard.

Berger, J. (1972), *Ways of Seeing*, Harmondsworth: Penguin.

Bourdieu, P. [1979] 1984, *Distinction: A Social Critique of the Judgement of Taste*, trans. R. Nice, London, Melbourne and Henley: Routledge and Kegan Paul.

Buck, C. (ed.), (1992), *Bloomsbury Guide to Women's Literature*, London: Bloomsbury Publishing Ltd.

Buckingham, D. (1987), *Public Secrets: EastEnders and its Audience*, London: The British Film Institute.

——, (1993), *Children Talking Television: The Making of Television Literacy*, London and Bristol, PA: The Falmer Press.

Camus, A. [1942] (1974), *L'Etranger*, Paris: Gallimard.

Cardinal, M. (1975), *Les Mots pour le dire*, Paris: Grasset et Fasquelle, translated as *The Words to Say it*, by P. Goodheart, (1993), London: The Women's Press.

Chodorow, N. J. (1978), *The Reproduction of Mothering: Psychoanalysis and the Sociology of Gender*, Berkeley: University of California Press.

——, (1989), *Feminism and Psychoanalytic Theory*, New Haven and London: Yale University Press.

Dawson, G. (1994), *Soldier Heroes: British Adventure, Empire and the Imagining of Masculinities*, London and New York: Routledge.

Duchen, C. (1986), *Feminism in France from May '68 to Mitterrand*, London, Boston and Henley: Routledge and Kegan Paul.

——, (1994), *Women's Rights and Women's Lives in France, 1944–1968*, London and New York: Routledge.

Dyer, R. (1979), *Stars*, London: The British Film Institute.

Eagleton, T. (1983), *Literary Theory: An Introduction*, Oxford: Blackwell.

Eichenbaum, L. and Orbach, S. (1983), *Understanding Women*, London and New York: Penguin.

Fallaize, E. (1993), *French Women's Writing: Recent Fiction*, London: Macmillan.

——, (1995), 'Reception Problems for Women Writers: The Case of Simone de Beauvoir', in D. Knight, and J. Still, (eds), *Women and Representation*, Nottingham: WIF Publications, pp. 43–56.

Felski, R. (1989), *Beyond Feminist Aesthetics: Feminist Literature and Social Change*, London: Hutchinson Radius.

Flaubert, G. [1857] (1966), *Madame Bovary*, Paris: Garnier-Flammarion.

——, [1869] (1969), *L'Education sentimentale*, Paris: Garnier-Flammarion.

Freud, S. [1909] (1977), 'Family Romances', in A. Richards (ed.), *On Sexuality: Three Essays on Sexuality and Other Works*, London: Penguin Books, pp. 217–25.

——, [1931] (1977), 'Female Sexuality' in A. Richards (ed.), *On Sexuality: Three Essays on Sexuality and Other Works*, London: Penguin Books, pp. 367-92.

Freund, E. (1987), *The Return of the Reader: Reader Response Criticism*, London and New York: Methuen.

Garcin, J. (ed.), (1989), *Le Dictionnaire, Littérature française contemporaine*, Paris: Editions François Bourin.

Hall, S. [1973] (1996), 'Encoding/Decoding', in P. Marris, and S. Thornham (eds), *Media Studies: A Reader*, Edinburgh: Edinburgh University Press, pp. 41–9.

Heath, S. (1986), 'Joan Rivière and the Masquerade', in V. Burgin, J. Donald, and C. Kaplan (eds), *Formations of Fantasy*, London: Methuen, pp. 45–61.

Heron, L. (ed.), (1985), *Truth, Dare or Promise: Girls Growing up in the Fifties*, London: Virago Press.

Holmes, D. (1996), *French Women's Writing, 1848–1994*, London: Athlone Press.

Knight, D. and Still, J. (eds), (1995), *Women and Representation*, Nottingham: WIF Publications.

Lejeune, P. (1975), *Le Pacte autobiographique*, Paris: Editions du Seuil.

——, (1980), *Je est un Autre: L'Autobiographie de la littérature aux médias*, Paris: Editions du Seuil.

——, (1986), *Moi aussi*, Paris: Editions du Seuil.

——, (1989), *On Autobiography*, trans. K. Leary, Minneapolis: University of Minnesota Press.

Lechte, J. (1994), *Fifty Key Contemporary Thinkers: From Structuralism to Postmodernity*, London and New York: Routledge.

Marcus, L. (1994), *Auto/biographical Discourses: Theory, Criticism, Practice*, Manchester and New York: Manchester University Press.

Mauger, G. (1994), 'Les autobiographies littéraires: objets et outils de recherche sur les milieux populaires', *Politix*, no. 27, pp. 32–44.

Miller, N. K. (1991a), 'Getting Personal: Autobiography as Cultural Criticism', in N. K. Miller, *Getting Personal: Feminist Occasions and Other Autobiographical Acts*, New York and London: Routledge, pp. 1–30.

——, (1991b), 'The French Mistake', in N. K. Miller, *Getting Personal: Feminist Occasions and Other Autobiographical Acts*, New York and London: Routledge, pp. 48–55.

——, (1992), 'Personal/autobiographical criticism', in E. Wright (ed.), *Feminism and Psychoanalysis: A Critical Dictionary*, Oxford and Cambridge, MA: Blackwell, pp. 306–11.

——, (1996), *Bequest and Betrayal: Memoirs of a Parent's Death*, New York and Oxford: Oxford University Press.

Mills, S. (ed.), (1994), *Gendering the Reader*, New York, London, Toronto, Sydney, Tokyo and Singapore: Harvester Wheatsheaf.

Mills, S. and Pearce, L. (eds), (1996), *Feminist Readings/Feminists Reading*, (second edition), New York, London, Toronto, Sydney, Tokyo, Singapore, Madrid, Mexico City and Munich: Prentice Hall, Harvester Wheatsheaf.

Moi, T. (1994), *Simone de Beauvoir: The Making of an Intellectual Woman*, Oxford and Cambridge, MA: Blackwell.

Morley, D. (1980), *The 'Nationwide' Audience*, London: The British Film Institute.

Mulvey, L. (1975), 'Visual Pleasure and Narrative Cinema', *Screen*, vol. 16, no. 3, pp. 6–18.

Neale, S. (1980), *Genre*, London: The British Film Institute.

Olivier, C. (1980), *Les Enfants de Jocaste*, Paris: Denoël/Gonthier.

Pearce, L. (1997), *Feminism and the Politics of Reading*, London, New York, Sydney and Auckland: Arnold.

Proust, M. [1913–27] (1954), *A la recherche du temps perdu*, Paris: Gallimard.

Radway, J. (1984–7) *Reading the Romance: Women, Patriarchy and Popular Literature*, 2 vols, London and New York: Verso.

Rivière, J. [1929] (1986), 'Womanliness as a Masquerade', in V. Burgin, J. Donald, and C. Kaplan (eds), *Formations of Fantasy*, London: Methuen, pp. 35–44.

Russ, J. (1984), *How to Suppress Women's Writing*, London: The Women's Press.

Sellers, S. (1991), *Language and Sexual Difference*, London: Macmillan.

Sheringham, M. (1993), *French Autobiography: Devices and Desires, Rousseau to Perec*, Oxford: Clarendon Press.

Smith, S. and Watson, J. (eds), (1998), *Women, Autobiography, Theory: A Reader*, Wisconsin: University of Wisconsin Press.

Stacey, J. (1994), *Star Gazing: Hollywood Cinema and Female Spectatorship*, London and New York: Routledge.

Stanley, L. (1992), *The Auto/biographical I: The Theory and Practice of Feminist Auto/biography*, Manchester and New York: Manchester University Press.

Steedman, C. (1983), *The Tidy House*, London: Virago.

——, (1986), *Landscape for a Good Woman: A Story of Two Lives*, London: Virago.

Suleiman, S. R. and Crosman, I. (eds), (1980), *The Reader in the Text: Essays on Audience and Interpretation*, Princeton: Princeton University Press.

Thomas, L. (1995a), 'Feminist Researchers and "Real Women": The Practice of Feminist Audience Research', in P. Drummond, (ed.), *Changing English*, vol. 2 no. 2, *Media, Culture, and Curriculum*, London: The University of London Institute of Education, pp. 113–29.

——, (1995b), 'In Love with *Inspector Morse*: Feminist Subculture and Quality Television', *Feminist Review*, no. 51, pp. 1–25.

Tompkins, J. P. (ed.), (1980), *Reader Response Criticism: from Formalism to Post-Structuralism*, Baltimore and London: Johns Hopkins Press.

Vincendeau, G. (1996), *The Companion to French Cinema*, London: Cassell and The British Film Institute.

Walkerdine, V. (1986), 'Video Replay: Families, Films and Fantasy', in V. Burgin, J. Donald, and C. Kaplan (eds), *Formations of Fantasy*, London: Methuen, pp. 167–99.

Wright, E. (ed.), (1992), *Feminism and Psychoanalysis: A Critical Dictionary*, Oxford and Cambridge, MA: Blackwell.

Young, M. and Willmott, P. (1966), *Family and Kinship in East London*, London: Penguin.

Filmography

Working Girl (dir. Nichols, USA, 1989).

Selected Television Appearances by Annie Ernaux

Apostrophes (France 2, 1984).

——, (France 2, 1988).

——, (France 2, 1990).

Aujourd'hui Madame: des auteurs face à leurs lectrices, (France 2, 1981).

Bouillon de Culture (France 2, 1992).

——, (France 2, 1997).

Caractères, (France 3, 1992).

Droit de Réponse, (TF1, 1984).

Féminin Présent, (TF1, 1981).

Index

language 48–9, 51, 82
transformation to middle-
class 6, 8–9, 14–15, 79–81,
128–9, 131–3, 164–75

women 92
writing, act of 42–3, 126

Young, M. 92